W9-ANY-173

Navaho Trading Days

1. Beyond the gorge of the Little Colorado lay the Western Navaho Reservation. As we followed the Navahopi Road eastward from Grand Canyon, we often stopped at this brush shelter of a Navaho friend.

Navaho Trading Days

Elizabeth Compton Hegemann

University of New Mexico Press
Albuquerque

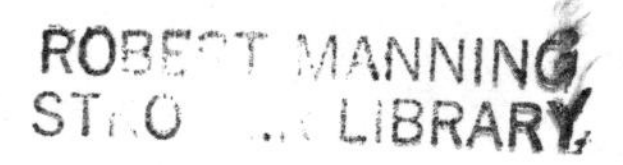

The Library of Congress has cataloged the first printing
of this title as follows:

Hegemann, Elizabeth (Compton) 1897–1962.
Navaho trading days. With photos. by the author.
[Albuquerque] University of New Mexico Press [1963]
388 p. illus. 28 cm.

1. Arizona—Soc. life & cust. 2. Indians of North America—Trading posts. 3. Navaho Indians. I. Title.
F811.H4 970.3 62-19922‡

Library of Congress [5]

First paperback printing, 1987.

CONTENTS

INTRODUCTION

As an old friend, I was delighted when Mrs. Elizabeth Hegemann of Albuquerque asked if I would prepare an introduction for her book, *Navaho Trading Days*. She predicated this desire on my long and intimate knowledge of and friendly relations with the Navaho Indians, comprehensive acquaintance with their vast Reservation, a majority of Reservation trading posts and white traders who had operated them since 1908. I warmly appreciated her invitation, and consented.

Elizabeth, daughter of Mr. and Mrs. William Clay Compton, was born March 20, 1897, on Indian Hill, a suburb of Cincinnati, Ohio. Her maternal grandparents, Mr. and Mrs. Charles G. Gove, were well known in Southern California and parts of the Southwest. She attended Miss Doherty's College Preparatory School in Cincinnati, spending many of her summers in Southern California.

On one of her annual trips to Grand Canyon, Elizabeth met Mike Harrison of the National Park Service. They were married in September 1925, residing in government quarters on the South Rim. I had known Mike for about two years prior to marriage; I first met his charming wife there about a year later. Both were much interested in Indians and had established very friendly relations with the Hopi, Navaho, and Supai working there or living in the South Rim area. Later they began motoring over the pioneer Navahopi road to the Western Navaho and Hopi Reservations—Elizabeth frequently, Mike when office duty permitted—to attend Navaho and Hopi ceremonies and dances, visit all trading posts enroute, and collect from traders and Indians, examples of Indian arts and crafts they especially desired to possess. Following their separation in 1928, Elizabeth made her home in Tuba City, primary trading and Indian Agency center of the Western Navaho Reservation, where she would be nearer her cherished Navaho and Hopi friends and their related trading posts.

In May 1929, the late Harry Rorick and Elizabeth were married. Before the end of that year they were preparing to purchase jointly the isolated Shonto Trading Post which they acquired and operated very successfully for the next ten years as a team, sharing equally in all related activities. Elizabeth's detailed chronological report of that experience and the accompanying pictoral record are the primary components of all aspects of her excellent *Navaho Trading Days*. Her marriage to the late Anton Hegemann took place after she had left the Reservation, and therefore he had no connection with the Navaho trading period.

A terse historical prologue is essential in context with any story relating to the Navaho Indians and their Reservation trading posts.

The Coronado Expedition of 1540, greatest in the annals of American exploration, after extensive and futile search for gold and other treasure, by right of discovery seized for the Spanish Crown most of the territory west of the Mississippi River. Juan de Oñate, fifty-eight years later as Colonizer, began the settlement of New Mexico, and after the bloody events of the Pueblo Indian Revolt of 1680, Diego de Vargas, the Conquerer, established the first Spanish sovereignty. Mexico next declared its independence from Spain, and New Mexico had a new master when General Kearny occupied Santa Fe with troops in August 1846, as one of the strategic moves of the Mexican War which ended with the Treaty of Guadalupe Hidalgo in 1848. This treaty gave the United States clear title to a territory larger than the original colonies, plus certain moral obligations toward and in connection with some 120,000 Indians in various stages of civilization and unrest, including the Navaho and Apache tribes.

In the settlement of the territory now embracing New Mexico and Arizona, the Spanish colonizers made certain, beginning in 1598, that settlers had horses, mules, sheep, goats and cattle to start their own communal herds. Later to enhance more friendly relations, provision was made for the like distribution among the long established communities of the sedentary Pueblo Indians.

From the time of introduction of such stock, the occasional raids of the nomadic Navaho and Apache bands accelerated rapidly and alarmingly. The Navahos and Apaches wanted horses and mules to expedite transportation and to facilitate and extend the range of their raiding expeditions. Navaho women needed wool and mohair for blanket weaving, and the tribe needed a mobile meat and wool supply. Cattle were of only secondary interest.

Despite repeated appeals of Spanish and Mexican settlers and all of the Pueblo communities, these raids were never restrained by Spanish and Mexican officials. Treaties later negotiated by American Army officials with Navaho chiefs to terminate such raids were promptly violated. By 1863, the raiding problem had become wholly intolerable.

Finally in 1864, after decades of unrestrained raiding, the Navahos were conquered by a large military force under Col. Kit Carson. There followed four terrible years of exile at Fort Sumner in eastern New Mexico which crushed the independence, self-confidence and morale of those who survived. The first contingent of captive Navahos started their homeward trek on June 18, 1868, and on November first of that year, Agent Dodd at new Fort Wingate formally assumed charge of the 7,111 Navaho Indians who were enroute via Fort Defiance to their homeland in northwestern New Mexico and northern Arizona.

The Navaho were a beaten people, determined at any cost to avoid another experience like Fort Sumner. The Navaho as a tribe had not only been defeated but subjugated. The Treaty of 1868 which ended that ordeal was never violated. As a result, they were receptive to commercial relations with the whites and to the primacy in their life with white men. Thus was the way opened for first establishment of white trading posts on their Reservation.

In contrast with the far earlier itinerant trader who transported rum, rifles, ammunition and trinkets into the camps of wild Indians, trading principally for their furs, the Reservation trader came among conquered Indians confined to reservations, and there built his trading post near dependable water supply, settled down to daily business at a fixed location which was also his home. Several pioneer Navaho trading posts were so established in the 1870's; a total of six by 1877; by 1943, the heyday of Navaho trading, a total of ninety-five traders were licensed.

The Reservation trading post became one of the most necessary and influential institutions of the Reservation system. The Navaho Reservation was so vast and so isolated that until the early 1930's, government officials had very little contact with the Indians, leaving the trader as the most important, often the only white man in the native community trading at his post.

To the widely dispersed Navaho, the trading post was not only a mercantile business but their trading, banking, information and local meeting and communication center. Up to that time the trader served his Navaho community as spokesman in the white man's world and became their protector. He was their counselor, advising in all business, governmental policy and personal affairs. Also he was their general factotum, giving medical help and burying their dead (which the Navaho deeply fear) and assistance in every matter where the white man was supposed to have special knowledge and skill.

Subsequently, under the federal relief programs beginning early in 1933, the government provided ample funds to support a great increase in

Navaho Agency administration, supervisory and technical personnel, and to inaugurate, Reservation-wide, the physical developments and control programs which so completely altered prior conditions and the old days of primitive atmosphere and isolation which prevailed over most of the Reservation.

Elizabeth Hegemann's experience as a Navaho trader spans this period of transition and changing conditions. She makes manifest her keen sense of affection and respect for Navaho and Hopi Indians and their cultures; the charm and glamor of the untouched Northwestern Navaho Reservation, as well as the implications of the transition. Her creed of dealing with the Navahos of the Shonto community is exemplary of best trader traditions. She delightfully commingles in her detailed story of trading and Grand Canyon days, the incidents and personalities that enhance interest. Many of these related incidents brought back memories to me of the people and places of those times that I used to know, and the events which transpired there. In synthesis, *Navaho Trading Days* is an outstanding record of her experience at Grand Canyon and on the Navaho Reservation.

Pictorially to illustrate and thus promote better understanding of the Navaho Country, Navaho and Hopi ways of life and related phases of her *Navaho Trading Days,* Mrs. Hegemann has selected and incorporated in her book, 318 captioned photographs taken by her. These are of particular interest in this context and of great documentary and historical value.

Until 1928 she used a 1919 3A or postcard-size Eastman Kodak, from then on a 3¼ x 4¼ Graflex. Subsequently, to insure greater permanence, she made new negatives of these photographs on 35 mm. film, Plus X Panchromatic, using an Exakta Model VX-IIa mounted on a Rowi copying stand. The enlarger used was a Leitz Focomat 1C, with a 5 cm. Elmar lens.

To the end that materials she had personally collected over the years shall be permanently available for public exhibition, enjoyment and benefit, or for related research purposes, Elizabeth Compton Hegemann has given:

Her entire collection of primitive Navaho jewelry assembled between 1916 and 1935 and comprehensively catalogued in detail by her; and a small collection inherited from her Grandfather Gove, of Southern California Mission Indian baskets bought near Pala, California in 1886, to Mission San Antonio, Jolon, California.

Her specimens of old Rio Grande tin work (over forty in all), assembled since 1948 from the Mary Austin - Frank Applegate - Fred

Harvey Company collections, have been given to the Southwest Museum of Los Angeles and to the Harwood Foundation of the University of New Mexico, in Taos.

The forty-nine old Hopi kachinas of the Bradfield-Vierra-McGill collection which she had acquired, were given by her in 1961 to the Museum of Northern Arizona in Flagstaff.

About eight hundred original photographs, none larger than post-card size, taken by her between 1916 and 1936 in Arizona, New Mexico, and Southern California, she presented to the Henry E. Huntington Library, San Marino, California.

JESSE L. NUSBAUM

Santa Fe, New Mexico
January, 1962

[PUBLISHER'S NOTE. Elizabeth Compton Hegemann died on April 8, 1962, after a long illness. Shortly before her death she approved page-proofs for this book, as well as the captions and order of photographs. During the last two years of her life, she performed the heroic task of making for the engraver's use her own new negatives and prints from her old photographs. During the process she invented darkroom techniques which solved some of the problems created by the condition of the early prints. Because these photographs are presented as historical documents, no attempt was made to retouch or disguise flaws in the originals. At the same time she prepared captions for the photographs, drawing upon notes, engaging in elaborate correspondence to ascertain names, dates and other facts, constantly aided by her remarkable memory. She also wrote the narrative text, which she looked upon as a highly personal document of recollections, rather than as a piece of scholarship. The editors have catered to Mrs. Hegemann's personal preferences in such matters as the spelling of place names and Indian words, and she was well aware that some of these have been changed by history or standardized by scholars.—*Roland Dickey*.]

1. GRAND CANYON

IN 1925 there was no need of a checking-station at Grand Canyon National Park for the few motorists who straggled in over the dirt approach road. A small sign simply requested motorists to stop in at the Park Headquarters to register. This was a log building with the Park Superintendent's Office upstairs, at the foot of the hill under El Tovar and Hopi House. Downstairs one Park Service Ranger was on duty, whiling away the hours between visitors by chatting with any local folks. I rolled slowly past on my way up to El Tovar and looking back in the mirror saw that the Ranger had disengaged himself from his chair and was gawking out the door at the driver who had had the nerve to pass him up. Then he relaxed as he recognized the red Buick (Sport Model 1923) with the California license, because I had been at both North and South Rims already that year and my dollar entrance fee was still good.

It was a beautiful September day when the high country around Williams, Arizona, and the South Rim was at its best. I had driven steadily, averaging a good thirty miles an hour at which speed no other car ever overtook me, with my dust cloud from the ungraded road drifting over the last of the yellow roadside flowers and the reddish brown of the scrub oak thickets. On the mountain sides the small patches of aspen were golden under the cloudless turquoise sky, and the thin air was exhilarating after the heat through the Mohave Desert. My tan corduroy riding breeches and flannel shirt were both in regulation men's sizes, because being tall and thin I scorned wearing their baggy feminine counterparts. These did not show any dust when I parked before the hospitable front door of El Tovar Hotel, although as usual I took off my wide brimmed felt hat to flap it free of dust. The smiling bellhop, Hopi Sam from Second Mesa, who came out to help with the bags, remembered me with a "welcome home."

One reason I decided not to stop at Park Headquarters was that I knew that Mike Harrison would be upstairs at his desk next to the Superintendent, J. Ross Eakin, an old career man of Geological Survey. And my early impression of Mr. Eakin had been that he was far too serious a man to appreciate his office hours being interrupted by any bit of light romance. Mike and I had not seen each other for a couple of months and it was rather common knowledge that we were to marry as soon as he could obtain a few days leave for us to get the license in Flagstaff.

Mike Harrison was born in Paterson, New Jersey, and after serving in the Army during World War I, had listened to the call of the West through civil service exams in the small but burgeoning National Park Service, and had been sent immediately to Grand Canyon about 1922. He took to it all like a duck to water and was soon riding his own cow pony, Tonto, with Western saddle and leather chaps through the rough piñon country, keeping up with the local boys who had figuratively been born in the saddle. Mike ran the Park Service office smoothly as he was an excellent secretary himself, and a year or so later was promoted to Chief Clerk when his force was expanded by a stenographer and a bookkeeper; a quite respectable office staff for a National Park in those days. Even the Park Engineer, M. R. Tillotson, had no assistant, and had only recently been able to move his family from their tent-house into regular quarters. We were lucky, perhaps by virtue of Mike's handling the papers in the office himself, and a set of these new quarters was reserved for us. But when I heard the tales of the other Park Service wives about their sojourn in the tent-houses reached by devious paths through the cedars, I began to feel that I had missed an experience.

Although I had known the Canyon for so many years, it had been only as a visitor for a few days or weeks at El Tovar. This time I became a member of the small group of "locals" as soon as I married Mike and we moved into our quarters. This was stepping across an invisible but very definite line of demarcation. The visitors and their business actually created the jobs for the locals and because of this they were more than welcome. But after the travelers had departed on the evening Pullmans or had fallen stiff and exhausted into bed after a trail trip, we could drop our cloak of professional hospitality and relax in the routine of our own local activities. These consisted of endless committee meetings and "auction" bridge parties where we laughed and talked between hands while consuming huge slabs of homemade cakes and cups of coffee. Afterwards while we stumbled homeward in single file behind the beam of a wavering flashlight, we could sense the silent void of the Canyon depths close by. No one could possibly live on the Rim and be oblivious to the Canyon, so beautiful and majestic in all moods, nor to the feeling of what little consequence our life might be when compared to the Canyon's millions of years of existence.

One Sunday morning on the El Tovar porch when Mike was wearing Park Service uniform but without his hat, he walked along with a couple of large Sunday editions on his arm. Black-haired and very slender, he looked far younger than his actual twenty-seven years. A tourist snapped his fingers and called, "Paper, boy!" Mike glared and then rushed home to put on his Park Service Stetson before returning to walk again the length of the porch, but by that time the tourist had bought a newspaper and did not deign to look up from its depths. Mike sputtered for days at what he thought had been a slur to his Park Service uniform.

Grand Canyon in the 1920's meant the tiny community at railhead on the South Rim, where all of those with National Park Service, the Fred Harvey Company and the Santa Fe railroad lived around the nucleus of the railroad station, El Tovar Hotel, and the older hostelry of Bright Angel. We lay supreme in our little world flanked by the great colorful depths of the Canyon and the miles of pine-covered plateau stretching south to the San Francisco Peaks. A single track of steel bound us to the main artery of travel at Williams, over which each morning came our precious water supply in tank cars on the regular freight train. That we locals who owned cars kept them jacked up for the five winter months not only describes the approach road of those days but also shows how dependent we were upon the Santa Fe Railroad. It was our lifeline. Nothing existed as yet in winter on the North Rim except the deer herds and the white-tailed Kaibab squirrels, so when we looked across that twelve-mile-wide chasm to the eight-thousand-foot level on a winter's night, not a light was to be seen.

Grand Canyon was taken over in 1919 by the youthful National Park Service, which had been established by Congress in August 1916 at the instigation of Stephen T. Mather, who had been asked to become Assistant to the Secretary of the Interior so that his exceptional talents could be devoted to this task. Without his foresight, means, and dedicated purpose, the King's River Canyon and the Grand Teton—Jackson Hole would not be as they are today. Until his death in 1930, Mr. Mather spent liberally of his own private funds for entertaining and doing necessary things for which there was no Congressional appropriation. He was the first Director of the National Park Service, while training his splendid young Assistant Director (Field), Horace Marden Albright, who was also the Superintendent of Yellowstone National Park. Part of his job was to interest others in the future of our national parks, and Horace Albright did that most successfully. He inspired John D. Rockefeller, Jr., among other things, to acquire enough land to protect the Grand Tetons, and to match the appropriations of North Carolina and Tennessee up to $5,000,000 to acquire nearly 500,000 acres for the Great Smoky Mountains National Park. When Mr. Albright made his inspection trips to other National Parks, there was always pleased anticipation in our isolated Grand Canyon village when we heard that "the Albrights are in." The Mathers were frequent visitors at the Canyon. At their little dinners in El Tovar, Mike and I were delighted to be included with the Eakins and Tillotsons. Often I wore an old Navaho silver necklace over a dark red velveteen blouse, and Mrs. Mather must have liked it because she bought a handsome, similar one from Mr. Spencer at Hopi House. That night we compared necklaces in the moonlight before the Mathers stepped into a Pullman at Grand Canyon station.

The South Rim had been managing its own affairs ever since the advent of the railroad in 1902, and particularly after Charles A. Brant opened El Tovar for the Fred Harvey Company in January 1905. Before that the few pioneers who brought their sightseers in by buckboard did everything in their own free and individualistic way. In 1923 there was still much talk by this contingent of the "good old days." A few of these pioneers had already passed on, among them Old Man Bass and Cap Hance. The latter, with his tall and taller tales of the Canyon, wintered alone in his cabin down on the plateau under Grand View Point, driving a few of his cattle down with him. Cap Hance had only one wish, that if he went to heaven it would contain the Grand Canyon within its environs.

Old Man Bass (William Bass) claimed to have made the first wagon tracks to the edge of the South Rim, and he was a hard-working trail blazer in what was to be the great tourist business of the future. He built a trail down to the Colorado River in the Big Thumb country and maintained Bass Camp, with good accommodations for small parties, which was some twenty-five miles to the west of the present Grand Canyon village. About fifteen miles to the east at Grand View, Pete Berry operated his log hotel in the summer for the stagecoach travel —two days with four-horse teams—from the Santa Fe railroad at Flagstaff. Another early pioneer was Sanford Rowe, commonly known as Old Man Rowe, who used to claim that he made parallel tracks to the South Rim with Old Man Bass, and got there at the same time if not ahead of him.

When I first stopped over at the Canyon prior to World War I, these men with their lively teams and assorted buckboards would jockey for position to meet the arrivals on the morning train in the dusty space by the station directly under El Tovar. Before the visitors could more than step from their Pullmans for a first breath of that cool, heady air, they were urged by authoritative voices to "Take this rig . . . right here . . . this way . . . this is the one you want!" I remember there was a lot of excitement in this rivalry and almost fist fights among the drivers in their long top coats. Finally everyone was loaded amid the backing of excited horses and the cracking of whips, and the buckboards rolled away with most of their passengers so groggy from the thin, high air of that seven-thousand-foot altitude that they had mind for little else.

After National Park Service gave a concession for all Rim drives and trail trips to the Fred Harvey Company, this last vestige of pioneer personalities came to an end. The locals who used to enjoy from the sidelines this morning wrastle of assorted rigs and horses with aggressive drivers in vociferous argument, were sorry the show was over. The Fred Harvey yellow buckboards with two cross-seats for six passengers and one with the driver, drawn by shiny matched bays or blacks in faultless harness, were beautiful to see twice daily drawn up for the Rim drive in front of El Tovar. Fred Harvey courtesy was now the order of the day with the railroad tourist business in full bloom. But by 1916 the crush of sightseers necessitated the substituting of large open motor busses—the White Motor Co.—which could hold several dozen persons on their cross-seats. However, the rackety motors and smell of gas fumes destroyed the peaceful beauty of the Rim drive as it was in the days of the horse-drawn vehicles.

Mr. Charles A. Brant, who never seemed to need a first name as identification, being known as "Mr. Brant" throughout the Southwest, always spoke of himself as an innkeeper. He was actually manager and major-domo of El Tovar from the opening in 1904 until his death there in 1921. He was a benevolent czar to all those who came under his jurisdiction, and his name lived long after he had been given the rare privilege of being buried at a beloved spot near the Canyon rim just west of Bright Angel. His dog and constant companion, Razzle, still had the run of El Tovar until death from old age, being looked after by Charlie Frazier, the former bartender who dispensed soft drinks from the rustic basement bar in Prohibition days. Charlie was a Negro, white-haired and wise in the ways of mankind, and a true friend of ours. Razzle's death is officially recorded as of August 16, 1928, but of Mr. Brant, only the year, 1921, is given.

My mother, Minnie Gove Compton, and her mother, Mrs. Charles G. Gove, had known Mr. Brant when he was a young clerk at the luxurious Montezuma resort hotel at Las Vegas Hot Springs, New Mexico, in the winter of 1884-85. They spent several months there as my grandfather Gove enjoyed the climate. My mother, in her tight-fitting Eastern riding habit with flowing skirt, had ridden horseback over the mesas. It was this same winter that my grandfather made his first trip to Grand Canyon, going north from Peach Springs through the Hualpai Reservation as the Flagstaff–Grand View road was blocked by deep snow. Many years later at El Tovar in a summer before World War I, Mr. Brant was amazed to find out that the Mrs. Gove to whom he was talking was *the* Mrs. Gove of Hotel Montezuma days when he had been a carefree young clerk. They had gotten out of touch in the years between. Mr. Brant was a charming and well-educated man from one of the Baltic provinces of Old Russia, and he added much to the pleasure of our subsequent visits to the Canyon. Unfortunately by the time I came to live there, only his memory was still alive among the older residents of the South Rim.

I lived there for the next three years, enjoying the daily life of meeting international visitors of note and getting to know them on an informal basis rarely possible elsewhere. They brought a breath and knowledge of the great global world which was often lacking in the Southwest before the jet age. On the periphery around us in the canyons and plateaus were the Supais, Navahos, Hopis, and Paiutes, who steadily pursued their ancient way of life and remained unobtrusive but always present. Altogether it was a fascinating and almost unreal background in which to make one's home, if all the beckoning potentialities were to be explored. Mike Harrison and I tried to do just that. We not only welcomed the new of which we were an integral part, but savored the old way of the pioneer life which was passing into history right under our noses. In our cramped government quarters, friends old and new gathered to meet kindred spirits who shared our enthusiasm for the Southwest. We listened to the reminiscences of the few remaining pioneers, to the early Indian traders, to the Navahos and Hopis who were our fellow workers, and assimilated something from everyone. The surrounding country became a part of us or at least we became an integral part of it.

We rode horseback a lot, Mike keeping his "Tonto" with the Rangers' horses and I borrowed one of these when they were not in use. Al Smith, a temporary Ranger who was married to the schoolteacher at Anita, owned a few horses. He drove them up one Sunday and we traded him an old .32 revolver and a five-dollar bill for a three-year-old range horse too weak from scanty pasture to do more than lean against the pole corral. It was about an even trade as that .32 would shoot around a corner and Al got rid of it mighty quick. And I almost decided to give the horse away while he was still on his feet, but the memory of that good five-dollar bill lingered with me. After a few weeks of feed and work with a currycomb, he began to resemble something equine. Eventually he developed into a nice riding animal, and his shiny black coat was a perfect foil for the Navaho saddle blanket and colorful bridle with reins of braided horse hair.

Another daily rider was Victor Patrosso (the manager of El Tovar and the older Bright Angel) whether for his figure or to get away from it all. His horse was the largest and fattest black-and-white piebald from the Fred Harvey barns, which he rode with an English saddle. Vic was manager for so many years that he became an institution, having succeeded Benedetti who took over after Mr. Brant's death. He was a bachelor who said he would never marry as long as his mother lived, and she lived until her nineties. He took an interest in everything and everybody, although his prestige could never reach that of Mr. Brant because now there was Park Service of which the Superintendent was considered the ranking person at the Canyon. But over the hotels and tourist accommodations Vic reigned supreme, and on a New Year's morning when he had returned to the Canyon one train earlier than expected, consternation spread throughout the large coffee shop of Bright Angel. The New Year's Eve party was in full swing with the staid employees of many years dancing on the counter tops—the floor was too rough!—when Vic's face was glimpsed at the front door. But he only waved his hat and disappeared. Next morning at seven, true to Harvey discipline, the coffee shop was open as usual.

Vic Patrosso was born in Italy and he used to tell how as a young immigrant he had begun as bus-boy with Fred Harvey and worked up through dining-car steward to superintendent of dining-car service and on to manager of El Tovar. Extremely loyal to the Harvey family, he would even attend personally to the chopped spinach for Willie Wee, the Pekinese of Marie Harvey Hall when she stayed at El Tovar; some said he even appeared with it at their suite with a napkin over his arm. Vic was well liked by all of us at the Canyon and he supervised a perfectly run dining room with a seven-course dinner for two dollars, correct in every detail. This was a treat for us who lived in the Park and could afford it. My mother would spend six months at a time in El Tovar so naturally Mike and I were frequent dinner guests. Vic's predilection for an Italian chef and assistants was understandable and their menu was excellent. If artistic or racial temperaments ever exploded, as when the chef chased Vic into the main dining room holding a long butcher knife at his back, it was considered as horseplay. Managing El Tovar was his whole life and in later years he never forgot the Canyon. Long after he and Frank Spencer (manager of Hopi House for thirty years) were both retired, he rang the doorbell at the Spencer's Boulder City home and asked with a bland voice when Frank appeared, "Could you direct me to Hopi House?" And once when I was dining at Victor Hugo's in Laguna Beach, I heard a punctilious voice at my elbow inquiring if everything were all right, to which without looking up I replied that it was. Then I heard a laugh and there was my old friend Vic, delighted to have played such a trick.

Much has been written about the original Fred Harvey; I would be the last one to write anything derogatory in the slightest way of the good he did in the West with his clean, decent eating and living accommodations in the Harvey Houses along the line of the Santa Fe Railroad. His sandwiches of ham or cheese with an extra slice of bread (three slices in all) for fifteen cents were known everywhere for their value. Of course he had to make his profit or he could not stay in business and therefore this story was told rather reverently by his employees and other denizens of the Southwest spaces. On his deathbed, instead of mentioning debts or bequests to his relatives, he was supposed to have murmured, "Cut the ham thinner, boys."

Our National Park Service quarters squatted under the tall pines on the slope south of the railroad station, four of us in a row—Chief Ranger, Chief Clerk, Assistant Superintendent, and Engineer. A sum between five and ten dollars per month was subtracted from our pay check for rental. At the time, Mike's salary was about one hundred forty dollars a month, so all deductions had great importance. Our heating system consisted of a woodburning airtight stove in the living room. It was an art to keep even heat in such a contraption. Either the fire went out or else it caught with such intensity that the round lid blew off with a burp and cloud of smoke to the ceiling. Our house cat, Tomaso Tabasco Chilipepper, disdained this stove after the lid had come down a tail's length away from him one time, and thereafter chose to snooze under the regular woodburning cook stove in the kitchen.

Halfway down the hill toward the Harvey Garage was the Community Hall, built about 1924 as a one-room building with a small stage at the end. Dances were held on Saturday nights with local talent such as Helen Colton or Doc Mellick at the piano. It was all in healthy thumpity-thump rhythm, and if he could tear himself away from the dance floor Mike would lean on the piano and raise his fine tenor voice in song. He could sing anything by ear, and just coming into popularity then was "Let Me Call You Sweetheart." Mike loved it and in the early morning he would sing it as he walked down the hill from our quarters to the Park Office. Unfortunately the path ran close by the cottage of a new employee who thought that the song just *might* be directed toward his wife. Poor Mike. When he heard about this through the Canyon grapevine, he was the most amazed person in the community, and said he guessed he'd have to pick another song or else pick another path to the office.

On one night a week we had movies, as this was still the great day of the silent films. The reel came up on the evening train to be run through the projector for this one show and then returned the next morning. While the film may have been silent, the showing never was, because the room was filled row-upon-row with wooden folding chairs which were prone to collapse with occupants at a tense moment. Coupled with this was the obsession of some of the tall, lanky cowboys who congregated in the back row, to perch on the backs of these chairs. When these collapsed, and at least one never failed to do so at each performance, the resulting crash was deafening. Besides this diversion, the film strip would always break once if not twice in the projector, while the poor operator made his repairs to a chorus of groans, whistles, and stamping. I think the community paid a dollar and a half to the fellow who volunteered for the job, and a movie that ran without interruption of any kind was something to be talked about for days.

It did not take much to amuse us. Our life was simple and little episodes were magnified and enjoyed. Tall, dignified Les Kennedy, long-time manager of Bright Angel hotel, had kept asking the NPS Rangers why they didn't do something about a family of young skunks that had been playing around the Bright Angel buildings—until the day when he watched with frozen attention the mother skunk followed by her six babies return to their hidden den directly under his own bedroom in the frame dormitory. From then on he declaimed that if any Ranger so much as scared that certain skunk family, he would have him, Les Kennedy, to reckon with right afterwards. With that sort of protection, the little skunk family grew up and moved on to other less populous fields.

Old Doc Jones, the resident Santa Fe railroad physician, prescribed castor oil and aspirin for any of our minor ailments, if we had them, and delivered a baby here and there. Our work and the climate must have kept us healthy, as I can't remember any of us complaining of more than a head cold, and then our only talk was "if we could only get out of this altitude for a few days." But Doc had another distinction; he was the only other resident in the National Park who dared keep a house pet, his old bulldog. Of course I had my Tomas of whom I was inordinately proud, especially when he wore his red velveteen Navaho blouse and tiny silver concha belt with great aplomb for our distinguished guests. Only once did he put me on the spot. It was when I had foresightedly locked him up in the dark kitchen closet while Horace Albright, of National Park Service, was paying his official call at my home. But Tomas' muffled yowls of protest penetrated even to the living room. Mr. Albright, although visibly amused, was diplomatically a bit deaf right then.

The Hopis who worked permanently at the Canyon were also patients of Doc Jones if they requested his aid, and so were the Supais who did manual labor on the roads and trails in the summer. Once a Model T tipped over, throwing out a middle aged Supai who landed unhurt except for one ear sheared off neatly by a limestone rock. He retrieved the ear, putting it in his pocket. Hours later he unwrapped this dust-covered object from his red bandanna handkerchief and gravely handed it to Doc Jones with a "You sew-um on, Doc." Doc Jones said afterwards it really hurt him to have to destroy such childlike faith in his own medical ability. The Supais had good horses, well-fed and trained for roping, and the men of the tribe were good cowhands. Without them, the one-day rodeo that we locals used to put on at the Canyon would have been pretty flat. Unlike the Navvies, they did not put their money in turquoise and silver jewelry, but they did invest it in expensive saddles and good horseflesh. Although the Reservation where they lived most of the year was some thirty miles west of Grand Canyon in the narrow side canyon of the Sky Blue Water, the families in summer would build cedar bark and juniper shelters up on the South Rim. Grandparents, children and dogs, could all be close then to the men who worked. But when peaches were ripe—those juicy, flavorful Supai peaches—they all returned to their canyon homes and orchards alongside the stream of clear, rushing water.

A few of the older women like Nellie Wottahommagie made finely woven small baskets and plaques with simple patterns in black on a white background. These plaques, like those of the Hopis, could be round or rectangular in shape and any size, but had to be practically *flat.* The Supai women's hair was cut square across the forehead and hung in a shoulder length bob above their stocky shoulders, while the men wore their hair cut short. This was very different from most of the Navahos of that period—both men and women wore their long black hair brushed straight back, to be looped and tied with yards of white cotton cord in an hour-glass knot called a *chonga.* One Supai woman, Old Mary, had become a regular pest around the Fred Harvey stable, tilted for hours in the one kitchen chair in the shade alongside the barn door. Now this chair was the foreman's until Mary pre-empted it without a by-your-leave, and he allowed he might as well regain possession before the summer was over. One day, after watching Old Mary settle her ample bulk and ampler skirts in his chair for the afternoon, he stepped inside the door where lay unobstrusive wires and pulled a switch. She leaped straight into the air and grabbing her broad behind with both hands, yelled, "Sumtin bite ass . . . bite like hell!" Then she took off down the road with skirts flying. The foreman sank gratefully onto his chair, tipping it further back, while a slight smile crossed his tanned face. She had taken the hint. Next time she tried to sell him one of her coarse baskets, he'd give her an extra dollar and they'd be friends again.

The stables sheltered the many mules used for the trail trips down Hermit and Bright Angel Trails, as well as the new Kaibab Trail across to the North Rim. These mules were first used for months packing supplies down to Phantom Ranch on Bright Angel Creek to familiarize them with the trail. Then the guides rode them until they were sufficiently wise and gentle to take care of the average tourist rider. The first wooden suspension bridge was constructed across the Colorado River near Bright Angel so as to develop Phantom Ranch. I remember riding over it with Bob Francy in 1923. I had ridden the Hermit and Bright Angel trails down to the river in 1916, wearing the long divided skirt of khaki that women trail riders sported in those days. Bob Francy, the Fred Harvey barn foreman, rode over at a slow walk, and when he and his mule were off the bridge, I crossed in the same manner. Likewise only one pack mule at a time was allowed on the bridge. As it sagged and swayed, the mules stepped on it gingerly, blowing gently through their nostrils and stepping off at the opposite end with evident relief. Unlike a horse, a mule will never hurt himself if he can avoid it. Of course the bridge was perfectly safe except for some unforeseen happening, and it was the only bridge of any kind in some thousand miles of the Colorado River. After about ten years of use, the unexpected did occur—a freak windstorm that twisted the bridge almost completely in two. Luckily no one was on it at the time. The story was that the men who built the bridge apparently had allowed for plenty of stress against the prevailing winds in the gorge, but not enough for any hard blow that might come from the opposite direction. As quickly as possible, National Park Service replaced it, in 1928, with a steel suspension bridge. In the meantime the caretakers of Phantom Ranch had to do a little pioneering themselves; for others it was a hard three days motor trip from the South Rim to the North Rim by way of Needles, California, or via Lee's Ferry if that were operating at the moment.

I made that arduous trip myself in the summer of 1925, when the main traveled route to the North Rim was from St. George through Short Creek and Pipe Springs to Fredonia and Jacob's Lake. At the North Rim itself there was only a log cabin for the Ranger Station and another one for the Rangers to live in during the three summer months. I was more worried about getting gas for my return trip to Fredonia than anything else, until one of the men said they could let me have a five-gallon tin at the regular price of one dollar per gallon. The auto traffic was absolutely nil and I was only there to meet Tex and Kitty Haught and Mike Harrison who had ridden across the Canyon. In less than ten years it was like a dream to return there with my own guests from Shonto, and find the luxurious accommodations in the Lodge operated by the Union Pacific railroad. In charge of the dining facilities was my old friend Tillotson's son, whom I had known as a young boy at Grand Canyon.

About 1928 tragedy did strike on the river, the culmination of a chain of events that I always believed had started with the shooting of a stray cat which had holed up under the Park Administration Building at the South Rim. A Ranger, Fred Johnson, offered to shoot it and did so, in spite of my protestations as to bad luck. That winter we heard he had slipped on some ice and broken his leg. Now that might have been enough to fulfill the prophecy. But the next summer when he and the Park Naturalist, Glen Sturtevant, with Chief Ranger Brooks, were rowing across the Colorado near Bright Angel, the boat capsized and both Johnson and Sturtevant drowned. It was well known that Johnson had always feared the river and this time it claimed him, whether the departed cat had anything to do with it or not.

Sturtevant was a grand guy. He and his wife with their two little boys lived only a stone's throw away from us in the pines. I remember the New Year's Eve—it could have been the last for him—when the Sturtevants, Tillotsons, Brooks, Coltons, Spencers, and Scoyens, gathered in our quarters for cider and cookies. This was in the heyday of Prohibition and none of us Park Service employees ever kept a drop of liquor in the house. But somewhere, somehow, that cider had been spiked a bit, and it did lend jollity to the occasion. Glen Sturtevant said goodnight with my Navaho silver bridle hung around his neck. He returned the bridle next day. Eivind Scoyen, as Chief Ranger, was our next door neighbor and a fine person. Born and brought up in Yellowstone National Park, it was natural for him to make a career of Park Service as Superintendent of some of our great Western parks. His wife was charming and witty, renowned for her stories—such as the time when she was a bride and in a fit of temper had thrown her wedding ring out the door in a snowdrift, only to spend the next hours madly sifting snow to recover it.

Hopi House on the South Rim just opposite El Tovar was where I spent many hours, not only to visit with the Navaho silversmith and his wife who were our friends, but to watch the visitors from the rest of the world as they went in or out. I would sit on a stone bench or near the blazing fireplace in winter, dressed in my Navaho skirt and blouse of crimson and black velveteen. Often I had wool cards in my hands so as not to waste a moment, and I always wore my necklaces and bracelets of heavy old silver or colorful turquoise and coral. Frank Spencer, the Fred Harvey manager for Hopi House during several decades, used to say that he always knew when I was sitting around, because his sales of silver jewelry increased. Hopi House itself was a de luxe curio or Indian crafts shop. No Japanese-made Indian curios were handled (if such were produced at this time) nor were the Denver and Albuquerque mass-produced items of Indian silver jewelry. Only true handmade silver jewelry from the Navaho, Zuñi, or other tribal silversmiths was sold, and the Fred Harvey name was protection enough for any buyer.

Stacks of beautiful Navaho rugs were there for the choosing and upstairs in a room not generally open to the public were kept the real collector's items in blankets, baskets, and ceremonial trappings, which Herman Schweizer had bought over the years. All of this buying was done from Albuquerque where he maintained his office, and shipped from there to the various Harvey curio stores along the line of the Santa Fe railroad. Frank Spencer might buy an occasional basket from a local Supai, but that was about all. Hopi House carried no articles for Indian trade, such as Pendleton robes, Stetson hats, shirts or Levis, sateen or velveteen yard goods. The local Supais supplied their wants from the Grand Canyon store of Babbitt Bros. Trading Co. The Hopis who worked at the Canyon bought their shawls, yard goods, and low-heeled shoes from the traders they knew back home under the Hopi Mesas or else in Winslow, where the assortment fitted their tastes. Of Navaho trade, there was none: they depended upon their Reservation traders and they very seldom rode up to the Canyon. When the Supai peaches were ripe, the Navvies might drift up in groups of two or three to do a little trading for them, saddle blankets principally, but that was strictly between Navaho and Supai. Hopi House was only maintained to cater to the visitors in furnishing the best of the Indian arts and crafts.

Among the passersby were many of the "names" of those years;

some would slip in quietly by themselves and others would be accompanied by their retinue. The Crown Prince of Sweden (now King Gustav Adolph) and his English wife, a Mountbatten, were still talking about the archaeological wonders they had been shown in Mesa Verde National Park by Superintendent Jesse L. Nusbaum (no *one* person was so closely associated with the creation of *one* National Park as was Nusbaum with Mesa Verde). Cliff Palace and the "steak fry" under the cedars were evidently the highlights of their entire Western trip. At Grand Canyon they were most appreciative of the Chief Ranger's effort to show them the geological wonders, and as a parting gift the Chief Ranger received a beautiful small Navaho rug. Upon unwrapping it later a ten dollar bill was found tucked inside, which created a minor household storm. His wife thought it would be a reflection upon his uniform to accept it, but he very rightly looked upon it as a kindly gesture from traveling dignitaries that should be taken in that spirit.

Almost every spring we had John Galsworthy on his way home to England after his winter in Tucson. In the midst of his *Forsyte Saga,* he traveled with his secretary and his tactful wife as a bulwark between him and the public. Drs. Sven Hedin and Roy Chapman Andrews discussed their past and present projects in Asia. Will Rogers, the Oklahoma humorist, with his lovely wife Betty and two irrepressible young sons, Will, Jr. and Jimmie, stopped over en route to California. A few years later at Tuba Trading Post, Will Rogers sat with us for meals at the long table, scarcely saying a word, but listening with interest to the terse comments of Jot Stiles and a few of the other locals. Maybe it reminded him of the days before he was famous and a Ziegfeld Follies star with his fancy rope act and extemporaneous remarks. George Palmer Putnam, the New York publisher, stopped off many different times for a few days' visit. He met some of the Reservation traders at my house, and was most interested in them and the Indians among whom we spent our everyday existence. The last time I saw him was when I had driven up from Shonto in later years, and he was on his way by train to San Francisco where he was to meet his wife, Amelia Earhart, at the end of the round-the-world flight from which she vanished in the South Pacific.

Those who loved the Canyon came again and again. To them, it was not "some big hole" or "a hell of place to fall into" to quote some of our casual tourists. William Randolph Hearst and Marion Davies arrived frequently in his private car in which they lived during their stay. Once we were invited for coffee and a chat, and although we were quite accustomed to the private cars of the railroad officials, this was something special and I remember the bowl of fresh roses which in our cold outdoors of piñon and sagebrush was indeed a breath from another world. Mr. Hearst—the Chief, as he was known to all—owned the Grand View Point acreage with the old hotel building, once operated by Pete Berry. Dick Gilliland was caretaker for Mr. Hearst, living in one of the old log cabins back in the pines from the Rim. In that way they were immune from the tourist busses at Grand View Point. Mr. Hearst planned to maintain all of this, including the old trail down under the rim to the copper mine, as an exhibit of turn-of-the-century life on the South Rim. But the National Park Service did not think there should be any privately owned property on the Rim, notwithstanding its altruistic purpose. As a patriotic citizen he deeded his magnificent Grand View location to the National Park, accepting in return an uninteresting tract back in the pines. It was during these negotiations that Mr. Hearst and Marion Davies came to the Canyon so often. Dick Gilliland and his wife were friends of ours, and as true Westerners they were loyal to Mr. Hearst and his interests, asking little in remuneration except for some creature comforts and the appreciation for a job well done. An unusually heavy snowstorm one autumn caught them with scant provisions, and they could not dig out of their home nor get through the drifts on the Grand View road. Phone calls to the Park Office at the Canyon brought them no information except that the scanty snowplow equipment would be busy elsewhere in the Park environs for several days. Then Dick did an unprecedented thing—he called the Chief direct at San Simeon—to say that they were snowbound and short of food. The telephone wires must have crackled immediately to Washington because within an hour that Park Service snowplow was pushing its way out to Grand View to relieve the situation.

George Horace Lorimer, the great editor of the *Saturday Evening Post* for about three decades, stayed several days at El Tovar each year to breathe that wonderful air, and perhaps to get away from literary agents. He did not indulge in trail trips but would walk for hours through the pines and out to the various points on the Rim for the spectacular views. No budding authors were lurking along these paths, although many of his own stable of authors stayed at El Tovar from time to time: Irvin Cobb, John P. Marquand, and James G. Blythe. The cartoonist and creator of *Canyon Kiddies,* Jimmie Swinnerton, was also among these. But Mr. Swinnerton—he always said the people who called him Jimmie were the ones who shouldn't—with his strong personality and inimitable stories of his personal experiences, was never a reticent individual. One of Mr. Lorimer's favorite companions was Helen Colton (Mrs. George Colton) of Verkamp's Curio Store on the Rim east of Hopi House.

She had been born in Prescott, Arizona, when Ft. Whipple was an active cavalry post inasmuch as Geronimo was still running around, and one of her schoolmates, the son of the Fort bandmaster, was the young Fiorello LaGuardia—later the well known Mayor of New York City in the 1930's. Helen had much pioneer Arizona history at her fingertips, but with all this and perhaps what was more endearing to Mr. Lorimer was that she had never had the slightest inclination to become "a writer." It was through Helen that I knew George Horace Lorimer and while he might not have shared my enthusiasm for the Navaho, their dress and jewelry, still he was sympathetic to my interests. As we saw him at the Canyon, he was a simple and likable man.

It didn't happen when Mr. Lorimer was there, but he probably would have enjoyed it, when, one morning the tall flagpole in front of Verkamp's on the Rim flew the American flag upside down, in the international distress signal. An agitated tourist rushed in to ask Helen Colton *what* had happened. Now she knew that George took great pride in raising and lowering the flag properly each day, but after one look she told the person not to worry, nothing had happened of tragic importance. It was just that her husband had been distressed that morning after a bit of celebrating, but she had not realized just how distressed. As George was one who liked to keep a bit of bourbon about the house even in Prohibition days, she had learned to accept it philosophically when a pint slid out of a Navaho rug she was showing to a customer. Without batting an eye she placed the bottle to one side, remarking that now her husband had lost another good hiding place, and proceeded with the sale of the rug.

Another who came to stay for weeks at a time, slipping in and out of the service entrance of the hotel, was Lincoln Ellsworth, the backer of many expeditions in Antarctica of which one was the Nobile dirigible flight in the 1920's. He would train for the rigors of these trips by hiking down one trail to the plateau at Indian Gardens and up the other one. He said he enjoyed the extreme contrast of this world of dry, hot color, and the white, snowy expanse of the arctic regions. Those three thousand feet of trail down and then up had put many a younger man out of commission, but Ellsworth thrived on it. No one would have known that he possessed great inherited wealth, with palatial homes in various parts of the world, when he stood around talking with a few of us locals, such as the Spencers and the Coltons. But let any aggressive or socially inclined stranger try to intrude and Ellsworth vanished into thin air.

All these were people who drew something from the Canyon, but there was one man who, in returning to the South Rim a few short years before his death, gave something to the Canyon just by his presence there. That was Charles Fletcher Lummis, who had tramped and ridden horseback through New Mexico and Arizona since 1882 and had created the word "Southwest" in its present usage during his years as editor of *Sunset Magazine,* and founder of the Southwest Museum and the Landmarks Club of California. Still slight and active, with his snow-white hair, he wore his traditional black corduroy suit with red cummerbund and a red cotton bandanna to keep his hair under control in our strong westerly winds. He felt that Mike and I were kindred spirits and we visited together in our small quarters at the Canyon and in his historical home under the sycamores near the Southwest Museum in Highland Park, Los Angeles. We showed him our prize pieces of old Navaho silver which we were collecting and kept hung on the wall in our home. And later in his home, he showed us four magnificent serapes from Saltillo, Mexico, from his collection. I believe these are considered to be the finest examples of that art. He loved the great earth country of the Southwest with its scattered groups of highly individualistic races, and his mind was as active as a young man's. In 1926 he went gaily down the Bright Angel trail on muleback with the regular party of sightseers. That night he held forth in our home on the sacrilege of the recent plane flight by Alger Graham into the Canyon depths. Mike just listened, not daring to admit that he had been in the plane with Graham. The spirit of Lummis was unquenchable.

This has been a cross section of those who came along our path at the Canyon in the 1920's, in the years when wagon trails were turning into traveled roads with the advent of the first hardy automobiles and the great development of the Southwest still in its infancy. In fact, when we drove around to the diggings near Mt. Elden where Dr. J. Walter Fewkes was working in the summer of 1926, I had the feeling that we were seeing the transition of one age to another. Not that the good doctor was inhospitable, because he did take the time to explain to us in layman's language just what he was looking for in the ruins, but I felt his faint bewilderment that a young Park Service couple upon hearing of his location east of Flagstaff, could come bouncing down on a windy afternoon over those long miles just for a little chat with him. He was still living in the style of past decades when he traveled to his locations in the Navaho or the Hopi country by slow wagon and team. Scarcely anyone knew his whereabouts nor would they have thought of following him for an hour's visit.

Frank Pinkley was Custodian of Southwest National Monuments then, and one of the men under him was "White Mountain" Smith, who held the job of supervising Petrified Forest. There were no signs or grand approach roads then, we simply angled south from Adamana following the "most traveled tracks" first right and then left. We drove around through the three forests in this same manner after carefully inscribing our names in the guest registry book on their screened front porch. Smith was glad to see us and we exchanged a bit of shop talk as to "leave" and how we were stretching it for this trip. Although there was no wind and the ground was dry, there was not another car in the whole Petrified Forest that day in 1925. As we rested on the big logs in the Rainbow Forest and looked at the beautiful colors in the pieces scattered over the ground, we could have filled the back of our car with specimens. But we resisted the impulse to collect even one scrap, as we felt it would not have been cricket for a Park Service man to do this.

PHOTOGRAPHS

2. Under the South Rim of Grand Canyon near El Tovar, the "Battleship" is clear of the steamy clouds rising after the night snowfall in December 1924.
3. Pines and junipers droop with wet snow in 1925 around our National Park Service quarters, as Mike Harrison holds our cat "Tomaso" high and dry on the front porch.
4. J. E. Kintner, the Postmaster, and Mike do some necessary shoveling on the main approach road near Grand Canyon Village that same winter.
5. Hopi House after a heavy snow in 1924, as seen from El Tovar on the South Rim. Frank C. Spencer, Manager of the Fred Harvey curio shops and Museum, lived on the top floor. At the right, above the rock steps, lived Paul Nichols and his wife, Jane Secakuku, Hopis from Second Mesa.
6. Tex Haught, of the old Tonto Basin family, as a National Park Service Ranger in 1924. His wife, Kitty, is on the left, while I hold the reins of Mike's horse, "Tonto."
7. My black cotton velveteen blouse and skirt was made in the authentic Navaho style of that period, sewn entirely by hand. Under the silver concho belt is a traditional hand-woven scarlet and black sash with fringe and ornaments. Wool cards are in my left hand.
8. My mother, Mrs. Minnie Gove Compton, on the path in front of our Grand Canyon quarters, leading Tomaso Tabasco Chilipepper. 1927.
9. Grand View Hotel shortly after Pete Berry, whom we knew well, had stopped operating it. This had been the terminus on the Rim for the horse-drawn stages from Flagstaff. The buildings and acreage on Grand View Point were the property of William Randolph Hearst in the 1920's.
10. A Supai summer camp of cut cedar boughs with pole and cedar bark shelter on South Rim in 1924.
11. Inside the circle of cedar boughs was their cooking fire with its pile of powdery white ashes, and sheltered spots where the Supai women prepared food and wove baskets.
12. Ranger Frank Winess makes his inspection of a more modern Supai camp, on the South Rim that year, with its large assortment of fat young dogs—good eating, so it was said.

2

3

4

5

6

7

8

9

10

11

12

13

13. One of the Fred Harvey guides rides across the wooden suspension bridge over the Colorado River in the early 1920's.
14. At the bottom of Bright Angel Trail was this suspension bridge over the Colorado River—the only bridge for a thousand miles north of Needles, California. I rode across it first in 1923, a year after its construction.
15. An unusual windstorm ended the career of the bridge in 1928. Nothing was on it at the time.

14

15

16

16. This cabin on the North Rim had belonged to the famed "Uncle" Jimmy Owens, who took Zane Grey on lion-hunting parties before 1910. It was the National Park Service ranger station in 1925. Rangers near the porch are Cox, Johnson, Brooks, and Winess.
17. A rare phenomenon at Grand Canyon appeared in the autumn of 1924, when a sea of white clouds filled the gorge almost brimful, while above was a clear blue sky. This lasted for several hours early that morning.
18. Mike Harrison, Charlie Etsidie (a Fred Harvey silversmith) with his wife and son, and an Interior Department official, 1928. Charlie's wife wears an old Navaho silver necklace of mine. A paved parking lot has taken the place of these hogans south of Hopi House.
19. A morning train of steam engine, baggage and "chair cars" ready to leave Grand Canyon Depot in April 1926; Mike Harrison, Mr. Galsworthy's secretary, John Galsworthy, and Mrs. Galsworthy stand next to me.
20. Charles F. Lummis, with a red cotton bandanna covering his snow-white hair and wearing his well-known black corduroy suit, makes his last trip down Bright Angel Train in 1926.
21. Tomaso surveys the Grand Canyon world back of our quarters as he sits on a western Navaho grey, black and white rug between two Second Mesa Hopi coiled baskets and a Kachina doll made in 1926 by Jason Honanie of Shungopovi.

17

18

19

20

21

2. *THE NAVAHOPI ROAD*

IN THE turn-of-the-century years, long before color film was available to every photographer, some of our greatest landscapists, among them George Inness, Louis Eakin, and Thomas Moran, came to paint their own interpretation of Grand Canyon. Their canvases, done with the skill of National Academicians, often showed an imaginative Canyon of mysterious depths, towering peaks, and flashes of heavenly light. But not many of these oil paintings were available, outside of private collections or museums.

Soon after World War I a Swedish watercolorist, Gunnar Widforss, came to paint in some of our national parks, and made his headquarters at Grand Canyon. A modest man of middle age, with a most engaging accent, he fitted right in with our small group. He was a meticulous craftsman, painting the Canyon as he saw it—and as we saw it—at various times of the day and under different weather conditions. The blue haze which is so much a part of the Canyon he transferred with great feeling to many of his canvases, and I felt that it appealed to him especially. Neither snow nor cold would keep him from perching with his easel at some point on the South Rim, but once after a two-day windstorm when he wanted to capture the effect of dust suspended in the air of the gorge, he returned to the village in what was for him a high state of temper. In a few last unexpected gusts of wind, his easel had been blown over twice, only to be patiently reassembled and his materials cleaned. Then when everything was going well and the light was exactly what he wished, an updraft surged by and left a tippy easel in a welter of pine needles, paint brushes and tubes. It was then he told us, "I queet."

He filled many commissions for the Santa Fe Railroad, the Fred Harvey officials, various hotels, and others like Lincoln Ellsworth, who felt that Widforss had created a niche for himself among the painters of the Southwest. To us, he was "Weedy," and his favorite form of relaxation in the evenings was a game of auction bridge with Helen Colton, Mike and me. Often we sat at a table in the soda-fountain room, sipping one of Charlie Frazier's chocolate sodas, while waiting for an opening bid from Weedy which not infrequently was "Von kluub—very veek."

One morning in May 1927, a terrifically excited Weedy stopped me near the desk of El Tovar with the exclamation, "He made it. He made it." Thus did I learn that Charles A. Lindbergh had landed at Le Bourget. The few sentences were on the type sheet by the registry desk, together with the stock market reports. To Gunnar Widforss it was a thing of enormous pride that a young American of Swedish parentage had been the first to make the solo flight across the Atlantic.

One morning in 1934, Widforss started out in his car for his day's painting. Only a few yards from his Bright Angel tent house he slumped over the steering wheel in a fatal heart attack. His sisters in Sweden preferred that his body stay in his American home, and he was buried in the Grand Canyon Cemetery.

George W. P. Hunt was still Governor of Arizona when I lived on the South Rim, as he had been re-elected to so many terms since Arizona became the Baby State in 1912 that he was looked upon as a perennial Governor. He was a man who believed in being folksy with a capital F, and the joke was that one could tell everything he had eaten in the last couple of days by the stains on his shirt front or vest, though there might be some repeats in the egg stains. In summer when he drove up with a carload of men from the heat and dust of Phoenix to view the Canyon and cool off a bit, he usually had on a business shirt with collar undone and a necktie pulled comfortably loose. This was all right if he wanted to go about that way—but not in the El Tovar dining room where the Fred Harvey rule was that men must wear coats, keeping a number of such black coats in light weight and various sizes available at the entrance of the dining room. The Governor knew this well and in the coolness of the Canyon air it certainly worked no hardship on any man and it did seem more in keeping with the polished silver and linens on the individual tables. But one day he did not feel like being a conformist and refused to put a coat on, only to be politely told by Vic Patrosso that he could not be served in the dining room there although they would be delighted to serve him in the Bright Angel Hotel where there were comfortable tables in the coffee shop. So it was this flying wedge of men in rumpled white shirts with neckties awry who bore down toward me on the narrow board walk along the Canyon Rim between El Tovar and the Bright Angel. As I recognized G. W. P. Hunt I wondered what had happened and stepped off discreetly into the dust and rocks to let them go by, and a few minutes later Patrosso came striding along to see personally that the Governor was given all possible attention in the coffee shop. But during many visits after this the Governor ostentatiously took his group of men to the Bright Angel. It was amusing to most of us at the

Canyon as we had seen men from all walks of life before entering the El Tovar dining room slip into one of the coats graciously offered them. As this was long before the day of the open neck, beautifully tailored sports shirts, these coats certainly improved the looks of the men in what was most obviously a tired business shirt. But Hunt enjoyed showing his complete disregard for such social amenities.

U.S. Senator Henry Ashurst of Arizona would spend a few days at El Tovar in the summers, usually accompanied by his wife and several friends and he was the epitome of courtesy to everyone. A tall, handsome man, we felt that he added a bit of distinction to our young Western state. The South Rim of the Canyon held the memory for him of a personal tragedy as his brother, William Ashurst, was buried in 1901 under the piñons not far from the head of Bright Angel Trail where the body had been brought up after a premature explosion in the tunnel of his mining claim a few hundred feet below the rim of the Canyon. Later, under Park Service regulations, the body was moved to the cemetery at Grand Canyon.

The Hopis who worked at Grand Canyon congregated in the living apartment at the south end of Hopi House on the second floor, where Jane Nichols kept house. She was a sister of Joe Secakuku of Sipaulovi, and her husband Paul was from Mishongnovi. Paul was in charge of the newsstand and curios at the old Bright Angel in the original log cabin with the crude stone fireplace, before which old Cap Hance used to sit and spin his tales. Jane fed the single Hopis at her family table, and took her part in the half hour "Hopi Dance" given for the tourists every afternoon at five outside of Hopi House. They ate in what might be called Hopi-American style, with very tasty mutton stews containing squash or onions, and with homemade bread of white flour made in round loaves with a thick crust. But for the true Hopi dishes from corn, such as *piki,* they had to wait until visits home at their own Hopi Mesa villages. Piki is the cornmeal gruel baked on a certain kind of flat rock, then quickly rolled while hot in a wafer thin layer to form a feather light stick about one inch by twelve inches long. The labor of grinding the corn to such fineness on the metates is backbreaking, and the spreading of the thin gruel by hand on the hot rock takes much practice and patience. When the piki sticks are piled high on a plaque, each color of red, blue, or white corn separately displayed, they are an important part of the gifts between families and clans at the ceremonial dances.

Whenever I needed a change of atmosphere from the dinner and bridge parties, I would climb the outside rock staircase to Jane's. She was always there with a smile of welcome, usually tending some kettle simmering on the wood stove, and we could sit on the kitchen chairs around the big table. Nothing was soft or luxurious about the place but soon any tensions I had, evaporated of their own accord as Jane's soft voice regaled me with bits of Second Mesa news. Inevitably it would lead to some forthcoming ritual in their villages, and we would talk on and on about the possibility of our getting out there. Paul Nichols could not get off, since the Fred Harvey employees of those days worked a split-shift seven-day-week, not even Christmas excepted. Mike could only get away from Saturday noon to Monday morning, so it sometimes meant that Jane and I had to go alone, leaving at home plenty of food cooked in advance. Even if we had to forego the pleasure of a trip back to Second Mesa, such as for the Bean Dance in 1927, a good chat with Jane always left me refreshed, for some of the quiet strength of the desert and her Hopi heritage flowed about me.

Jason Honanie of the Quahongwa family from Shungopovi, and his wife Norma, a young Navaho girl, were frequent companions of ours. Her family came from Burro Springs south of the Hopi Mesas and she and Jason did not meet until they both were young adults attending Sherman Institute in Riverside, California. They lived not very far from us among the Santa Fe quarters in the piñons as Jason worked for the railroad. They were a very happy couple who tried to combine the best of their Hopi and Navaho traditions or customs with the way of life they had learned at Sherman. My plea with Norma was to let her beautiful black hair stay long and straight, and not to wear it short with a permanent. There was no beauty operator then at the Canyon, but there was a man barber who would give those of us with short hair a necessary trim. Our latchstring was always out for Jason and Norma, and I remember their baby, Laverne, being twirled in my large Luiseño Indian basket on the floor by Tawaquaptewa, the Chief of Old Oraibi who was over for a visit. He sang ever so softly that favorite among Hopi children the "Little Squirrel Song." And about the second time he heard it, Mike was singing it also in that minor key.

Jason carved and painted with exquisite skill authentic Kachina dolls from the dried root of a cottonwood tree. He would only make a few of these a year which he would present to his friends. Every little detail would be perfect, from the bulging eyes to the dance rattle in one hand or whatever that particular deity should carry. Norma, no doubt wishing to show her inherited skills, set up a Navaho loom in a corner of their tent-house and set to work, and it was this that inspired me to learn Navaho weaving. Although having been familiar with Navaho rugs, I had never made a study of the necessary basic work such as the carding and spinning of raw wool and the work of setting up the warp on the loom with the heald sticks.

That spring I bought several longhaired fleeces of both black and white sheep from the Navahos we knew in Coconino Basin. These fleeces were bulky with sand and burrs and were heavy to handle when wet, although they weighed less than five pounds dry. I washed them thoroughly in my kitchen sink regardless of what that strong sheep smell did to the rest of the house. Then there was "carding" to learn, the same as our great-grandmothers had done in Colonial times, and the more difficult art of learning to spin a tight and even yarn on the Navaho hand spindle. This was made of a light wood, both round disc and two-foot-long slender stick. Piece-by-piece I acquired this necessary equipment from various Navvies we knew, and they showed their interest in the Belecana (any white-skinned person) woman who wanted to work as they did, by parting with these treasures. A spindle or batten with the right smoothness and balance is treasured for decades by a good weaver. Charles Amsden's book, *Navaho Weaving,* was of help also with its diagrams, although it was not so much knowing how to do it, as learning to do it well through continuous practice. The young Navvy girls go through this same experience.

To set up a Navaho loom in our Park Service quarters was a project in itself, inasmuch as there was an insecure plasterboard ceiling, and one was not allowed to drive a nail into the floors. But we did manage it with cedar posts wedged between ceiling two-by-fours and the floor, with cross-poles bound top and bottom in true Navaho style. I had tanned sheep skins with warm thick wool on the floor where I sat in front of it. Altogether, when the warp was in place with the pattern begun at the bottom, interspersed with the balls of white, black, and red handspun yarn and the batten sticks, I thought it made a pleasing addition to the house. Some of my neighbors thought otherwise as they held their nose against the sheep smell and complained that they had lost a good fourth at the bridge table just for *this.* As my work progressed and I continued to wear Navaho dress with more and heavier pieces of old pawn silver, I became rather well known in the El Tovar lobby. Mr. Carl Gray, President of the Union Pacific railroad then, once told me that he not only approved of a young person doing such, but that he wished he had one like me up in Glacier Park. That did help to assuage the look-down-the-nose of a few of the Park Service wives. Probably, to put it kindly, I had been born twenty years too soon.

In making the intricate diagonal or diamond-weave saddle blankets I learned by experimentation what an infinite variety of patterns could be created by the rotation in which I pulled the three heald sticks. I never attempted a large one but I did make a small one for Tomas to lie on; also a soft rug, known as Day-u-gi in Navaho, of natural beige and white wool, which I timorously showed to Mr. Spencer at Hopi House only to have him say to bring in some more like it and he'd sell every one. I was amazed. But with my other duties I simply did not have the time for all this handwork, and rested on my laurels for awhile after completing a regulation Chief Saddle Blanket of authentic old design in natural black and white with a touch of red. Unfortunately this was burned in the Shonto house fire of 1940 after I was no longer living on the Reservation, and only photographs of it remain. Because I was the only Belecana whom they knew that had learned to weave as they did themselves, the Navvies began to speak of me in my Grand Canyon days as the Woman who Weaves—Est-san-ysht'lo. Thirty years later when meeting once again my old friend, Maxwell Yazzie, of Tuba City, he used that name which had followed me from the Canyon to Shonto and even beyond for two decades.

Because of these Navaho activities I was probably the most consistent user of the Navahopi Road down into the Western Navaho Reservation except for the Harvey Cars on their one-day trip to Tuba City. The Navahopi road meandered across country, scraped out with pick and shovel where necessary across the small canyons, to abruptly leave the high plateau by a dugway blasted from solid rock and so steep and narrow that it was known as Waterloo Hill. A car had to creep down in low gear or up in low gear, it was all the same, and if the motor quit or any stray obstacle was met, then it was indeed Waterloo. Another spectacular spot was where the faint tracks barged suddenly around a sharp promontory where straight down a thousand feet was the bed of the Little Colorado, with the car's wheels a couple of feet from the unprotected edge of that sheer drop. It was such places as these that made twenty miles an hour a good average running time for the whole trip.

In 1923 and 1924, when the Fred Harvey Company opened up the first passable road between the Canyon and Cameron at the Little Colorado Bridge, Sanford Rowe used a few teams with Fresno scrapers, and a Navvy crew for pick-and-shovel work over the thirty-five miles of cross-washed plateau that sloped from seven thousand feet at the Canyon to nearly four thousand at Cameron.

It was a needed connecting link between the Grand Canyon community of tourist accommodations and the primitive, colorful Western Navaho country. While still in the Park east of Grand View was a tortuous, pine-studded stretch of road known as Long Jim Canyon with only a few spots wide enough to pass in its whole length. In late afternoon the whole covey of high, open-seated, canvas-topped, Harvey busses would be making their return run from Desert View with their passengers for the evening train. The trouble for me was that often at this same time I was heading away from the Canyon toward the Reservation, so I had to keep my eyes peeled for those swaying canvas tops through the trees, because those drivers on schedule would not give ground for anyone. When I saw them coming I simply took to the timber wherever I could stop and watch them go high-balling past with their passengers frantically holding on as they slide from side to side on the cross-seats, and never feeling sure whether they all looked at me with envy or compassion. Long Jim Canyon passed into history in 1929 with the advent of a new graded road.

East of Desert View in Coconino Basin lived Old Man Rowe in his one-room log cabin among the cedars just off the Navahopi road. Sanford Rowe, pioneer and alleged maker of the first tracks to Rowe's Well at the South Rim, decided that the country was getting too crowded for comfort after the railroad came in 1902 and the National Park Service in 1919. He moved eastward to the edge of the Western Navaho Reservation where a dug well in the limestone strata would give sufficient water for his scanty needs and there was endless wood right around him just for the cutting. These took care of his simple wants. We knew him pretty well and he enjoyed our stopping in with bits of the latest Canyon news although he really cared little about what did go on there and not because he was embittered that money was being made by others (not by us in NPS) where he had failed to reap much fame or fortune from his hard pioneer labor. Far from it, he was simply disinterested in the modern way of life, and gave the strong impression that he was absolutely at peace in this world of his own choosing. He knew that he would die there in contentment and he did.

The story of our friendship is hardly complete without the episode of the black horse we bought from him for forty dollars. It handled well around his place but back home at the Canyon turned out to be a balky old jughead, and we continued to complain about it each time we saw him. Finally he said to ride it back and he'd give us a couple of Navaho rugs instead. Out of courtesy we let him pick the rugs from a few in his cabin, most of which were moth-bait anyway. Nevertheless he joshed us about its being "the fust time he'd ever los' out on a hoss-trade." Be that as it may, I bought from him several very old and primitive Navaho silver bracelets at the low cost of the sugar and coffee he had loaned against them over a year before. He was glad to get rid of such stuff, but black horses he really liked.

Where Coconino Basin dropped off to the east and overlooked the entire sweep of Painted Desert to the faint blue mound of Navaho Mountain on the skyline, was the brush shelter of a young Navaho, Eugene Gordy, and his blind wife. The Navahopi road angled close by and when we saw his high-seated little buckboard there, we knew he was at home. They could only stay on this part of their range in the thunderstorm season when the rock tanks held sufficient water for the sheep as although the sagebrush browse was always abundant, available water was the problem. Eugene's wife could not have been more than twenty, but trachoma had already done its work; her red and swollen eyelids with the constant discharge left her without enough sight to weave on her small loom except by sense of touch. They had a baby girl and a little boy to whom Eugene was extremely devoted. These children handled everything their mother touched, including the rags she used for her itching eyes. But what could we say when we knew she was unable to see what they were doing and Eugene was herding sheep most of the day or bringing back water in their small keg laboriously filled from a shallow rock tank? Things could not be kept uncontaminated when they had to be used by all and rarely washed. I felt sorry for Eugene as he was a good Navvy, trying his best to look after his young family even in the face of tragedy. He helped his wife with the weaving, which eked out their livelihood, by getting the warp in position and then arranging the proper sequence of the colored balls of yarn that she had spun herself. This confined her work to straight line patterns or plain saddle blankets. When they shifted their home twice a year with their sheep, he had to take her in the buckboard because in that piñon country she could get into plenty of trouble on horseback. In former days there would have been an older or a younger wife to help with the duties of the hogan, and perhaps in this case the old Navaho custom of plural wives would have proved beneficial. But Eugene had been away to boarding school and was living in the new way approved by Nahtahni, the Indian Agent at Tuba City.

This whole thirty-mile stretch of country from the Coconino plateau to Tappan Springs near the present Highway 89 was like a prologue to the three-act play of the Navaho Reservation life itself. This vast Reservation with its hidden and scattered population stretched endlessly to far horizons over hundreds of miles of unfenced desert and canyon. We drove, perforce, so slowly across the rocky ledges and sagebrush slopes of those uninhabited miles that we literally became a part of the landscape as our car softly creaked and groaned under its load of extra tires, gas, oil, shovel, ax, tarp, food and blankets. These were pearls without price when needed in that land of lonesome trading posts and scattered hogans. Everything was taken note of as we crept along, if I bounced over a certain ledge too hard a mental note was made to try it at another angle on the return trip or else go around it. When a Navvy had driven his horses to water at a rock pool, it was a pleasure to stop and watch him sit his horse like a good herder far to one side. While the horses drank their fill he was motionless until the last one had finished, then wheeling his horse he gathered them up and started pushing the herd along once more. There was not a sound except for the soft thud and scrape of unshod hooves as they crossed the flat beds of rock.

A bunch of sheep busily nibbling the sagebrush near the road would be appraised in the springtime to see if many had been sheared, as that would be a newsworthy item at the next trading post. Somewhere with the sheep would be the small herders, usually too shy to do more than show their wind-blown hair above a clump of brush. The Navvy boy or girl in charge of the flock might be close to ten, with one or two younger as helpers. They would take the sheep from the hogan corral early in the morning, the smart old goats leading the way, and not return with them until sunset. These children knew where and how to drive the flock to water and to keep them spread out grazing the rest of the day, except for the noon hours when the sheep would bunch up in any good resting spot. Even at this early age the Navvy children accepted the responsibility of staying with the sheep during the heat or cold, wind or rain, and sometimes a small herder could be seen carrying in his arms back to the hogan a lamb which had just been "dropped" out of season. In those decades on the Navaho Reservation it was a pastoral life and the mainstay of the family was the lucrative herd of sheep and goats. The members of the Navaho Tribe owned over a million head of sheep and goats by 1930 and this was twice what those sixteen million acres of arid plateau country could adequately support. The sheepherders and their parents did not comprehend this situation as it was being discussed in Indian Bureau circles; they only knew it was harder and harder for the sheep to find any grass or sagebrush to eat.

With the long afternoon shadows the homeward trek began, the spicy smell of freshly trampled sage rising in the air as the sheep and goats trooped along behind the lead Billy with his clanking brass bell. From windward came the smell of piñon smoke bringing with it a message of mutton stew, fried bread and Arbuckle coffee for the hungry little sheepherders and they hurried their pace. Soon their charges would be safe within the pole corral and they could join their family around the cook fire in the center of the hogan floor. Their day's work had been done when they checked in with every last ewe, lamb, and Billy accounted for in the home corral. After dark the glow of a hogan cooking fire reflected through the smoke-hole could be seen for some distance on a clear night, as often it was the only light as far as eye could see. Such a sight could be a beacon of help or shelter in an expanse of empty miles to any trader stuck on the road, provided it was not shining from old Calamity's hogan in the mud flats named after him south of my future home at Shonto, or some other such crotchety character.

22. Jason Honanie wore an Eagle Dance costume in the daily afternoon performance given for tourists at Hopi House. Jason and his Navajo wife, Norma, were neighbors and good friends of ours at Grand Canyon. 1924.
23. Jason and Norma's daughter, Laverne, with her first Christmas tree at Grand Canyon, 1925, surrounded by her familiar Kachina dolls and Butterfly headdresses standing erect in the snow.
24. My own Navaho style loom in our home at Grand Canyon in 1927. From my handspun yarn and warp I was weaving a rug of an old "Chief saddle blanket" design.
25. Elsie and Anna May Secakuku, Jane Secakuku Nichols from Sipaulovi, and Peter Honeayeva. Three of them were ready for an afternoon dance at Hopi House in which Hopi children did not participate in those years.
26. Close to the Navahopi Road in Coconino Basin, this Navaho sweat house faced east. When hot rocks were placed inside with a little water poured over them and the doorway blanketed, it gave a cleansing steam bath.
27. Sanford Rowe, a pioneer on the South Rim, at his cabin near the Navahopi road in Coconino Basin, describes how he lined out the route from the Grand Canyon plateau down to the Western Navaho Reservation. 1927.

22

23

24

25

26

27

28

29

30

28. East approach road (Highway 64) traversed the length of Long Jim Canyon in 1925. This road in the narrow, pine-studded canyon was abandoned in 1928 for a graded, parallel route.
29. The edge of Navahopi Road is at the right of the Navaho girls on burros who are herding sheep.
30. Navaho sheep, some black and light brown, and goats graze on the brush of Coconino Plateau above the gorge of the Little Colorado seen in the distance. 1926.

31

32

33

31. With Eugene Gordy's family in their summer shelter of cut juniper boughs on the eastern edge of Coconino Plateau.
32. Outside hang skeins of yarn to dry and sheep pelts to sun. Eugene used the buckboard alongside to move his blind wife from winter to summer home.
33. The old Navahopi Road ran very close to the edge of this gorge, about a thousand feet deep in the otherwise level plateau. Water flow in the gorge was irregular and always full of silt. 1927.

34

34. He doesn't mind the closeness of my Kodak, but she isn't quite sure. These young Navahos stopped beside the Navahopi Road while driving their horse herd up to higher country. 1927.
35. "Waterloo Hill" at the right is where the old Navahopi Road climbed up the limestone strata among the piñon, a low gear road all the way. The Navahos, with pack burros, followed a shorter horse trail.
36. The young Navaho, his wife and brother-in-law wore buckskin moccasins. The tall, peaked hats the men wore were high style in those years in the Western Navaho Reservation.

35

36

37

38

39

37. Out of the deep shadows and into the last light on the higher country, the horses picked their way slowly. They were never fed and they competed with the sheep for existence on the dry range.
38. A natural rock tank holds plenty of water for the tired, thirsty horses to drink in the early evening while the Navaho at the left sits his horse patiently. 1926.
39. The Navaho starts herding them along, although the horses are loath to leave the water.

3. *TUBA CITY*

WHEN Mike and I used to go down to Cameron from the Canyon in 1926, Stanton Borum was the partner with Hubert Richardson and there was just the one stone and frame trading post building. A few tenthouses and the like took care of the ones who worked there as well as a passing transient or two. It was all informal and friendly and we ate at one table on the screened porch at the north side of the trading post building. If a car drove up and stopped, everyone stopped what he was doing to see who it was; such was the pace of life on the future Highway 89. Scarcity of water was the great problem. Later on, in WPA days when the springs near Tappan were developed, Cameron had plenty of water and the first bathroom which we were all shown with great pride. No more could Hubert accuse his wife, Mabel, and me of exchanging all the gossip of the desert while we sauntered slowly to and from the old privy near the rim of the Little Colorado. It was peaceful there in the evening with all of the Painted Desert spread out before us. There was so little traffic, even past Cameron, that when Preacher Smith married a young couple in the center of the bridge over the river, not one car had to be flagged down. After a wedding supper with everyone on the porch, the bride and groom retired to the trading post where they slept on a stack of Navaho rugs. This was the wedding, Reservation style, of Wes and Billie Case of Grand Canyon.

The Moencopie Valley below Tuba City spread out between eroded mud cliffs with Hopi fields of corn and melons filling it from rim to rim for several miles adjacent to the village of Moencopie. The Navahos managed to have a few fields with some hogans close to the northwestern edge, which the Hopis may have felt was an encroachment on their rights. As this is all Navaho Reservation, the Navvies probably felt they were being generous in allowing the industrious Hopis to farm there at all. This was one of the background problems which the Western Navaho Agent faced perennially. If there was ever a slack day in the Agency office this situation could be counted upon to fill the vacuum. The old road from the Agency to Flagstaff wound around the edge of Moencopie village on easy, sandy grades, with pleasing vistas of the horse corrals, peach orchards, and mud-roofed rock houses grouped around their small plazas. To save mileage a road was cut down the side of a mud hill directly into the valley by Agent C. L. Walker, and it was known locally as "Walker Hill," fine in dry weather, slick as grease after any moisture. Even those most skilled at driving in mud avoided its steep grade with a reverse curve and went the long way through the village. But one middle-aged school teacher just learning to drive her Maxwell, started down confidently after a light shower. Her car slid at the top and as she froze on the wheel, it took off straight down the steep hillside. There was enough brush to keep it upright and at the bottom of the gully the motor died as the car stopped in the soft mud. Without touching a gear or the ignition, she walked to the nearby Kerley Trading Post where a Hopi trucker had been watching the performance with open-eyed amazement. Soon she and the Maxwell were seen on the fast-drying road again, neither apparently the worse for wear.

Tuba City was the hub of all Western Navaho activities as it was the site of the Agency with its boarding school, hospital, and general offices. In the years prior to 1934 the Agent worked directly under the Indian Bureau in Washington, there being no Window Rock or general Navaho agency in the Southwest. It was Jacob Hamlin, the Mormon pioneer, who named it Tuba City after his good friend Tuba, a headman of the Hopis. The site has passed through two different phases, first as the Mormon settlement of the 1880's, and then, after 1901, as the Indian Bureau's Western Navaho Agency. The Navaho name for it is Tqonah-nés-disi, Tangled Waters, descriptive of the Tuba City mesa where springs flow in many directions around Moencopie and Moenave. Irrigation ditches with tall Lombardy poplars on each side of the dusty main street in 1925 showed that it had once been a Mormon town. It was this private ownership that enabled Babbitt Bros. of Flagstaff to buy a few acres for a trading post at the entrance of the street. This Tuba Trading Post was the largest and most substantial in the Western Navaho Reservation for decades, being operated for Babbitts at various periods by Samuel S. Preston, Jot B. Stiles, and Earl Boyer. Always a big wool post with much sheep- and cattle-buying in the fall season, it was the pay checks from the Agency that brought steady year round business. At one time in the 1920's Buck Lowry ran a small post under permit at the dead end of the main street, and under the hill in Moencopie Valley a permit was granted to John Kerley for a post which is still run by one of his sons. After Walter Runke resigned as Agent in 1920 as the aftermath of the unfortunate Taddyteen shooting affair, there were several superintendents in charge until Harvey K. Meyer came as Agent in 1923 and stayed until relieved by Chester L. Walker in 1926, who remained until his transfer in 1933.

On the Fourth of July, 1926, there was a grand celebration at Tuba combined with what was the end of the boarding-school year, when the Navaho parents rode in from afar to take their children back to their hogans for the summer vacation. It was a time of great excitement for all. An informal parade was held in the morning, the Navvies bedecked in their best Pendleton robes and silver jewelry lined up two-by-two out in the sagebrush, before riding up the main street ahead of the school boys and girls dressed in their various uniforms. Watching these pass with uncomprehending eyes were clusters of non-school Hopi and Navaho girls in native dress, a few sitting comfortably on burros. I had made the several hours drive down from the Canyon for the event, and took my place among the spectators standing in front of Tuba Trading Post.

Jot Stiles strolled along the line of the parade seeing everyone and what they wore, not to admire their costumes, but as he said, to spot those who owed him money. Jot was a trader the Navvies really respected. He had grown up on the southern edge of their Reservation, spoke their language and understood their way of thinking. When it came to cattle and sheep buying time no Navvy could fool Jot in the same way a couple of them had fooled the Cow Springs trader. These Navvies sold that trader the same cow three times in as many weeks, cutting it out from the trader's herd at night and having a different Navvy bring it in the next day. The young Navvies could not help bragging about this exploit, which was fun to them, so the story spread far over the sagebrush telegraph. Some traders on the Reservation without previous ranching experience would not buy stock from their trade at all, but this policy worked a hardship on both sides. The trader buying sheep or cattle in October, according to Indian Bureau regulations had thirty days in which to drive them off the Reservation. This could mean fifty to one hundred fifty miles of scanty grazing and scantier waterholes to a railroad shipping point, with always the chance of hungry sheep getting into a batch of poison weeds. These weeks were a period of worry and responsibility for even the best of stockmen-traders.

In the fall of 1928, after Mike and I had written finis to our marriage, I lived with the Stiles at Tuba trading post for many months, often making trips around to Shonto, Kaibeto, and other outlying posts. Many interesting people came to Tuba for the day or for overnight but of course the number did not compare to the stream of daily visitors at

Grand Canyon. It was a transition period for me from life in a famous National Park into the free, simpler life of the vast Navaho Reservation.

On the mesa east of Tuba were signs of an ancient civilization with lines of foundation stones and pottery shards over a considerable area attesting to a sustained occupancy. Anahsazzi is the Navaho name for ancient peoples, covering all prehistoric cultures, and I always found it a most convenient and all-encompassing word to use. Burials of Anahsazzi were sometimes partially exposed by a sandstorm and it was after one that the Stiles and I drove out on a Sunday to walk around the old ruins. Jot was not particularly interested in Anahsazzis in general as they had no sheep or cattle to sell, so while Marge and I turned over shards in the hope of finding a whole ladle or a tiny pot, he idly amused himself by stacking some scattered bones and a skull together. Shaking his head with a trace of a smile, he said, "If my Navvy trade could see me now, I wouldn't have one of 'em left." However, he did let me snap a picture as he sat hunched over the skull and cross-bones of that unknown Anahsazzi.

Our Navvies at that time were still very superstitious about touching the dead or having anything to do with burials, old or new. So when a Navvy had an epileptic fit in the bull pen of Tuba Trading Post, it called for quick action on the part of the trader. Jot was behind the counter at the time and as he watched the rest of the Navvies almost tear the front door apart in their scramble to get out, he vaulted the counter, grabbed the fellow's legs and pulled him outside. If he had died inside, the whole trading post and contents would have become *chindi* in Navaho eyes, a terrible thing to happen to a large stone building with thousands of dollars worth of merchandise on the shelves. No Navvy would knowingly come near a *chindi* location nor touch anything later that might have come from there. We told Jot that he probably passed a few Navvies himself while dragging that sick one out the front door.

C. L. Walker, the Agent in these years, was a career Indian Bureau man who thought he had learned the ropes through long experience with both regulations and Indians. He used to quote a saying that, "the 'regulations' would make a crook out of any Agent who tried to do a competent job." Anyway, he believed he knew how to run a good agency and he did not care much for well-meaning interference in his administration, whether it might come from Louisa Wetherill of Kayenta or John Collier of the Indian Rights Association. When Collier made frequent visits to Tuba City to talk with some of the locally known Hopi and Navaho dissidents, Agent Walker ordered him and his party off the

Western Navaho Reservation—at least that is the way the story went—and as Agent of the Western Navaho Reservation he had full power to do this and to forbid their return.

No one dreamed then that John Collier would be named Indian Commissioner in 1933 by Harold Ickes, the newly appointed Secretary of the Interior, because Mr. Ickes had expected the commissioner's job for himself. But when this did take place, we heard that Walker was packing his suitcases. As he was a civil servant in good standing the worst he could anticipate was a demotion by transfer, and whether by coincidence or not, he was transferred almost immediately to Ft. Peck, a small agency on the frigid Canadian border. In the next few years I worked more closely with the Collier administration in the Indian Bureau than I had with the previous one. After 1933, when Harry Rorick and I had been established several years at Shonto, both of Collier's sons and their wives visited us there. They were as sincerely alive to the welfare and future of the Reservation as we were. It was only a question of combining the theoretical with the practical, and a trader had to be as practical as the Navvies around him.

North of Cameron, the Gap was the next trading post on the road to Lee's Ferry at the Colorado River. The Gap received its name from a break, or gap, in the long north-south formation of sandstone cliffs at this point, and was operated for years by Joe Lee, a grandson of the old Mormon, John D. Lee of Mountain Meadow massacre fame, for whom the Colorado river crossing and ferry were named. Joe stayed at the Gap post and traded while his partner, J. C. Brown, ran the business end in Flagstaff from his cigar and newsstand opposite the railroad station, where he could incidentally peddle some of their Navaho rugs. The paved Highway 89 now follows a route slightly to the west, where other owners have a new Gap Trading Post. The old Gap post is no more and Joe Lee has also taken off on the good Mormon trail; he died in the Pioneer's Home in Phoenix. He liked to talk of the days when his grandfather had hidden out by the Colorado River before he was finally tried and executed in 1876. Joe was at home in a dim trading post full of Navvies, speaking their language fluently and taking an interest in their various family affairs as it broke the monotony of his own bachelor existence in an isolated spot. When I first met him he had long lost all his front teeth, but his smile was engaging. With stray tourist travel beginning to creep past the Gap with the future Highway construction, he bravely faced up to the future. Agent Walker found this out one day by chance when phoning Joe at the Gap over the rickety Agency line. Joe's voice sounded so strange that Walker could not believe he had him on the phone and kept trying to clear the line until Joe said with a final effort, "It's me, Mr. Walker, and tain't the line, it's mah new store teeth."

About seven miles north of the Gap in a growth of juniper and piñon under the Echo Cliffs was a small Babbitt Bros. trading post called Cedar Ridge. It was called a "dry post" because it depended on the scanty rainwater from tin-roofed buildings to fill the cistern, and needed water hauled from the Gap a good deal of the time. The tracks of the road to Lee's Ferry ran directly in front of the door, and it was the last stop in civilization for a long, long way north including the dangerous crossing of the Colorado by ferry. Earl Boyer was the trader at Cedar Ridge for a number of years and his wife well knew the rigors of the Lee's Ferry crossing as her first husband and another man had lost their lives when a rope broke and their truck went under. As with the Gap, the new Highway 89 passes to the west and a new Cedar Ridge post is there, but it could not retain the former flavor of the last outpost to the north which was embodied in the old post. It is strange what a haven to people such an isolated post was, with no phone nor even mail connection. In an emergency there was only the trader upon whom to rely. It must have been his presence—come hell or high water, a trader is always at his post—plus the availability of food, water, and maybe gasoline, that inspired this sense of security. In the same way people were to descend on Shonto during my years there, in emergencies dire and otherwise, feeling that once they were at the trading post all their troubles would be solved.

By 1928 there was a scraped road, graded more or less in spots, to the Colorado River where the new bridge over Marble Canyon was being built. The day was already past when J. C. Brown, going to the Gap, had to make his own tracks after a summer rainstorm. The bridge would span the sheer cliffs about five miles south of the old Lee's Ferry location. But several months before the bridge was completed, the Ferry was lost when the river was in full flood—the ferry was in reality a shallow wooden scow with boards laid across the top which was just wide enough for a car or wagon. Coconino County owned and operated the ferry at that time because it was the only link within the state of Arizona with the so-called northern strip, but naturally they did not want the expense of replacing the ferry for just a few months usage. So for several months in 1928 the northern strip of Arizona was as cut off by the river from the main portion of the state as it had been in pioneer times.

Just then Hubert Richardson had a couple of people out with a pack outfit going from the Navaho Mountain country over to House Rock Valley. With the ferry suddenly gone, the problem was how to negotiate the river crossing. One of the men at Lee's Ferry who had known the river all his life, said he would swim the mules over even though the water was high and then take the people and packs over in his rowboat. Hubert told us this was agreed upon and as I was living in Tuba I offered to drive him up early in the morning thinking that with my new Graflex I might get some pictures of this last pack outfit crossing. After grinding down in low gear over the narrow ribbon of road dug from the rock cliff on the south side of the river, known as Lee's Ferry Dugway, we met the pack outfit at the bottom on the sandy, alder-filled bank of the Colorado where there was scarcely space enough for us to turn the car around. They had heard us coming more than a mile away as they were all congregated there in the hot, damp air of the river, partially in shade as yet although the hot sun was gilding the tops of the high cliffs. Packs lay in heaps and the riverman held his rowboat snubbed to a rock, while some seventeen mules and a white mare milled about near the edge of the water. The white mare was supposed to go first and the mules to follow, but she had no such intention. Finally a young, strong mule accepted the challenge after a long look across at the opposite bank. At once he was swimming frantically with only his nose, eyes and ears above water. The others followed. At a distance their long, erect ears looked like the horns of goats as the mules swam rapidly, guided by the rowboat from dropping with the current too far downstream. They had to reach the one sandbar on the north side or be lost in the rapids below. As the skillful boatman brought them to land, the white mare was the last to climb out, still showing her disdain for the whole enterprise. While the stock dried off, the two people and the packs were rowed across. When all were safely over, Hubert and I began our return trek up the dugway for the last time that I ever drove it. Within a few months the new Marble Canyon Bridge was completed, and the dugway with the Lee's Ferry crossing receded into the dust of history.

In the early 1920's there was still a very ancient ceremony known as the Rabbitskin Robe Dance, which the Reed Clan in Moencopie gave periodically. Elsie, the handsome Navaho wife of Walter Lewis, had told me about it. Walter was a Hopi from Moencopie who owned a couple of trucks and carried the mail under contract from Flagstaff to Tuba. They lived with their young children on the Tuba mesa just above Moencopie village in a squat, stone house with space around it for his trucks inside a barbed wire fence. Walter was a fine-looking, pleasant mannered Hopi as well as a good business man. We liked them very much.

When Elsie told me that I had better come down on a certain day in that late spring of 1927 if I wanted to see a ceremony, I was pretty certain what it would be. After stopping at her house on the mesa, Elsie and I went over the rim to where we could see some of the dancers taking their position in the center plaza, and sure enough they were wearing the grotesque-looking rabbitskin robes. A few small groups of Hopis were lounging against the sides of the houses and we sidled in alongside one of these. No one paid any attention to us as they were seemingly intent on following the oft-repeated words of the chant which had already begun, The chanting was very low, not much above a humming sound.

The robes worn by the round dozen of men participants made them look huge because the thin strips of rabbitskin with the fur left on, dried, twisted, and then woven, made a thick and bulky covering. Nothing was done artificially to increase their height as in the Zuñi Shalako, and the greyish-brown robes swathed the men from neck to ankle. The masks had reddish-brown faces with round rings for the eyes and nose, while in the back was a huge, glistening pompom of greenish-black feathers. Possibly the numerous roosters roaming the plazas of Moencopie had donated their best tail feathers to this good cause. Worn high about the shoulders, topping the rabbitskin robes, were white cotton ceremonial shawls with deep bands of red, black, and green wool. These, and the red fox skins worn hanging in the rear where the tail should be, gave the necessary color contrast to the muted desert sand tones of the dominant rabbitskin robes.

As the day wore on, the ceremony became a bit monotonous with just the chanting of songs in certain groups with the costumed figures standing in one or two lines. Late in the afternoon two old women in ancient Hopi dress with offerings of sacred cornmeal on plaques knelt in front of the entire line for the duration of a chant. The Clan Priest in a white shirt and black corduroy trousers directed the movements and the chanting with unhesitating authority. I noticed that he was not an elderly man as is usually the case in such Hopi ceremonies, but that he wore his hair in the old style with bangs and short side-pieces, the back hair long and tied in a knot with a red wool, handwoven garter strip.

This was one of the most solemn Hopi rituals that I had ever witnessed. It contained nothing for the children, therefore the spectators were mostly adult Hopis. Evidently it had not been advertised by word of mouth, as even in the late afternoon there were no Navahos or Agency employees straggling down from Tuba. We joined one of Walter's relatives for a meal of mutton stew in their home; but there was no general feasting nor carrying about of woven plaques with gifts of pink, blue, or white *piki*. Perhaps that explained the absence of Navvies, who had a good nose for such festivities when there was general feasting.

Not at the time of this ceremony but later on, I examined one of the rabbitskin robes where it was kept by a Hopi family in a large wooden chest at their Moencopie home. The narrow skin strips had been sewed with sinew end to end, forming a long string which was then used for both warp and woof in a loose, in-and-out weave. It was quite similar to those fragments of rabbitskin garments made by Cliff Dwellers. I could not find out when these Moencopie robes had been made, but judging from appearances at that date (1927) they had been brought over from Old Oraibi when a few families of the Reed (Pakab) Clan decided to live permanently in Moencopie. This was after 1902, although some of the men had come over each year to plant and tend their crops in this fertile valley with running water. Perhaps the Mormons living in Tuba and later the Western Navaho Agency there, gave these Hopis the necessary feeling of security to attempt making a permanent settlement at Moenkopie. This was Navaho country: they were sticking their head in the lion's mouth. Historically speaking, the small village of Moencopie could be called very young compared to Shungopovi and Old Oraibi, but a bit older than the very recent Hotevilla or Bacabi. And during the 1920's at least, the Moencopie Hopis played a leading role in the economic life of Tuba with their hauling of freight for the traders to the Western Navaho, and contracting the mail runs even as far as the biweekly Kayenta route. This passed by Shonto for several years and Edwin Kaye and Robert Lewis, both long gone, were our dependable friends. They got their trucks through in spite of snow and mud or wind and sand. The Reservation was their home and our home, and we depended upon each other.

40. Billy Bass—a son of the pioneer, W. W. Bass of Grand Canyon—and I visit with a couple of Navahos out looking for horses near Tuba City in April 1926.
41. A stream just below Tappan Springs in a hidden canyon. Stone walls of an old cattle rustler's hangout remained in 1925.
42. Everflowing Tappan Springs, named for Col. Tappan, U.S. Army, who camped there in 1857, lies a few miles to the south of the Little Colorado and west of Highway 89. A Navaho home with sheep herd is above the rim.
43. The bridge, completed in 1911, was named for U.S. Senator Ralph Cameron of Arizona, and eliminated the dangerous quicksand of old Tanner Crossing on the Little Colorado.
44. In the doorway of Cameron Trading Post, April 1926, are Mike Harrison, Ida May and Stanton Borum, Goldtooth Charlie, and Hubert Richardson. At that time Hubert and Stanton were partners in the Cameron, Kaibito, and Leupp trading posts.

40

41

42

43

44

45

46

47

45. Seven-Mile Wash, was actually the Lower Moencopie. Anyone going north or east in the Reservation had to ford this wash seven miles north of Cameron. It was first bridged in 1928.
46. The main road from Flagstaff to Tuba in Moencopie Valley often was blocked by a slow-moving band of sheep and goats.
47. Two old Hopis in a typical Moencopie home of that time, with *ristras* of chile in the fall, and pieces of mutton or goat meat hung to dry on the high lines. Fresh corncobs on the tarp attract the ever-hungry dog. 1923.
48. Moencopie, westernmost of the Hopi villages, as it looked in 1925 from the edge of the old road from Tuba to Flagstaff.
49. Moencopie Wash, east of the village, where a Hopi herds his sheep.

48

49

50

50. The rare ceremony known as Rabbitskin Robe Dance was given in May 1927 at Moencopie. All participants seemed to be elderly, including the two women with their offering of blue cornmeal on plaques.
51. The Rabbitskin Robe ceremony was given only in Moencopie by the Reed Clan, and not in any other Hopi village. About twelve men and two women participated.
52. The Dance Priest who took personal charge of the entire ceremony is in a white shirt, blue corduroy pants and moccasins, with his hair worn in the old-style Hopi fashion. The dancer at the right signals with his whisk of yucca leaves to others taking position. Most of the dancers wore silver *ketohs* (bow-guards).
53. The figures appear huge because of the bulky robes of dried, twisted and woven rabbitskin strips, but nothing artificial was done to increase their height. The Hopi women and children in the background merely paused for a moment on their way past. This ceremony was not for children.
54. The two women wore old dresses of handwoven black wool with a dark red design at the hem. The shoulder shawls were also old and of white handwoven yarn with red and black bands on the edge. The impression of age and solemnity was dominant throughout the ceremony.

51

52

53

54

55. Irrigation ditches with tall trees lined the main street of the former Mormon town of Tuba City, settled in 1873, which was, in 1925, the Western Navaho Agency.
56. Moencopie fields with their Hopi melons and corn. Mrs. Emory Kolb of Grand Canyon, whose husband is one of the well-known early explorers of the Canyon, stands next to me.
57. From the Tuba mesa, the road to Flagstaff passes Kerley Trading Post at the foot of Walker Hill. This road was always deep in either dust or mud.
58. Navaho men and women riding up the main street of Tuba in the Fourth of July parade in 1926, had refused to dress up in feathers "like Indians."
59. A few Hopi men dressed up to take part in the parade. The one with the striped cap and painted body is authentic in portrayal of a Tewa clown. A Fewkes photograph of 1891 at Walpi shows this exact costume.
60. The Four-H Club and Red Cross were represented by Hopi school girls from Moencopie. The other girls in old native dress walked in the last of the parade, with the scrawny burros at the tail end.
61. Jot Stiles, trader at Tuba Trading Post, solemnly piles together the Anahsazzi bones scattered on a surface ruin east of the Agency, and hopes that none of his Navaho trade will see him. 1928.
62. Mr. Simpich of *National Geographic Magazine* and Mr. Adams, photographer, with Harry Rorick beside a Fred Harvey Transportation car from Grand Canyon, on a special trip in 1927. Mike Harrison in Park Service uniform, with Jot Stiles on his left. Sandy Hassell in doorway and Bill O'Brien—in Stetson hat at left—were Jot's assistants. Marge Stiles stands behind her son Roger with his Navaho playmate.
63. Tuba Trading Post, owned by Babbitt Bros. of Flagstaff, was built of gray stone in fortress style. By 1927, additional living quarters and guest rooms had been added.

55

56

57

58

59

60

61

62

63

64

64. A Navaho family on its way to a "sing" on the mesa west of Tonalea in 1926, takes its small bunch of sheep along.
65. Mike Harrison and our car are beside the Gap Trading Post in 1926 on the main road to Lee's Ferry and Utah. Joe Lee, a grandson of John D. Lee of the Mountain Meadow Massacre, was a trader here for many years in partnership with J. C. Brown of Flagstaff. The present Highway 89 and the new Gap are west of this location.
66. In 1926 these tracks were the future Highway 89 and were just north of the Gap near Cedar Ridge in the "little painted desert" of eroded mud hills.
67. Highway 89 now is west of this little painted desert region where the old road skirted its edge.
68. Cedar Ridge Trading Post early in 1926. The only road to Lee's Ferry and Utah ran in front of the post near where my car is parked under the piñon. A scaffold for tramping wool in the large sacks is built at the right of the platform. The trader at that time was Earl Boyer, who ran it for Babbitt Bros.

65

66

67

68

69

69. Crossing the Colorado River with a packtrain of mules at Lee's Ferry, 1928. Mules with a white lead mare are being driven into the river on south bank at the foot of the Lee's Ferry dugway. There was no other way to cross until the completion of Marble Canyon Bridge in 1929. The small wooden scow on a pull-rope that served as the ferry, had capsized a few months previously. Coconino County would not replace it for the few months usage prior to completion of the steel bridge.

70

70. Herded in over his depth, a smart young mule takes the lead towards the opposite shore. The young Mormon in rowboat keeps downstream to hold them on course. In that hot summer morning the steam from the mules rose over the cold water.
71. In the middle of the current the mules start downstream and the man rows hard to turn them toward the only possible landing on the sandbar.
72. The boatman has turned the mules directly across the current to the sandbar.

71

72

73

73. The weary mules climbed out on land after their tussle in the swift muddy water with the white mare one of the last. The red sandstone of the gorge already was reflecting the heat of the sun.
74. The last trip over was with the boat loaded with packs, saddles, and the two riders.
75. Marble Canyon Bridge over the Colorado River with Vermilion Cliffs in the background a few miles south of the old Lee's Ferry crossing. When the last steel was laid in 1929, an era of pioneer living in northern Arizona came to an end. Lee's Ferry dugway went out of existence, and the shifting tracks of the road south to the Gap and Cameron became paved Highway 89.

74

75

4. *THE ENTAH*

An Entah or Squaw Dance, always given in the summer months, was an integral part of the old Navaho way of life. It fulfilled many physical wants as well as spiritual needs. The patient for whom it was given primarily and whose family paid the expenses, seemed only an incidental part of it. The family, consisting of Clan relatives also, after deciding to put on an Entah, would pledge a certain number of sheep or goats to be butchered—often large, old ones. This depended on the wealth of the family and the number of Navvies expected to attend from afar. The necessary coffee, sugar, and flour would be procured by the selling of wool or rugs, or pawning jewelry with the nearest trader. For this reason, he was usually the first to hear of the prospective Entah, and if it were held close enough to his trading post, he would contribute a suitable amount of these staples himself, because for several days his transient Navvy trade would be good with skins, saddle blankets, and cash.

The Medicine Man who had been summoned from perhaps as far as fifty miles away had complete charge of the spiritual side of the ceremony—from the chants over the patient inside the Medicine Hogan on the first day until the final blackening of the body, and Killing of the Scalp, on the third day. In the old days when the Entah was considered a War Dance, given for the purification of the person who had slain an enemy or who had seen an enemy killed, it was of much importance. As even then it was confined to the months when thunder rolled across the Navaho country and the nights were pleasant for singing and dancing until the dawn, the patients to be purified had to wait through the winter months despite any mental hardships.

For a real get-together by the Navvies from other sections of the reservation, an Entah was supreme. This was before the day of the Tribal Council with its official delegates and annual meetings at Window Rock. The Navvies would gather in groups, perhaps sitting on their horses, and talk of sheep and grass and water conditions on their home range. There was no hurry, what with free food to be had at the cookhouse for the next three days of the Entah. No man had been elected to anything.

If anyone was listened to with respect, it was because he had earned well that position of trust in the Navaho community. Groups would disintegrate only to form again around other individuals. It was a good time for the government stockman of that district to be on hand, and he usually was. He would talk with the more influential Navvies in a friendlier, more casual way than he could in weeks of meetings in his office or in distant trading posts.

In the morning when no outside ceremony was taking place, there was usually another large group—of different makeup—somewhere in the immediate neighborhood. This was centered around a bunch of Navvies, squatting with their heads close together, surrounded by a ring of onlookers lounging in their saddles on horseback. It signified that gambling was in progress with dice, cards, or whatever they might lay their hands on. Navvies have been inveterate gamblers way back to the days of their primitive moccasin and stick games. The moccasin game is very old, and played only in the hogan on winter nights. Two pairs of moccasins are half-buried in sand with a pebble hidden in one, and the two opposing sides take turns in guessing where the pebble is—the counting is very intricate with one hundred two points necessary to win—and one game can easily last all night.

The Indian Bureau regulations did not allow gambling on the reservation, nor were traders allowed to sell playing-cards or dice. But in this case it was wise for the stockman to take no notice, for if he said anything the game would only shift to some out-of-sight spot on the mesa. Better to let them alone where they were and keep a casual eye on what was taking place. The Navaho policemen, if they were there, probably felt the same way. Only Nahtani, the Agent, could not afford to countenance it, and that is why he very seldom attended Entahs except for an hour in a more or less official capacity. In those years, the word of the Agent was law within his jurisdiction, and he had to uphold the dignity of his position. Considerable turquoise and silver jewelry, saddle blankets and even saddles, changed hands among their Navvy owners without any issue being made of it. Because it was a gambling debt and not a family possession, much of this would end up in trading posts as pawn for as much of a loan as the new owner could wangle from the trader. An old trader could spot a gambling debt bracelet almost as soon as the Navvy pushed it across the counter top to pawn.

The so-called "cookhouse" built of cottonwood boughs placed on end in a rectangular shape just high enough to move about in was a busy spot for the distaff side of the Navvy families giving the Entah. Located not far from the Medicine Hogan for convenience in feeding the guests, great quantities of fried bread were made from white flour and baking powder, and fresh corn roasted in the husks. Only the melons needed no preparation as they were eaten outside in the shade of a wagon or some other cool spot. The sheep and goats for the feasting were killed outside the cookhouse. I have seen a large buck sheep dragged to the door, have his throat cut so that the blood from the jugular vein gushed into a large enamel pan, then his head removed and his legs cut off at the knees, all in a matter of minutes. Next, his skin would be pulled off and pegged out on the sand to dry. The meat, cut into small pieces, went into the stew pot, while the succulent ribs were soon sizzling over a bed of red coals. Fresh lamb or goat ribs cooking over pungent cedar ashes has a mouth-watering aroma, particularly Reservation meat where the sheep and goats fed all their life on sage and other flavorful shrubs. I remember once at Shonto when Vic Patrosso, the Manager of El Tovar, looked at our roast on the table and said flatly that he never ate lamb. But as there was no other meat within fifty miles and he was hungry, he gingerly tried a slice. Shortly thereafter we heard him asking to have the roast lamb passed again, saying he had never tasted anything as good as this meat.

Entahs are three-day-and-night affairs and I cannot say that I ever attended a single one straight through from start to finish. That would have been an endurance race, and I much preferred being fresh to enjoy special parts of it. I liked the bustle of activity around the Medicine Hogan on the first day while the rattlestick, or Sacred Stick, is being made and marked with appropriate ceremony. On the second or Camping Out night, the two groups of young Navvies hold their competitive singing bouts, and everyone else lies around the fires under the star-filled black sky. Last but not least in the cold gray of the desert dawn, the hundreds of mounted Navvies move through the sagebrush as the little Queen carrying the Sacred Stick on high, comes galloping with her escorts around the Medicine Hogan.

This last event took place on the morning of the third day, and before noon the ceremonial blackening of the patient's body and that of his assistant was accomplished, to be followed by the Burial of the Scalp at the prescribed few hundred paces from the Medicine Hogan. Probably in the Entahs I witnessed in the 1920's and early 1930's in the primitive north central part of the Navaho reservation, an old Paiute scalp or a piece of one was used; there must have still been enough of these available. None of us was supposed to get very close to it when it was buried and then "killed" again by an arrow or gunshot by some old Navvy hired for this purpose. Somehow the actual "Killing of the Scalp" after its burial did not affect me as much as it should have, perhaps because I was not on the Reservation in the early years of Don Lorenzo Hubbell, Sr. He was quoted as saying that whenever a trader had been killed, there would always be an Entah held shortly afterward.

The Mud Dance which takes place as a sort of finale on the afternoon of the last day, is a release for high spirits in the impromptu humor of the "Mud Clowns." Although the beginning is supposed to be serious with the touching of hands on the patient where he sits with the Medicine Man in front of the Hogan, culminating in his being tossed bodily high in the air then caught and stretched out face downward on the ground to loosen the hold of the evil spirits within which are causing the trouble. To force them out of the body, the Mud Clowns run lightly in their moccasined feet up and down his spine. I never had any doubt that the patient after this treatment would feel much relieved.

The preparations for the Mud Dance were not secret. The ten to twelve men participants would strip to gee-string and moccasins, then head for the mudhole. In Shonto Canyon, a very little digging created a fine mudhole in the wash itself. However, in dry country a wagon would be used to haul a fifty-gallon keg from the nearest spring; the water would then be allowed to trickle out into a hole dug a couple of feet deep in the adobe. The men would gather around and, picking up handfuls of mud, smear their bodies from face to ankle, and the backs of their neighbors. They wore no masks such as the Zuñi or Hopi Mud Clowns do, and their long black hair was twisted tight in the usual chonga knot. After being coated with mud they gathered in the Medicine Hogan to climb out one-by-one from the smokehole, although again they might choose more direct action and approach the patient in front of the Hogan after merely trotting around the brush shelter. After they finished with the patient, there was usually a little boy in the family group who also was tossed in the air, and what boy wouldn't like that? Then the rougher fun began when the Mud Clowns on their horses took out after a reluctant Navvy who was trying his best to escape such treatment. In all of this, the women were left severely alone. Navvy women always seemed to possess great natural dignity and saw to it that the men treated them with bodily respect, at least in public. But I secretly wondered if such a stout old matriarch as Hosteen Tsayutcissi's wife would not have been a match for any Mud Clown who dared to tackle her.

The horse races which took place informally every afternoon at these Entahs of the 1920's were run on any flat stretch of ground, and played their specific role, for the result of these races determined the value of some of their favorite race horses before a sale or swap. A Navvy's race horse was babied, and even if not grain-fed, would be led the many miles to the Entah while the Navvy rode his second-best horse. There were plenty of side bets on these races, besides the incentive of the store shirt or sack of flour given by the trader. All of this was a decade before the necessary horse reduction program due to overgrazed land, when the horse population of the Navaho Reservation was close to 40,000.

An occasional footrace might be announced between three or four men who had been arguing for hours as to who could run faster. Strange to say, it was mostly mature men who competed in this and it drew the most wildly cheering spectators of all. Foot races were most popular among the Navvies who lived around the Hopi Mesas or Moencopie, perhaps from the inspiration of the Hopis who had been known for centuries as fleet and tireless runners. The footrace that I photographed at an Entah near Moencopie Valley was amusing because the one Navvy who refused to strip down to gee-string and bandanna but ran in his rolled up Levis, was the winner. And he was the oldest to boot.

Some writers who have made special trips from afar to see an Entah have written that no Navaho is supposed to sleep during the three nights of this ritual. If this is so, then I've stumbled over many a Navaho wrapped in his Pendleton robe after dark, giving a fine imitation of being sound asleep. And it was not alcoholic stupor, because at that period in the isolated parts of the Western Navaho country, drinking was not yet a problem. Some enterprising Hopi with a truck load of melons would throw on a few cases of soda pop to sell—that was all. We could be thankful for the hundreds of miles of desert trails that separated us from the railroad towns and/or the bootleggers during those Prohibition days.

Too many writers have relied on what one Medicine Man said, interpreted to them through one individual, for most of their information as to the customs and ceremonies. It was easy to be misled by a natural bias of the Navaho, even an unconscious desire to circumvent the prying mind of an outsider. When so recently the Belecanas had been the hated enemy of the Navahos, why should the Navvies suddenly wish to share the innermost secrets of their tribal mythology? Most of us who lived on the Reservation did not blame any Navvy for the evasiveness or double-talk that probably occurred in many instances.

People who had lived for decades among the Navahos knew this. No one was more careful about making definitive statements as to the spiritual or mental complexities of Navaho life than Sam Day or Lorenzo

Hubbell, Jr., who had lived all their lives among them. I preferred to absorb my information piecemeal from listening to such men as these whenever they did express themselves on the subject. Sometimes at Shonto I felt that the Navahos we knew well, often dropped little kernels of truth in a casual way, but never in answer to direct questions. When the spirit of obtaining information to be recorded was apparent, then the opaque veil would fall quickly over those things which could, or should not, be revealed to a Belecana.

76. At an Entah ceremony in the early summer of 1926, west of Moencopie Valley, a group of young Navahos gossip during a break in the festivities.
77. To feed the hundreds of Navaho guests at the Entah, many sheep and goats were slaughtered daily. By the brush cook shelter of cottonwood boughs, the buck's throat has been slit and the bright red blood caught in a blue enamel pan to make blood pudding.
78. This buck sheep is being dragged to the cook shelter for slaughtering and the woman owner directs the proceedings.
79. The buck's carcass has been hung up on tied poles and quartered, ready to be roasted in the stone bake oven. As this Entah was south of Moencopie, the oven was a concession to neighboring Hopi customs.
80. At sunrise on the third day of the Entah, the Little Queen with her escorts gallop in from the distance and ride around the Medicine Hogan. A young girl of the family, or clan, has been chosen for her good looks and dependability in the role of "Little Queen" as she must be responsible for correct handling of the Sacred Stick she carries.
81. Hundreds of mounted Navahos ride through the sage, following the official group that is now leaving the Medicine Hogan soon after sunrise on the third, and last, day of the Entah.
82. Horses and wagons stand outside the oblong arbor of leafy cottonwood boughs which sheltered fires for cooking mutton stew, fried bread and coffee.
83. The door of the cooking shelter was a gathering spot for visiting Navahos.
84. A few headmen of the local Navahos arranged for the first horseraces at this Entah in 1926 by choosing the judges for the event from among Navahos of known integrity.
85. Some Navaho spectators change places and put on a little show of their own.

76

77

78

79

80

81

82

83

84

85

86

86. Long-haired, moccasined Navaho riders in a relay race on the afternoon of the last day of the Entah.
87. Rounding the far turn in a bunch, the bareback riders sway with their horses. They race across the open mesa with no track or post to guide them.
88. Changing horses and saddles in one of the relay races.

87

88

89

90

91

89. Preliminary ride through for the "chicken pull," to let their horses know the spot where their riders will lean from the saddle to grab the raised corner of the buried burlap sack. As Navahos had no chickens, such a substitute was necessary for the game.
90. The Navaho on the gray horse reaches to the ground for the "chicken neck," —the corner of the sack.
91. A footrace was rare among the old time Navahos. The older man—who had refused to strip—won the race with his Levi's rolled to the knees.

92

92. The horse in the center has a "squaw saddle" with a rounded pommel studded with lines of decorative brass tacks, used by the Navaho women.
93. These Navahos are on urgent business at the Medicine Hogan. The two sticks carried by the woman will be used in the ceremony.
94. As there was no nearby waterhole, the mud for the Clowns was made by pouring water from the barrel into a shallow depression. The old man in high moccasins with a row of silver buttons, and old-style white pantaloons split to the knees is in charge.
95. The seven Mud Clowns properly bedaubed, in gee-strings and moccasins, run around the brush shelter to grab the patient sitting in front of the Medicine Hogan.
96. Here they have picked the patient up and hold him above their shoulders, while the Medicine Man, or Hatothli, sits sedately on the ground.
97. Thrown high in the air, the patient shows his exultation by his outstretched arms.
98. The real fun begins when the Mud Clowns want to treat a few of the Navaho spectators. A Clown climbs on his horse to help run one down.

93

94

95

96

97

98

99

99. End of the Mud Clown ceremony is a rousing dance, round-and-round in a circle. The old Navaho at the right with a bandanna tied over his hair enthusiastically dances all by himself.

100. Sand and dust sweep across the ground, filling eyes and nose with the fine alkali powder during a sandstorm that began in the early afternoon. There was no place where man or beast could take shelter.

101. The Entah gathering is engulfed in the full sweep of the afternoon sandstorm. Soon everything, from clothes to food, would be filled with grit.

100

101

102

102. At daybreak on the fourth day the weary Navahos start homeward in all directions of the compass. Another Entah is over and the Enemy slain.

5. *THE HOPI MESAS*

THE HOPI MESAS watch over the fifty miles of undulating desert to the basin of the Little Colorado from where they lie as the southern outcropping of Black Mesa, like giant rocky fingers spread a few miles apart. These three promontories of cream colored sandstone are known as First, Second and Third Mesas. They were named in that order because the eastern one was closest to Keams Canyon Hopi Agency and came therefore to be known as First Mesa.

First Mesa interested me the least of all because it always had been the most accessible to the Agency and the best known to outsiders, particularly at Snake Dance time. But there were specific attractions there, among them Nampeyo, the unsurpassed pottery maker of those years, with her eye for gracious form and her use of very old Hopi designs. There was Tom Pavatea's trading post in Polacca at the foot of the Mesa, where really good Hopi pottery and baskets were handled for the white trade, both wholesale and retail. At a little distance was a squarish house amid bare grounds, the home of one of the unsung authorities on the Hopi country, Mr. A. H. Womack. This man from 1905 on had worked patiently with the Hopi men to find new sources of water around their arid mesas and to develop better what they already were using. His great practical knowledge of topography and stratification was known and respected, and when I first knew him in the 1920's he was a fixture in the country, known locally as the water witch.

Second Mesa was the one I knew best, although this was relatively the most inaccessible. Many of the Hopis from Second Mesa worked, or had worked, for the Fred Harvey Company at Grand Canyon in that little community on the South Rim where I lived for several years. There was Joe Secakuku, and his sisters from Sipaulovi. Jane, the wife of Paul Nichols of Mishongnovi, was a special friend and we had good times together. From Shungopovi there was Hopi Sam, and Jason, and we were as welcome in their homes on the Mesa as they were in our little Park Service quarters at Grand Canyon. The Hopis of Second Mesa knew it whenever I came into their country, because from their villages on high they had an eagle's view of the great open flat below where the twisting ribbon of the approach-road lay. My red car was unique and they could recognize it crawling along the dusty tracks, down into the cross-washes, and up again with a larger dust cloud. By the time I had parked at Toreva and laboriously climbed the foot-trail, some of them would be waiting to greet me.

The few tourists of those years usually bypassed Second Mesa as they struggled westward from Walpi across the Polacca, Wepo, and Oraibi Washes respectively, to New Oraibi and thence down to Winslow and civilization. The three villages perched on top were the place to see the unspoiled Hopi life of that era. Their Snake Dance ceremony always fell on a later date than Walpi's, so that it could be enjoyed in peace and quiet with perhaps Lorenzo Hubbell, Jr. and the Indian Agent from Keams Canyon as the only non-Hopi spectators. Even they might not climb up that long, rocky trail to Shongopovi for their Snake Dance, because in those years only a wagon could traverse the route across the mesa from the north to this very old village. Shongopovi was ancient and a very large pueblo when the Spaniards first came into the country, establishing a mission there as well as at Awatovi but making Sipaulovi and Mishongnovi only *visitas*. It was the brave Franciscan Friar at Shongopovi who willingly gave his life in the great Pueblo Rebellion of 1680.

I knew very little about Hotevilla, although the road from Blue Canyon to Oraibi passed close by it. It was a new village created in the fall of 1906 when a defeated faction split off from Old Oraibi. The Hotevillans wished to be let alone and were the followers of an old fanatic, Youkeeoma. In those days they were called the Hostiles, but now that they have become reconciled to modern ways they are called Conservatives.

The road was a rocky track that dropped off the mesa to the north of the Hotevilla cornfields and peach trees under the rim, and then angled west for the big Dinnehbito Wash crossing. After this, the road went north over the mesa until descending into Blue Canyon, which was itself a very long gash of brilliantly colored rock strata in the heart of Black Mesa. A wash, and incidentally the road, wandered between walls of white rock in what seemed an aimless way, but it was the only direct north-south route in this whole central part of the Western Navaho Reservation. It was much used by Navahos, traders, and Indian Bureau employees up through the 1930's.

One spur of Blue Canyon can be seen today on a short detour from the Howell Mesa road: Coal Canyon, not far from Moencopie, where layers of black coal appear among the red and white sandstone formations. This coal was of good quality and the Hopis hauled it under contract for years to Tuba for the operation of the steam plant in the Agency.

Oraibi, the Third Mesa, to me meant Lorenzo Hubbell, Jr., because his home and trading post in New Oraibi under the hill was always a first stopping place. In warm weather we camped in the deserted day school yard where there was a water hydrant, but ate breakfast with Lorenzo at the big round table in his kitchen. Giant cups of coffee, with fried eggs and green chili comprised the usual breakfast. And if the heap of green chili was not large enough to completely submerge the fried eggs, I heard about it promptly and explicity from Lorenzo. Bread and bacon were afterthoughts, and glasses of water were never put on the table. Water took up space the stomach needed for coffee.

Lorenzo was a large man with dark brown hair and a rather fleshy face. His voice was very soft and husky; his slow way of speaking was well suited to the Hopi and Navaho trade. He was punctilious in greeting his callers in their own language, whether it was Hopi, Navaho, Spanish, or English, as he was fluent in all four. Sometimes I spent the whole day in his dim, inner office where he sat behind his desk, just watching him handle the various personalities and races who had business with him. His Navaho name was Nahkai-tso, Large Mexican, and Lorenzo was justly proud of his Mexican ancestry because his grandfather Hubbell's wife came of a wealthy and prominent family of Chihuahua, Mexico. And Don Lorenzo, Sr., in his turn, married a girl of Spanish blood from New Mexico who, until her dying day, refused to use other than the Spanish language. At least that is what a couple of her children told me. So the rippling Spanish of Nahkai-tso was his first love and his birthright, but one might say that his second love was the Navaho language which he had also learned as a child.

On about the third visit that Mike and I made to Lorenzo, Jr. at Oraibi, he kept leading the talk around to racial backgrounds and languages. Finally I sensed what he was driving at—Mike's slender build with his regular features and black hair gave a very definite impression of his belonging to the Spanish-speaking group in the Southwest. But Mike continued to speak in generalities and avoided any direct personal reference, as these were the years when the Ku Klux Klan was flourishing and those of certain groups had learned to be reticent. At last Lorenzo, Jr. could stand it no longer and asked directly if he were not of Spanish background. Mike knew the time had come to be equally honest and he said quietly, looking him in the eyes, that he did not have one whit of Spanish about him as he was just plain Jewish; his parents had emigrated from Poland when it was under Russia and pogroms were annual events. Poor Lorenzo, Jr., felt terrible as we could see and apologized, saying he had never dreamed that Mike was other than Spanish-speaking but afraid to say so and therefore he had wanted to help him out. Then with his usual tact he added that he and Mike had a great deal in common as they both could understand the feelings of the minority groups in the Southwest.

Lorenzo Hubbell, Jr., was a trader of traders. He would greet a Navvy who came from a distance with a long hand-clasp, like a lost brother. If he had brought in wool with him, Lorenzo would then give him a bit of an edge over the top price it was bringing elsewhere. Naturally the Navvy would be delighted and the sum would be jotted on a trade slip—the ubiquitous brown paper bag in most trading posts. No, Nahkai-tso never forgot his old friends. Then ever so gently he would remind the Navvy of a debt owed these many years, perhaps because of forgetfulness? What customer could resist such diplomacy. And after this old debt had been duly subtracted from the trade slip, then the remaining sum could be traded out with the clerks in the trading post.

This was an enjoyable matter of hours while each purchase—ten cents or ten dollars—was marked off the slip. The sacks of flour and sugar, the canned goods, new pails or coffee pots, topped with yard goods in bright colored folds, would be stacked and ready to be carried out to the wagon. Some of the women would be wearing brilliant-hued Pendleton robes selected from the piles on the trading post shelf. These blankets have been manufactured for years in Pendleton, Oregon, of pure virgin wool from the flocks of fine sheep in that part of the country. Primarily they were made for the Navaho trade, and every trading post in or near the Reservation had to stock them. Navvies preferred Pendleton blankets above any other. Those with wool fringes were called shawls, and those without, robes. A straight-line pattern of Pendleton shawls and blankets was designated "Beaver State," and these were one dollar more retail. We Belecanas living in the Southwest used them on our beds and couches, and over the seats of cars in winter.

When a Navaho family was finally loaded up for the two- or three-day journey home, Lorenzo would appear to add a small gift for some absent member of the family whom he remembered. Each year some Navahos would drive their wagonloads of wool around nearby traders and across miles of rough country, right to the door of Nahkai-tso at New Oraibi. Rival traders used to say that "old debts" were frequently a figment of Lorenzo's imagination, simply because he overpaid them for their wool. Be that as it may, the Navvies were satisfied. It was well known that he would hold their pawn for years and pay good prices for their rugs if he knew a family well. He told me that he believed in the eventual worth of these Navaho rugs, even though in Depression Years the traders were overloaded with them. Time has proved him right.

In later years, during springtime at Shonto when some Navvy lugged his first Pendleton of wool—forty pounds perhaps, carried in a Pendleton robe folded lengthwise and sewed together with yucca strips so it would hang across the back of a horse—we would be told how much per pound Nahkai-tso was paying. That was as sure as the first robin, inasmuch as we were the closest post to the north of Hubbell's own Piñon Trading Post. "Closest" in this case meant an arduous fifty miles or more, even on horseback, over the steep north face of Black Mesa and then across Blue Canyon (Boko Dot-klish) and Dinnehbito Wash. Long Salt lived in this country between us and Hubbell, and in some years he brought to us at Shonto his three sacks of wool—the nine-foot long regulation wool sacks that hold from 300 to 350 pounds of light Navaho wool. We could only guess that he owed too much just then to Nahkai-tso, as his pawn with us was not heavy.

Harry and I did much wholesale business with Lorenzo, and our relations were always of the best. He knew that I felt a kindred spirit with the Navaho people, even as he, to a greater extent, had always been one of them. He knew we were at Shonto not only to make our living, but because we liked being among Navahos and a part of the Reservation life. The knowledge Nahkai-tso had of the Navahos was so deep and profound that it could not lightly be written down or told to outsiders. The superficial students of the Navaho have been the ones to write prolifically of Navaho customs and traits, and they are soon given the label of being "an authority on the Navahos" by the reading public. But with Lorenzo it was different, and with the possible exception of Sam Day, no one had a more fundamental inner grasp of Navaho thought, religion, and ritual of daily life. Much of this died with him.

Under the tip of Second Mesa below Mishongnovi is the landmark known as Corn Rock because it resembles two huge ears of corn standing on end. It is a good place to sit and breathe the thin air that comes across the desert from the San Francisco Peaks, blue on the horizon to the southwest. When one looks down at the valley just beneath, the cornfields are in irregular patches with the hills of green cornstalks as tiny polka-dots, and the occasional burro with his bulky load moving slowly like a tiny black beetle. Some of these burros have had their long ears cut off short, because they were caught stealing corn and must be punished for life. So the Hopis said.

On the Mesas there are some spots very sacred to the Hopi people. Each village has its own location for burials, for certain shrines such as that of the solstice, and for the burying ground of the eagles used by certain clans in ceremonies. No paths lead to these spots, and they are quite unobtrusive. I respected these private and sacred symbols of the Hopi faith. A prayerstick or *baho,* decorated with a few inches of handwoven white cotton cord holding a fluff of eagle breast feather, may be placed with a prayer in front of a shrine (perhaps Spider Woman) in the same spirit that one of us lights a candle in church. Whenever I saw high in the Mesa rim a crevice heaped full of stones with a broken pottery bowl or an old enameled pan on top, I felt the same reverence as for a marble tomb in the midst of sweeping green lawns. After their life under the open sky in the heart of this land of their ancestors, what a perfect place it was for the Hopis to rest eternally.

Sipaulovi, that gem of an old Hopi village, sat on its own rock pyramid just to the north of Mishongnovi. The rectangular plaza, surrounded by one- and two-story houses, filled the level space on top. Jane Nichols' single-story house faced south and nearby at the northwest corner of the plaza was a deep and narrow passageway between two houses. It was completely covered with cedar poles and brush, over which was a small terrace and storage with a tiny, high window. Through this passageway, there was only the tremendous sweep of sky to be seen and far below, the pastel tones of the distant desert. I much preferred this entrance of the plaza at Sipaulovi to the much-photographed Last House at Walpi, which it resembled. Carl Oscar Borg's watercolor of this Walpi house was given me as a present at Grand Canyon in 1925, and is now in the Museum of Northern Arizona in Flagstaff.

To the north and east of the village, opposite the main approach trails, were little paths leading down under ledges of rock. Each family was assigned a certain location which was used carefully, as these spots were the outdoor toilets of those days. There was not as yet a privy in the Mesa villages. I always went to the one assigned to Jane's house. Corn cobs, the first toilet paper, were much in evidence, and there was never any offensive odor as the sun and wind of that dry mesa land swept over the ledges, not to mention the energetic chickens. When it was green corn season, these chickens really had a picnic and scavenging buzzards did their bit also, to be followed by the heavy summer rains that washed the ledges bare. Thirty years later with more civilization has come a rash of privies that cover the rocky slopes in front of Sipaulovi and Mishongnovi. The doors are kept shut and padlocked, and I wondered if the keys ever were lost. Anyway they are a mark of progress, presumably.

In October of 1927 Jane Nichols and I drove over from Grand Canyon to stay in her house at Sipaulovi, because she wanted to see the Lalakonti, Woman's Basket Dance, at Mishongnovi in which her husband's sisters would be taking part. In the morning we walked the mile by trail between the villages in the cool, dry air and arrived at the Mishongnovi plaza just as the group of women participants walked past to take up their positions in line. Each carried in her hands a Second Mesa coiled basketry plaque, differing in size, color and pattern. The women wore cotton housedresses under their fringed, brightly colored shawls of thin wool; although a few of the conservative ones did wear the ancient Hopi dress of two lengths of black handwoven wool with narrow red borders, worn with one shoulder bare, and belted around the middle with a red, handwoven sash. Over this was worn a ceremonial white cotton shawl with a wide band at top and bottom of an embroidery-type pattern woven into the woof with black and red or green wool. The Hopi men wove the white shawls on wide, upright looms in a tight weave of diagonal or diamond design. This was men's work, often done in the kivas, and women took no part in it. Their crafts were basketry and pottery. Most of the women wore buckskin moccasins and leggings of white doeskin wound round and round to the knees. I used to think that if a rattler ever made the mistake of striking at this arrangement he would end up as a sadder and wiser snake.

For the first part of the ceremony, the women formed an elongated circle open at one end, with a half dozen little girls there. Every woman held her plaque upright in front of her so that it showed to best advantage, while the songs were being chanted. A few plaques had the symbolic kachina design, but more had the corn or the butterfly pattern. One that caught my attention had the Paiute-Navaho wedding basket design, which is rarely done by the basket weavers of Second Mesa.

Two maidens were beautifully costumed in the white embroidered ceremonial shawls, and around their necks were thick strings of shell wampum, turquoise, and coral. They must have borrowed every single necklace owned by their family. But the distinguishing mark of the Lalakonti ceremony is the single, large curved horn of pure turquoise blue worn over the left ear. This is balanced by a pinwheel arrangement of feathers on the opposite side, and the whole headdress is topped by feathers, which looked to me like eagle tail feathers. It was not a solemn dance and all the women and girls seemed to enjoy themselves immensely. When the time came for the giving away of their plaques, a big crowd of men and young boys gathered in the plaza. Because these plaques would be thrown high in the air in all directions, to be caught by the nimble or lucky ones, this was the high spot of the whole ceremony for the small fry. The dance lasted for most of the day with time off for a meal, and judging by the Hopi men lining the rooftops they liked the unusual experience of being spectators while the women and girls performed the rites.

In Jane's house, like the others around the plaza in those years, there were no beds, tables, or chairs. A couple of low wooden stools and a stone banquette on one side of the room sufficed. The walls were white, and the floors were of clean, hard-packed adobe, with no clutter of possessions anywhere. Suspended from the ceiling near a wall was a long, cedar pole, upon which was hung the family shawls and blankets, and by the open hearth stood a few well-used cooking pots. The house had a separate storage room for corn, pumpkins, dried squash strips, seeds, and other foods always kept in reserve by the thrifty Hopi.

All the family slept on the floor on sheepskins of long, thick wool, which were not only warm but quite soft. Every morning these sheepskins were carried outside, shaken thoroughly, and hung in the sun for a couple of hours. Later they were rolled with skin side out and stacked in a corner of the room. Being tall, I needed the skin from a large buck sheep, otherwise I would be half on the hard mud floor, so Jane found a very large black one for me and I slept next to her on the floor of the main room. Others were stretched out around us for men, women, and children, and we were wise to have chosen a spot away from the front door traffic area or we would have been stepped over all night long. One night after settling on my sheepskin I saw a last flame from the fireplace reflected from the eyeballs of a freshly killed goat's head, reposing a couple of feet away. In the gloom I had not noticed it when I picked my sleeping site.

When I stayed with Jane for the Nimán Kachina Dance of 1927, the big thunderheads were beginning to pile high above the horizon with their promise of rain for the Hopi crops of corn, squash, and melons. The small children of Sipaulovi felt this electric excitement in the air, while the older women padded barefoot in and out of their houses with smiling faces, as they carried woven trays heaped with cornmeal or squash blossoms which are splendid in mutton stew. The smell of roasting or boiling meat was in the air, and doubtless the carcass of that buck whose head had rested close to me all night, was filling several pots and adding his bit to the general aroma.

103

103. At Old Oraibi, in 1927, Flora, a granddaughter of the Chief, Tawaquaptewa, gave me her finished Kachina plaque, and the one being woven, to hold. The desert wind was blowing so hard I could scarcely hold the plaques steady.

104. Old road running north through Blue Canyon, 1927. This was the only route between the Hopi Mesas and Red Lake on the road to Navaho Mountain or Kayenta.

105. The road winds along a side wash down in Blue Canyon.

106. The bluish white cliffs almost meet in this spot where the Buick stands in the road in 1926. The drought of the 1930's caused such erosion here that it became impassable.

107. A bit further along, the canyon widened and it was easy to follow the sandy bed of the wash.

104

105

106

107

108

109

110

108. From Blue Canyon on the north the road came down to this crossing of Dinnehbitoh Wash. Because of its long drainage this wash could remain "up" for days when no car would dare attempt a crossing. It was almost dry when I took this picture in 1927 on my way to Oraibi.
109. This blow sand was a problem in the fields below the western edge of Third Mesa near Hotevilla, which had been founded in 1907 by a dissident faction from old Oraibi called "Hostiles." 1928.
110. Looking down on the Hopi corn patches under Hotevilla from the edge of the Mesa. Erosion control has been started in the small wash at the right. In the middle distance is the Dinnehbitoh Wash. 1928.

111

112

113

111. At the southern edge of Third Mesa, looking north at ruins of Old Oraibi. These houses were left vacant in 1907 when their Hopi owners departed to form their own new pueblos of Hotevilla and Bacabi farther back on the Mesa.
112. Old Oraibi from the south, in 1926, showing vacated and semi-demolished homes of the "Hostiles." The handhewn doors and frames were placed in their new rock houses in Hotevilla.
113. The steps up to the house in Old Oraibi, with Flora holding her baby girl. Summer 1927.

114

115

114. Some homes in Old Oraibi in 1926 where inhabitants belong to the "Friendlies" faction under Chief Tawaquaptewa.
115. Friends of mine, and relatives of Jason's, at Shungopovi on Second Mesa asked me to take this picture of their family group: Eunice and Shirley with their little children, another brother and sister, and their parents. Their house shows very old construction in its rock apertures and cedar vigas. Their dress was typical of this in-between period of the early 1920's.
116. Under Third Mesa in New Oraibi was this unpretentious warehouse of mud and poles belonging to the trading post of Lorenzo Hubbell, Jr. Inside were stacks of beautiful Navaho rugs, tens of thousands of pounds of them. Outside are seen the usual trading post scales and the ubiquitous soda pop boxes. The visitor's wardrobe trunk looks sadly out of place.
117. East of Third Mesa was the treacherous Oraibi Wash which had to be crossed to reach Second and First Mesas and the agency at Keams Canyon. I didn't quite make it this time, in 1927. Norma sat in the car while Jason walked to get help.
118. The main road winds through the Hopi cornfields south of Second Mesa. 1926.
119. Second Mesa is in the distance, with Sipaulovi on the center pyramid of rocky ledges. This was the main road between all the Hopi Mesas and their Keams Canyon Agency in 1926.
120. Jason and Norma Honanie going down the trail from Shungopovi to where my car was parked at the bottom. They were taking back Hopi clothes, green corn and melons, to Grand Canyon.
121. Shirley and his wife Eunice from Shungopovi wore their best clothes when visiting at Grand Canyon, in contrast to those worn at home in this same year of 1926. Norma's baby, Laverne, is in my lap.
122. Two main streets in Shungopovi and a Hopi man that Jason said was one hundred years old. In 1680 the people killed their Franciscan friar in the general rebellion there.
123. Numerous broad stone stairways led to the upper levels of this Shungopovi street in 1926. Ladders and entrances through the roofs were no longer necessary for protection.
124. The square kiva with a ladder through the roof remained true to custom. The numerous wagons at the right testify to the reliance on an agricultural economy in 1926.
125. A Hopi grave on the edge of the mesa with pottery bowl and enamel pan which had held nourishment for the departing soul. 1926.
126. I climb the trail to Shungopovi ahead of one of Jason's nephews, who could have taken it at a dead run.
127. Hopis from Shungopovi with laden burros going down to work in the fields under Second Mesa.
128. Wagon road below Mishongnovi with a four-horse team on the way down to Toreva.
129. Near Toreva a Hopi irrigated his tiny garden by lifting bucket after bucket of water into a rock tunnel that sloped in that direction.
130. Peach trees blooming near a spring at the foot of Second Mesa. 1926.
131. At the tip of Second Mesa, under Mishongnovi, is the well-known landmark of Corn Rock which looks like two ears of corn standing on end. 1927.

116

117

118

119

120

121

122

123

124

125

126

127

128

129

130

131

132

132. Snake and Antelope kivas on the southwestern edge of Mishongnovi.
133. Early on an October morning in 1927, these Hopi women and little girls of Mishongnovi hurried with coiled plaques in hand to begin their Basket Dance in the plaza.
134. Hopi plaid shawls over gingham dresses were interspersed with the traditional handwoven white cotton mantles with their borders of black, red, and green wool for the Basket Dance at Mishongnovi in October 1927.
135. The housetops held plenty of men spectators, and small boys swarmed in the plaza to catch coiled plaques thrown in the air as gifts to the people.
136. Beautiful headdresses of eagle feathers and one turquoise-blue horn at the left ear were worn by two young women. These maidens are referred to as the Lalahkonti.

133

134

135

136

137

138

139

137. This is still a serious part of the ceremony, but the Hopi man at the left dances a few impromptu steps of his own. The men seemed to enjoy this woman's dance as it is customarily they who dance and the women who watch.
138. A few Hopis in lower Mishongnovi hurry to be at the kiva when the runner arrives. The Hopi boy in white underwear had run up the mesa trail from the distant valley. 1926.
139. In the summer of 1927, these Hopis were running as part of a ceremony under the direction of the Dance Priest (in plaid cotton pantaloons and dark shirt) on the mesa top under Mishongnovi.

140

140. A Hopi shrine for the solstice with eagle feathers tied to slender reeds by twisted white cotton cords. The feathers fluttered continuously in the air of the high mesa. The reed sticks were about three feet high and usually had four feathers on each. 1927.

141. A boy from Second Mesa gazes at the Spider Woman Shrine where *bahohs* lean against the rocks and dead sagebrush. These *bahohs* are prayersticks made from two short sticks wrapped with handwoven white cotton cord and a downy eagle feather attached. 1926.

142. This deep rock shelter was said to be the home of the Masau Kachina, who may appear at any time of the year among the Hopi Mesas as he does not live in the San Francisco Peaks with the other Kachinas. 1926.

141

142

143

144

145

143. Sipaulovi plaza with the *kisi* in place for the Snake Dance. The Hopi child has been sent to chase away the inquisitive rooster who is eyeing the *kisi* at the right—a shelter of erect cottonwood boughs with thick green leaves. Under it is a sunken receptacle in which snakes are placed during the public part of the Snake Dance ceremony. 1926.

144. A view showing Jane Nichols' house at the north end of Sipaulovi plaza. Many ladders were then in use. On the day of the Snake Dance my camera was wrapped up in my car as I did not wish to offend my Hopi friends. 1926.

145. High on the edge of Second Mesa was this Hopi shrine with its dozens of *bahohs* carrying fluffy white eagle feathers. One of the two small sticks in each bundle is notched at the end. 1927.

CHIEF JOE SECAKUKU
HOPI INDIAN (YELLOWFEET)
INDIAN CURIOS
WELCOME

146

147

146. Joe Secakuku's first store at Canyon Diablo, where the then rough and rocky Highway 66 made two right-angle turns over a narrow bridge. Cheap painted gourds hung in one window, but the other was filled with beautiful examples of prehistoric Pueblo I and II pottery. Joe Secakuku and Mike Harrison are in the doorway. 1926.

147. At Canyon Diablo store in 1926 with Harry "Indian" Miller at left—he had given me his bobcat to hold—and Joe Secakuku on the right. Miller was an Apache. He later moved his "zoo" on Highway 66 to Painted Cave near Lupton.

148

149

148. Looking south from the doorway of Jane Secakuku Nichols' house in Sipaulovi.
149. The entrance to Sipaulovi plaza at northwest corner. 1926.

150

151

150. A neighbor of Jane Nichols on Sipaulovi plaza asked me to take her picture with her son. 1927.
151. Sipaulovi clings to its own rounded pyramid of rock. The rash of outhouses on its slopes had not yet appeared in 1926.

The night before the final day of the week-long ceremony, Jane said we must all go to bed early, and I noticed that our room was full and that they closed the solid wooden front door. This was because sometime during the night the Kachinas would visit the plaza without their masks and nobody was supposed to see them. Only the old man, the Kachina Father appointed for that year, would be there to welcome them. After I was half asleep, maybe around midnight, they came. Jane punched me in case I had not heard, but neither of us budged from our sheepskins. As the Kachinas moved about the plaza in groups chanting their songs ever so softly, the sound of their rattles and the swish, swish of moccasined feet seeped through the thick door in little spurts of sound. Soon it was quiet again and we all went to sleep.

Everyone in our room was up at the first grey light of day, with sheepskins stacked, and coffee was drunk quickly from the few enamel cups passed around. Although the coffee had that peculiar flavor of Arbuckle's, it was strong and plenty hot for the coffee pot sat right on the cedar coals. Jane whispered to me, "They come now. Let's go." So I followed her through the open passageway to the top of the trail, not forgetting to pick up my Kodak. The sun had not yet topped the distant mesa rim on the eastern horizon, and the valley was still cloaked in the muted tones of grey and brown. Suddenly little figures in white, green, and red appeared far below us under a rocky cliff, and in single file began to move swiftly up the trail. I struggled to do the best I could with the camera, thinking of the moving objects and the lack of sunlight, with my F7.7 lens and no tripod.

A tall Nimán Kachina, his waist encircled with spruce boughs, led the line, flanked by the Kachina Priest and the Kachina Father. Then came more of the Kachinas in their bright yellow and blue masks, topped with the high feathered headdress of the conventional Nimán Kachina costume. Their arms were filled with green cornstalks, melons, and pumpkins, and their silver *ketohs* (bow-guards) shone against the brown skin. A half dozen Kachina Mannas followed the others up the trail. These Mannas wore the ancient ceremonial woman's dress with the embroidered shawls of white cotton, and even masks with head-covering to simulate expertly the whorls or squash-blossom hair dress of a Hopi maiden. Only their uncovered hands and the unusually large moccasined feet gave away the fact that they were men.

Because the Kachina Priest was blessing each Kachina and Kachina Manna with a pinch of sacred meal before he entered the plaza, there was a little wait in line. This was lucky for me as I could photograph close up, even if it did happen to be the backs of some. Once in the plaza, they formed in two parallel lines after depositing their cornstalks in various piles with much rustling. The chanting began as usual, low and then gradually louder, to the accompaniment of the brown gourd rattles, while the sides of the Sipaulovi plaza gradually filled with the local Hopi family groups from white-haired ancients to babies in arms.

When the time came to give away the presents, the Kachinas went singly or in pairs to the four sides of the plaza so as not to overlook anyone. The gifts for the children were presented with quiet dignity, and the small brown faces broke into happy smiles at such attention from these mystical Kachina beings. A little girl being especially favored might receive one of the flat, simplified replicas of a Kachina that had been carefully made by one of her relatives—perhaps a clan great uncle.

Then the Kachinas and Kachina Mannas walked down to their cave to rest, after which dishes of food on woven plaques were carried down the trail to them. The families repaired to their own homes to eat copiously of mutton stew with hominy, *pikami*—the tasty dish of cornmeal stewed with sprouted grain, and raised white flour rolls. Trays of the special red, blue, or white corn *piki* were carried on handwoven Second Mesa plaques into other homes as gifts. *Piki* takes time and patience to make: grinding by hand of dried corn into fine meal on the metates; then the spreading of watery batter in two installments to form a wafer-thin layer on a flat, hot stone. When this batter curls at the edges and loosens from the stone, it must be quickly picked up and folded into a long, tight roll. This is repeated again and again until the *piki* rolls can be stacked high enough to fill a plaque. The pure corn flavor of *piki* stick rolls is truly delicious, and the crisp texture is enticing to tongue and fingers alike as the rolls are eaten held in one hand.

Jane and I were starved, and dipped into the large pot of mutton stew with our fingers along with the members of the family. The pot had been placed in the center of a mat on the floor around which we were all seated. Although there were some large spoons available, the trick was to seize a protruding piece of meat so as not to get burned and transfer it quickly to a bit of bread and then into one's mouth. After this feast I stretched out in the shade of the house awhile with a bandanna to hide my face from any pestiferous fly. It was peaceful and quiet as the soft Hopi voices rose and fell within the houses.

With the coming of afternoon, the Kachinas returned. This time in the group there were two young Hopi brides, girls who had married within the last year. Jane wanted to see this part for a niece of hers was one of the brides. The girls knelt for quite a part of the ceremony, and the Kachina Priest passed along the line giving them the Sacred Pollen blessing. When the final chant was finished as the sun dropped low, the Kachinas walked briskly out of the plaza in a single file on their way to the Kachina cave where they discarded their blue spruce boughs. Later they went to the kiva. But no Kachina figure would be seen again in Sipaulovi until after the winter solstice when the cycle of Kachina dances would begin once more.

Very early the following morning there was another rite to be fulfilled: the young captive eagle who had looked out so proudly from his perch on our neighboring roof-top had to be sacrificed. The Kachina Clan member to whom he belonged threw a blanket over the eagle and squeezed his throat, quickly and mercifully, so that his spirit might be freed to go home. After ceremoniously being plucked of all feathers while surrounded with tiny plaques, his body was buried near the village in the clan's private burying-ground for eagles.

152. At first grey light of dawn, the Kachinas have left their cave and are coming up the trail to Sipaulovi behind two priests. The last day of the "Home Dance" of the Nimán Kachinas had begun on July 30, 1927.

153. On the roof of this house was the captive eagle who was nurtured until the end of the Nimán Kachina Dance when he would be ceremoniously sacrificed to carry the message back to the Kachinas' home in the San Francisco Peaks. Held by a rawhide thong on one leg, his sheltered perch was on a second floor balcony. 1927.

154. The lead Kachina walks swiftly with only spruce boughs and a gourd in his hands, while behind him are others moving at a slower pace with arms full of green cornstalks and melons.

152

153

154

155

155. Standing on the trail just below the northeast entrance to Sipaulovi plaza, a Kachina Manna—a man dressed in woman's clothes—looks critically at me and my camera through the eye slits in his deerskin mask.

156. A Nimán Kachina wearing around his neck and swinging from his hip the distinguishing mark of this costume—the blue spruce boughs from Black Mesa.

157. While the Kachinas wait in line, the boughs of blue spruce attached to their waists wave gently at the slightest movement. A red fox skin is hung at the back.

158. The Kachina Mannas are Hopi men in head masks with artificial whorls of hair, women's handwoven shawls over black woolen mantas, and high doeskin moccasins. They wait to enter the plaza where each is blessed and touched with sacred corn pollen by the Dance Priest.

156

157

158

159

160

161

159. Armloads of corn have been thrown to the ground in the plaza and lines are forming as directed for the first chants. The Dance Priest is at the head of the line of Mannas, each of whom holds a large hollowed gourd. The Clan Priest stands at the left.
160. Clan Priest and Dance Priest stand side by side at the left. Both lines of Kachinas and Mannas are moving into position.
161. Here the Mannas have reversed positions as the Dance Priest and Clan Priest move along the line giving their blessing again with a pinch of sacred pollen.
162. The Mannas kneel down while the Dance Priest goes along the line of standing Kachinas touching each with sacred pollen.
163. Cornstalks have been pulled to the sides and distributed to the spectators—the families of Sipaulovi. I was the only non-resident.
164. One Nimán Kachina moves alone in majesty across the plaza to the fortunate recipient of his gifts.

162

163

164

165

165. Four Nimán Kachinas go their respective ways across the plaza with their gifts for the children of their families and friends.
166. The spectators—old men, women, and children of Sipaulovi—await with pleasure as the Kachina stoops to distribute his armload of gifts.
167. Towards high noon, lines form again, with the Mannas still gripping large pumpkin gourds. The white-haired Dance Priest, in Hopi dance kilt with store checked shirt superimposed, is still directing the chants.

166

167

168

168. Seven Kachina Mannas holding large pumpkin gourds and a whisk of spruce, stand in front line.
169. The black and white wooly sheep pelts at the right hand corner are for the Mannas to kneel upon. The Dance Priest is still dispensing the sacred pollen from his small medicine pouch.
170. The Kachinas turn to form a solid front, while five of the Mannas kneel facing them. At the end of the kneeling row are two small figures. These are girls—brides of the last year—who are to be blessed in this part of the ceremony. One of these was a niece of Jane Secakuku Nichols.

169

170

171

172

171. A few of the old and young from Sipaulovi watch the Kachinas in a new grouping in one corner of the plaza. The Clan Priest and the Dance Priest are making their rounds.
172. The line of Kachinas leaving the Sipaulovi plaza to return to their cave, followed by the Mannas.
173. Piles of discarded blue spruce boughs could be seen piled at the entrance of the Kachinas' Cave after the dance was over. Sipaulovi, 1927.

173

6. *NAVAHO MOUNTAIN*

It was April of 1926 at Grand Canyon when the Fred Harvey Transportation Company, sent one of their cars on a scout trip to Rainbow Arch where Ray Williams, the Santa Fe Railroad photographer, was to take photographs for a brochure. Several of their special drivers also went in the car to familiarize themselves with the Navaho Mountain country, and this official party kindly let Mike Harrison and me tag along in our red Buick.

Even though we left the Canyon very early in the morning, the spring thaw was in progress and we fought mud all the way to Coconino Basin. Curly Ennis drove the lead car to break trail and I followed in his ruts. Once near Rain Tank he was sliding broadside into a narrow cattle guard fence crossing, but at the last second he straightened out and I did the same behind him, holding my breath. He said afterward that he "sure came near to widenin' that gate." As we dropped down the Navahopi road over Waterloo Hill in low gear, the air became warm enough for us to peel off our top layer of sweaters. Checking in at Cameron with Hubert Richardson who owned Rainbow Lodge, we were told to keep on going as they were expecting our party up there tonight.

Where we had fought spring mud at the Canyon, we now fought spring blow-sand around Tuba and it was heavy pulling all the way. It was early afternoon when we reached Red Lake Trading Post (Tonalea) where our cars created much excitement. Red Lake was a Babbitt Bros. trading post twenty-five miles east of Tuba, halfway down the slope of a sandy mesa above what was a lake in wet years and a dry waste in others, which was most of the time. It was a bare, unattractive location that only rattlesnakes must have loved because they multiplied and thrived there. The O'Farrells used to kill them in the warehouse and as they slithered past the open door of the trading post, all as part of the day's work. Johnny's wife would use the boiled flesh for sandwiches; it looked and tasted like tuna. Many a traveler gagged a bit after eating a delicious tuna sandwich when he was told that it was freshly killed and boiled rattlesnake meat. Cora O'Farrell used to thread the spinal column before boiling it clean to make attractive, articulated bone necklaces. Although Red Lake and Begashibito (Cow Springs) had rattlesnakes galore, Shonto did not have them. As to why, not even the Navvies knew, but apparently no self-respecting rattlesnake would even allow himself to be caught dead in Shonto canyon. Even snakes have their preferences. Red Lake was known far and wide as a "dry post," and one of Johnny O'Farrell's famous stories was how he had to take a bath, scrub the kitchen floor and wash his clothes, all with one bucket of water.

I bought a length of turquoise-blue cotton plush, 2½ yards for $7.50, for a Navaho blouse which the O'Farrells said a Navvy woman would make by hand in the three days before our return. Then we manned the cars and took off east down the trail which I was soon to know by heart, winter or summer, day or night. The best thing about Red Lake was the view to the east and north where the southern rim of White Mesa looked like cornstarch above the undulating miles of green-blue sagebrush. The Elephant's Feet with their well-delineated toes flanked the narrow tracks of the road to Kayenta, with the stern brow of Black Mesa in the distance. On this trip the three Harvey drivers in Curly's car had their rifles across their knees taking pot shots at jack-rabbits. But Curly was trying to make time, at a twenty-five mile-per-hour clip, near the Elephant's Feet when he plunged into a tiny cross-wash, throwing men and rifles into the air. Coming along behind, Mike and I could see daylight between the three of them and the seat, while only the steering wheel kept Curly down. This warning gave me the extra moment needed to step on the brakes and save the car springs.

When we reached the higher altitude again in the rock country between the Navaho and Paiute Canyons, I began to tire and Billy Bass drove for me. There was no Inscription House post then and as we kept going north we were too busy following the dim tracks over the endless rock beds to look at much scenery. A daub of white paint on the rocks at crucial spots (put there by Richardson) or dim scratches from the steel rims of Navvy wagon wheels, were the only markers to tell us where the road was. Once or twice Curly's car would stop and slowly back up because he had reached a dead end and was once more looking for the road. All this was above the seven-thousand-foot level and it was beginning to get dark. We pulled on our top layer of sweaters once more.

It was long after dark when, stiff and tired, we finally arrived at Rainbow Lodge high on the shoulder of Navaho Mountain. The cars were left among the cedars and we trooped in to eat the hot food that Susie Richardson was keeping on the stove for us. We were to start with our pack mules early in the morning, one extra mule being assigned to

Williams for his heavy cameras and attendant equipment. We had to go over the old trail and traverse the extremely narrow Redbud Pass, which only a few years later was eliminated by some of the first Navaho CCC projects. We rode steadily all day and were rewarded by our first glimpse of the arch of Rainbow Bridge in the warm reddish light of the low sun. Whenever Williams stopped to photograph and set up his view camera on a tripod, I stood behind him and took the same shot with my postcard-size Kodak. He got a real kick out of this, and kindly suggested the best exposure for me to use. In gratitude I helped him carry some of his bulky equipment. It was a thrill to see the arch grow larger as we progressed down the canyon, and the feeling increased when we signed the registry book in the tin box under the sheltering end of the arch. My name was No. 553, in the book, of those who had seen the arch since its discovery sixteen years before by John Wetherill and Nasjah Begay. Its symmetry and warm reddish brown color made it truly beautiful. All the next day Williams photographed while some of the party went on top of the bridge and, as usual, lost the seats of their trousers in sliding down to it. Next morning we were ready to leave early with the mules for our climb up the trail to Rainbow Lodge for one more of Susie Richardson's wonderful meals.

We hated to leave Navaho Mountain, but jobs at the Canyon called and once again, soon after sunrise, we were on the road. This time we could see what was around us as we crossed the flat mesa to the south. The Anahsazzis evidently had found the climate and location here suitable because there were plentiful groups of surface ruins. Some had walls two and three feet high still standing outlining square rooms with fine thin-stone masonry. A few of these we could see had been excavated in former years, perhaps by Dean Cummings of the University of Arizona. The shards on the ground were mostly of the coarse patterned black or orange stripes on red of the Kayenta culture and of what we called in those years Pueblo III.

In daylight we could see what we had missed on the way up—the tremendous canyons of sandstone on each side of the rock road as it twisted and squirmed through twelve miles of almost impassable terrain. In fact we were so close to Navaho Canyon on the west that in one spot, after stopping the cars, we had only to walk a hundred feet before peering down into the depths. This branch had no gradual beginning; the box canyon plunged a thousand feet in sheer drops of several hundred feet each, where fair-sized piñon trees clung like bushes in the cracks. A tributary of this Navaho Canyon drainage system that eventually emptied into the Colorado above Glen Canyon was Neetsin, which came in from the southeast. The cliff dwelling called Inscription House was in Neetsin, and I planned a later, more leisurely trip to see this. As it was, our return trip went easier because there had been no windstorm in the last three days. My blue plush Navaho blouse was ready for me at Red Lake as promised and just after dark on the fifth day we pulled into Grand Canyon and home.

As is often the way with places comparatively close to home, I didn't get down to Inscription House for almost two years, although in the meantime I had packed up Tsegi Canyon and seen quite a bit of the Mesa Verde country. I had my Graflex tied with thongs above my right knee and it was not the most comfortable thing for the steep, twisting trail into Navaho Canyon. My Pendleton tied behind the saddle and my full Navaho skirt seemed much more at home in these surroundings. But I forgot the discomfort when focusing through the square ground-glass plate instead of guessing distance with my 1919 Kodak and hoping for the best. The trouble was that the Reservation people of those days did not like being photographed, any more than did the horses and sheep who became spooky when the Belecana smell reached them. While trying to take pictures unobtrusively I was always getting their backsides in the finder as they stood, or moved away from me. I had to take a lot of ribbing about being the best photographer of "rear ends" in that part of the state.

Inscription House cliff dwelling is not large and sprawling like Keet Seel nor strikingly beautiful like Betatakin, but it is intimate and charming in its own gracefully curved promontory. The cave is perfectly located, easy of access, and looks out over the grass- and brush-filled valley between the smooth red sandstone walls of Neetsin Canyon. When an early summer rain passed over, little cascades of silvery water slid down over the sloping rocks of the opposite wall, while we sat in the dry dust of the cave. It did not seem as awesome as the giant Tsegi Canyon.

Some people have expressed doubt as to the authenticity of the 1661 date in Inscription House. But I knew "Sister" Wetherill well and she has told me how she and Malcolm Cummings, digging aimlessly as ten-year-olds might, had exposed the etched date and other letters in the cliff wall of the inner room. They called to their fathers at once to come see. Dean Cummings and John Wetherill brushed the wall with care and several other Spanish words came to light. But the etching had been so shallow that it was hard to decipher them all—only the date of 1661 was deeply cut. In later years it had been freshly scraped out a bit, probably by someone wanting to photograph it—it looked that way when I took a picture of it in the spring of 1928.

174

174. Under the White Arch on southern edge of White Mesa after a light snowfall. 1928.

175

176

177

175. In salt flat just below Red Lake Trading Post, looking west over the sandhills toward Tuba. The old stone post dates back to the 1870's. Our main road to Tuba and Flagstaff lies in foreground. Travelers from Kayenta and Navaho Mountain also had to use it. The automobile tracks go past the door of the trading post, but the horse trail shows up over the sandhills at the right.
176. White Mesa from the southeast with the wagon road that we were following in the left corner. 1928.
177. The Arch of White Mesa resembles a flying buttress, and in the sunshine the rocks appear white. This was a grayish day with snow melting on the rocks and darkening their color.

178

178. A couple of miles east of Red Lake the old road ran right between the Elephant Feet in the 1920's. These sandstone landmarks were outcroppings of the south strata of White Mesa. Black Mesa is in the distance at the right.
179. This branch of Navaho Canyon known as Neetsin contains the small cliff dwelling which Cummings and Wetherill in 1911 named "Inscription House." Water is flowing after a summer rainstorm which gave the red sandstone a silvery cast. 1928.

179

180

181

182

180. Under Inscription House and above the bed of the wash a Navaho dog and burros enjoyed a pool of rainwater. Slippage from the foundation walls of the cliff dwelling with fifty-odd rooms is on the bank of wash at the right. It was very easy of access in 1928.
181. The odd part of Inscription House is the cornucopia-shaped sandstone promontory in which the cave lies.
182. On the cliff wall of one of the inner rooms is the date 1661 next to almost obliterated words in Spanish, as photographed in 1928. John Wetherill's daughter, Ida, told me personally how she and Malcolm Cummings had first seen these deeply incised figures in 1911.

183

183. The T-shaped doors and the remnants of wattle-work partitions were all fairly well preserved as yet in the spring of 1928.

184

184. Our car tracks on the road to Navaho Mountain north of Inscription House are in the foreground. This Navaho with long hair in a chonga knot and a Pendleton rolled on the saddle behind him stopped to ask where we had come from. 1927.

185

185. Living near the rim of Navaho Canyon with a handful of goats was this poor family. Her only ornaments were a few safety pins on her blouse, but she smiled happily when I put my own necklace on her for the picture. 1928.

186

186. On the high ridge between Paiute and Navaho canyons, this Navaho woman waits by the pile of cedar posts her husband has cut for a trader. The baby is in the old style *awae-tsal* cradleboard on a white goatskin, with a head-throw of soft tanned doeskin. This mother is well-to-do, as shown by her "two-bit" buttons and coral beads with turquoise *jah-cloh*.

187

188

187. A rather typical Northern Navaho living between Paiute and Navaho canyons. His long hair done up in a "chonga," he wears a silver squash blossom necklace and large concha belt of mine. 1928.
188. The trader painted white dashes across the rock beds to indicate the location of the road on the high ridge between Paiute and Navaho canyons. A Fred Harvey car from Grand Canyon is making this trip in 1927.

189

190

191

189. Navaho Mountain as seen from the south. The Navaho name is Hiding Place of the Enemies, or Not-is-ahn. A band of Northern Navahos hid in its trackless canyons to escape Kit Carson's roundup in 1863.
190. The original building of Rainbow Lodge which burned some years ago. In 1926, S. I. and Susie Richardson ran the Lodge. Our cars—the Fred Harvey Packard and Pierce Arrow, and my red Buick—are parked in a tiny clearing.
191. In April 1926, the official Fred Harvey party starts with mules and packs for Rainbow Bridge—Tsay-nonna-ah in Navaho. Ray Williams, photographer, with Curly Ennis, Harry Rorick and Billy Bass of Fred Harvey Transportation. Mike Harrison and I were asked to go along.

192

192. Dropping down into rough country, the trail goes south of this landmark known as "Squaw Saddle." 1926.

193. The old route through Redbud Pass in 1926, just wide enough for a pack animal, was abandoned a few years later.

193

194

195

196

194. On the sides of these sandstone canyons, wind and water worked to create new arches.
195. One of our first glimpses of Rainbow Arch from far up the canyon.
196. Wherever Ray Williams set up tripod and view cameras for his official advertising photos, I sidled along behind and snapped with my Kodak, F 7.7 lens.

197

197. While the rest of the party went on top, Ray Williams photographed below from many angles. In return for carrying some of his equipment, I benefited from his expert suggestions.

198. A registry book was kept in a tin box under one end of the Arch. When I registered on that April day of 1926, just sixteen years after John Wetherill first saw the Arch, my number was 553. Only half that number had been visitors—the others were "repeat" signatures of guides and packers.

199. After we left the Arch on the third day of clear blue skies, great white clouds piled up above the snow-covered slopes of Navaho Mountain. April 1926.

198

199

7. GANADO & CHIN LEE

St. Michaels, Arizona, was once known for two things: first, the Franciscan Mission with Fathers Anselm Webber and Berard Haile, O.F.M., and second, the home of the pioneer Sam E. Day family. The Franciscan Mission nucleus had a school and a hospital dispensary when there was nothing else of that kind in the neighborhood. But it was for the work of these Friars in the phonetic spelling of the Navaho language, with the printing of the first Navaho-English vocabulary to be followed by other such valuable contributions as the *Ethnologic Dictionary,* that St. Michaels became widely known. I had the pleasure of meeting Father Berard at St. Michaels about 1926, and Father Anselm in Gallup sometime after 1918, when he was attending one of the numerous conferences regarding Navaho Reservation boundaries, and I was stopping at the Harvey House there. A short distance from the Franciscan Mission was the Day homestead on a slight knoll among the junipers, although as it happened, the Day family were Protestants. They had moved here from Chin Lee and operated a trading post during the lifetime of Sam E. Day, Sr. But his son, Sam Day, Jr., did not care much for trading as he had too many other things to do, including his job of Deputy U.S. Marshal which gave him considerable standing in the community. Then there was the marriage to Kate, his handsome Navaho wife. Their boy, Little Sammie, in 1926 was a bright, attractive youngster who resembled his mother.

Sam Day, Jr., told me that during his young years playing under the cliffs of de Chelly and del Muerto canyons, his one ambition was to get into Massacre Cave. Due to erosion and rock falls it was perhaps more difficult to get up to that ledge then than it had been back in 1804 when the Navaho women and children hid there from the Spanish soldiers. Finally, when in his late teens, he made it with a Navaho of his age, by using lengths of good rope and climbing over that natural wall at the front of the ledge behind which the Navaho women had felt so safe. And they would have been, so the story goes, if one old woman who had been a slave of the Spanish could have resisted the impulse of screaming a taunt at them.

According to Sam, no human had set foot there since the last human life had ebbed away in 1804 from the effect of ricocheting bullets. The gashes these had made on the upper side of the inner wall looked quite fresh in spite of the lapse of time. Chipmunks had found shelter there and left telltale signs of empty piñon shells. Layers of fine dust had drifted over the shrunken skeletons clothed in the black woolen weave with red border of the ancient style squaw dresses. Moccasins, narrow woolen belts, piñon pitch water bottles and heaps of corn cobs were all there to show that the women had been prepared to stay until the Spanish soldiers had left. A few bodies were lying separate as if they had crawled there in their agony, but many others lay in heaps where they had fallen after a mortal wound. There were at least fifty of these skeletons, really bodies mummified by the high, very dry air of that protected cave.

I was allowed to see and handle priceless relics from the Massacre Cave of Canyon del Muerto, where Sam kept them in two old round-topped trunks in his room. This room was still designated as his although he lived most of the time in his nearby hogan with Kate. His mother saw to it that the New England atmosphere was maintained, with the old-fashioned bureau and high headboard of the walnut bed dominating the room. The contents of the trunks seemed a bit incongruous when they were spread out on the Victorian walnut bed, especially the mummified remains of a tiny girl wearing the little squaw dress of tightly woven wool in which she had been killed. This was one of the pieces missing, so I was told later, after the Brooklyn Museum bought his whole Massacre Cave collection. The curator had hurried to buy it because he had heard that items were being disposed of and he wanted to preserve it as an entity.

Mrs. Day, Sr., sat in her large kitchen with its wood-burning stove, a bare kitchen table and chairs. The cupboard was almost bare too; she seemed to live on the air and her vitality, with her slight frame and knot of snow-white hair to delineate her eighty years. But whenever I dropped in, she would want to put on the tea kettle for a hot cup and maybe boil an egg she had just brought in from the nest. In return I would mail her presents from Grand Canyon—small jars of fancy jams —and her note of thanks spiced with local news would always follow.

The roll-top desk of Mr. Day, and his chair covered with old Navaho rugs were kept as he had used them, rocking chairs in the same room had small footstools in front although the floor was deep in Navaho rugs. This was the living room where blooming flowers on the deep sill of the south window completed the homelike atmosphere. Whether

Sam Day, Jr., ever missed this in his adopted life within the hogan, where there was little furniture and no pictures or flowers, I did not know. But since then I have slept in hogans at Shonto for months on end, and there is a restful simplicity within the ceiling and walls of smooth, unadorned cedar logs, without decoration of any kind to distract. A few clothes might hang from a wooden peg and an airtight stove kept the bed company, but these were strictly utilitarian objects and did not distract the mind. With the ever-present cedar smell in a snug, round hogan, there arose the feeling of being a part of the earth. To look out of the doorway at the rising sun—all hogans face east—or the full moon in early evening, was to feel a part of the earth and the encompassing universe. I could well understand how Sam Day, the Belecana, was happy in a hogan with Kate and their son.

Mrs. Day, Sr., liked to reminisce of the days when they had gone with wagons from the Rio Grande settlements to far off Canyon de Chelly to open a trading post for the Navahos and to make their home in the Reservation country. This took place in the 1870's, and after they had been well established they heard through the Navahos that a man had settled about fifty miles to the south of them near where the old Navaho headman, Ganado Mucho, lived. This man was spoken of as Nahkai San, Old Mexican, which was their name for Lorenzo Hubbell, Sr. He could not have been old at the time, but the beards or mustaches worn by most of the Belecanas made them appear older than they were to the clean-cheeked Navahos.

Mrs. Day told me also that when her son, Sam, was born in their Chin Lee home, that there was only her husband and a Navaho woman to take care of her and that "it almost killed me." Sam was supposed to be the first white child of white parents born in the Navaho Reservation. During her later years, Mrs. Day was loyal to Sam while she respected his Navaho wife, Kate, but no more than that. Each of these women had her inherited culture. Kate took pride in her own neat hogan and her weaving of fine rugs, and used the Navaho language. Mrs. Day kept her New England background and used English, although she understood Navaho. I have heard it said by a few who were capable of judging, that Sam Day thought and spoke in Navaho as no other white man could, not even excepting Lorenzo Hubbell, Jr. If a group of Navvies were talking or singing with Sam Day in a hogan, it would have been impossible to tell from without that one voice was that of a Belecana.

When the Santa Fe railroad built the new Harvey House at Gallup about 1925, they had the walls of the lobby decorated with authentic symbols and figures from Navaho sand-paintings. It was named El Navaho, and Sam Day was asked to preside over a Blessing Chant, such as is given for a new hogan. It was a great event in this part of the Southwest, and the blessing must have been effective as El Navaho became one of the most popular of all the Harvey Houses on the line. It is a pity that it had to be a victim of the motor age traffic of four-lane highways. Now that it has been torn down, nothing more than a memory remains of those years when a cross section of the Southwest—traders, Hopis, Navahos, Zuñis, Indian agents, Forest Service supervisors, and National Park superintendents—passed through its hospitable doors.

The northwest Navaho country was the very last to be settled; the areas around Chin Lee and Ganado were the first to be settled. These were closer to the cavalry outpost at Ft. Defiance, and much more accessible to the new railroad as it pushed west in the early 1880's past Gallup and Winslow. Their background of longer civilization was evident when we used to visit them in the 1920's, and we felt the difference in the Navahos as well as in the traders. The latter in some posts already had traditions to uphold, and the Navahos were starting their first innovations of short hair and store shoes. Depending upon whom we might be talking to, it was either old man Hubbell or old man Day who had been the first to open his respective trading post at Ganado or Chin Lee. Tom Keams, the English sutler who followed the cavalry and stayed to open his trading post at what is now Keams Canyon, was undoubtedly the first. But Keams sold out to return to England, dying a couple of years later, while both Hubbell and Day lived to a ripe old age and died in their adopted land of the Navaho.

So much has been written about Ganado by famous people and prominent writers that I hesitate to add even my two-bits worth. But I was not a visitor as I lived in the Navaho Reservation country, on the edge of it at Grand Canyon to be exact, but up to my neck in it at Shonto. I slid in and out of Ganado over those ubiquitous mud roads the best way I could; and it was the Steamboat Canyon road—well known to me —about which Lorenzo Hubbell, Jr., used to tell this story. He had taken a woman writer who could not drive a car—it might have been Laura Adams Armer—out with him to see a Navaho ceremony. On the return trip he got stuck in an extra muddy spot on the road, and had to cut brush to give traction to the rear wheels. Then he pushed, but this did not do any good without someone to let in the clutch and step on the gas at the same time. So he told the writer to get behind the wheel and do just as he said. Then Lorenzo, being a large man, gave a mighty heave to the back of the car and heard the motor roar as the car lurched forward. But then instead of stopping, it zig-zagged wildly down the road through the sagebrush flat. He yelled and waved and then ran after it, sliding about with great clods of adobe sticking to his shoes. He had visions of being left stranded miles from nowhere while the car returned by itself to Ganado. Finally the car slid and stalled in a clump of brush where the panting Lorenzo caught up with it—the dazed writer still with her foot on the gas.

Lorenzo Hubbell, Jr., was a big trader during World War I and the next decades. He had bought the Keams Canyon Post from old Tom Keams, later reselling it. Then he bought the Oraibi Post and this became his home until his death many years later. Also he owned with Ed Thatcher the post at Pinon in the middle of Black Mesa where there was no close competition and the wool trade was heavy. To reach Pinon by car in the early 1920's was very difficult over the tracks that angled northward from the back of Oraibi Mesa. No sign, not even an Arbuckle board with a painted arrow, showed the way to Pinon, because Lorenzo did not want any strangers snooping around. I well remember his speechless look of surprise one day at Oraibi when he casually asked what I had been doing, and I answered just as casually, that I had been up at Pinon for the day. But times were changing and Pinon could not remain an isolated kingdom much longer. Eventually another post run by the Navaho Tribe did open there but it was not a success, and I believe it was sold to a family of traders operating from the Mormon country around Farmington.

Lorenzo's posts, or those he controlled, were far flung, from the Hopi Buttes to the Colorado River at Marble Canyon in the north. When the new bridge and highway opened there in 1929, the old trader, Buck Lowry, opened a place at the north end of the bridge, but it was owned by Lorenzo. In addition to these, he had a wholesale office and warehouse in Winslow, and for a few years he maintained a retail store in Hollywood as an outlet for his Navaho rugs. But he told me once, spreading his expressive hands, that it was so much easier to expand than it was to contract. This was during the depression cycle when he wanted to get rid of a few posts. The main drain on Lorenzo's finances, according to common talk, was Ganado—the old home and trading post in which his two sisters and his younger brother Román held equal interest. A handsome and attractive man, Román never seemed to be a money-maker like Lorenzo, Jr. A profit at Oraibi might have to buy a carload of flour for Ganado; or so the local chit-chat had it.

Román Hubbell had married a very pretty girl who had come west first as secretary to Don Lorenzo, Sr., when he held an important appointive position in Washington for a few years. When she and Román decided to marry, so I was told, they had the Hopi marriage ritual performed at Oraibi before the civil ceremony took place. There were two sons of this union, one of whom died in World War II. John the remaining son, looks more like his grandfather Hubbell than like his father, but prefers the academic world to that of the Reservation. True to the Hubbell tradition of speaking Spanish, he goes a step further and is a Professor of Spanish in university circles. When stopping in at the old Ganado home in recent years, however, I have seen him trading behind the counter while back on a visit, using as perfect Navaho as if he had never been away from the Reservation. His grandfather would have been proud.

There was an aura of history and permanence about Ganado that no other trading post could achieve. It was not only the long dim store with high counters, whose only light came through two barred windows at the front; it was memories of other times. Herman Schweizer of the Fred Harvey Co. placed the first big order here for Navaho rugs ever given to any trader. A Navvy after an argument concerning a wagonload of wool, tried to kill Lorenzo, Sr., who was saved only in the nick of time by his good Navaho friend, Many Horses. It was at Ganado that metal rounds of "trade money" instead of U.S. coins were used for many years. This kept the Navaho trade at home because such trade money was worthless any other place—probably no trader with less standing or heritage in the community could have gotten away with it. When the newer Babbitt Bros. Trading Co. looked at the scheme and liked it well enough to try it in some of their posts, it did not work—too many complaints from the Navvy customers. Some traders joined forces to have a ruling made that it was illegal to use "trade money" on the Navaho Reservation, so the practice stopped at Ganado.

The long living room in the main house showed its culture in the walls covered with canvases from some of the finest painters of the Southwest, its overflowing bookcases, and the ceiling filled with a solid mass of Apache, Pima, Paiute, and Hopi baskets. Over the fireplace hung a large oil painting of Lorenzo, Sr., and from the north windows could be seen Hubbell Hill just beyond the garden plot and the wide wash. From this distance nothing was visible on the top except the few stunted cedars and round boulders, but that was the private burial plot of the family. Lorenzo, Sr., and his wife were buried there, to be followed by a daughter and Lorenzo, Jr., and in 1957 by Román.

Like the John Wetherills of Kayenta, the Hubbells of Ganado wanted to be buried in the country they loved. At times all of them had lived in towns where they did business and knew many people, but they never forgot that they were an integral part of Kayenta or Ganado. That was the difference I sensed between the Wetherills, the Hubbells, and the Days, in their kinship and understanding of the Navahos, and those who in spite of having traded many years among the Navahos, never felt close to them as people. These latter were the traders whose first thought, whenever they retired, was to live far from the Reservation.

South of Ganado on the Chambers road was Klagetoh Trading Post, that was run for a time in the 1920's by an artist, Nils Hogner. He had fixed it up in rather an artistic, rustic style, utilizing desert plants and rocks about the house, all of which was in complete variance with the traditional Reservation trading post run by a Western trader. Teckla, a Navaho girl, was his wife. She was slender, wearing her beautiful Navaho costume with distinction, and besides that she was very smart. The saying was that without Teckla there would not have been much to Klagetoh. At the long dining table where meals were served to anyone they knew, she presided with dignity, and I was sorry to hear that the marriage broke up after a few years and Hogner left the Reservation to return East. As I remember, Teckla belonged to a wealthy and well known clan in that district, who owned many sheep, cattle, and horses.

This was still the horse age and we would often stop in the road to let a wagon and team pull around us, as in rough country they could maneuver far easier than we could. Wagon wheels as yet were in active duty under the wagons and not standing in stiff rows as decoration in front of some so-called "trading post" on a four-lane highway. Horses were an asset to own no matter how scrawny they might be, and in early spring days the Navvy men could work off excess energy by breaking a few broncs.

In those days between Ganado and Chin Lee there were several primitive roads which might be followed depending on the weather. One was through the wild and lovely Nazlini Canyon. This was the favorite haunt of small black bears. In later years whenever one of these bears was seen on Black Mesa near Shonto, where they were relatively unknown, our Navvies always said that he must have come from Nazlini. Although Navahos would not kill a bear because of their belief, he was never out of sight of watchful Navvy eyes.

At Chin Lee itself, Cozy McSparron held forth, where he was well known as a trader from World War I years. The Day family, who were the pioneer traders at Chin Lee, had long since moved down to St. Michaels. Cozy and his wife took in paying guests for meals and rooms, and in summer were beginning to do quite a business with Indian

Detour cars of the Santa Fe Railroad. That was in the late 1920's, when these cars with courier guides were very popular with select groups. About that time Cozy's trading post and guest accommodations were given the name of Thunderbird Ranch and publicized as such. This struck many of us locals as rather pretentious and touristy, but probably in a brochure the word "Thunderbird" sounded more picturesque than "Cozy's place at Chin Lee."

When Mike and I were there in the fall of 1926, Cozy showed us a good spot to throw our bedding rolls and make our campfire. We carried extra wood in the car. We planned on staying several days because we wanted to see what Dr. Earl H. Morris had uncovered that summer under the White House cliff dwelling in Canyon de Chelly. Dr. Morris was backed by the American Museum of Natural History, I believe, for this exploratory work, and had been there with an assistant and a couple of Navvies for several months. As we rode up on horseback, the Navvies were working with a Fresno scraper and two-horse team pulling away the mound of dirt at the east end of the ruins, where the inside wall of masonry was about three stories high at one spot. Dr. Morris was concentrating with whiskbroom in the fine dust next to this wall, and with his glass goggles and improvised mask we scarcely recognized him.

The present danger was that the water in the canyon had commenced to flow against this side, and unless the channel could be changed these ruins would soon be undermined and washed away. This was one reason Dr. Morris had been urged to make this study and recover all artifacts possible, and a long stone jetty was built out into the bed of the canyon to deflect the flood waters towards the opposite side. The jetty was about five feet high and in the succeeding decades did a very good job of protecting the White House location. Quicksand was the hazard when we rode back and forth, and continues to be so today. It depends upon time of year and amount of rainfall. Sometimes it is bone dry, and again a truck driven by local Navvies will get stuck in quicksand and be slowly sucked under.

200

200. This Navaho was out looking for horses south of Hopi Mesas in the late fall of 1926. The man did not mind posing, but his wife—listening to Mike Harrison's spiel—had no idea she was in the picture.

201. Northeast of Fort Defiance, this lake held plenty of water in the summer of 1928.

202. The wide Chin Lee Valley, southeast of Chilchinbito, 1928.

201

202

203

204

205

203. The main road in 1926 near St. Michaels, Arizona, as it wound across the arroyo bridge and mud flat toward the "Haystacks," between Fort Defiance and Gallup.

204. Mrs. Day, Sr., wife of the pioneer trader Samuel E. Day, in front of her screened porch at St. Michaels with her son Sam Day, and his young son, Sammie. Mike Harrison is at the left. 1926.

205. In 1928 Thatcher's Trading Post, owned by Lorenzo Hubbell, Jr., was the only habitation at Pinon, in the center of the great Black Mesa.

206. Black Mountain Trading Post, owned by Lorenzo Hubbell, Jr., was an ugly, utilitarian sort of place, but trade was good there in those years. The trader, a cousin of Lorenzo's, stands on the rocks next to Mike Harrison. Spring, 1928.

207. Garcia's Trading Post at Chin Lee. We bought a five-gallon tin of gasoline from the store, as hitching racks there had not yet given way to a gas pump.

206

207

208

208. In the summer of 1926, Dr. Earl H. Morris was excavating the old ruins under the cliff dwelling known as the "White House." A team of mules on a very long rope was pulling the Fresno scraper which a Navaho guides along the foundation wall just above the dry bed of Canyon de Chelly.

209

210

209. Earl Morris, in goggles, is doing a little shovel work himself, wearing the breeches and high laced boots of those times. Mike Harrison squats to watch the Navaho assistant.

210. Four men of Morris' crew are at work among the rubble of the three-story buildings directly under the White House. The long breakwater of rock and wire had just been built out into the wash to divert the water from undermining the entire ruin.

211

211. The breakwater photographed from in front of the ruin. As the canyon bed was completely dry, I tied my white horse on the stream side of the rock wall. September 1926.
212. North of Klagetoh in the spring of 1928, some young Navahos were picking out a bronc to break after first running the bunch into their pole corral.
213. On foot and swinging his rope, a Navaho tries to force the horse of his choice out of the milling bunch.

212

213

214

214. The horses not wanted are quick to make their break for the open range.
215. The Navahos let the bronc roped between them get rid of some energy.
216. After the horse begins to tire, they "ear and tail" him while the saddle was cinched tight.
217. Then the Navaho jumped on, losing his hat in the act, as the little bronc began crow-hopping.

215

216

217

218

218. The road to Ganado, north of Klagetoh, in 1928.
219. The Hubbell Trading Post at Ganado, where in 1926 gasoline was sold from fifty-gallon drums. Román Hubbell is walking out of the picture at the right.
220. Hubbell Hill lies across the wash northwest of the trading post home. The wife of Don Lorenzo, Sr., as well as his good Navaho friend, Many Horses, were already buried on the hilltop in 1926. In 1930 Lorenzo, Sr., was buried there, as were, in later years their sons Lorenzo, Jr., and Román.
221. The sheep dip near Ganado was very different from that at Shonto. There were fewer goats and bigger herds of "bred-up" sheep. I borrowed a horse to ride over the wash for this picture as I would not attempt it in my Buick parked near the vat. 1926.
222. Horses and wagons were still the mode of Navaho transportation in 1926, even at Ganado.

219

220

221

222

223

223. Old-time Navahos using forked sticks to push the heads of the sheep under water so that the last tick would be killed by sulphur and tobacco solution. The woman wears moccasins with the high leg wrap of white deerskin.
224. The chute is full of incoming sheep, so the Navaho men and women have scarcely a moment to rest. It is a man's heavy work, but as the women own the sheep they want to keep their hand in the proceedings too.
225. Where the road dropped down into Nazlini Canyon in 1926, Román Hubbell and Mike Harrison sit down for a chat. A Navaho sweathouse of stone is on the rim at the left, facing east over the wide valley below.

224

225

8. *KAYENTA & THE WETHERILLS*

KAYENTA, known as Tqo-doh-néshjay to the Navahos, is a location under the lee of small rolling mesas with the mass of Black Mountain to the south and to the north the sweep of Monument Valley guarded by Agathla and Nashja (Owl) Rock. The real spot known as Kayenta, a corruption of Tyende, is a few miles away on Tyende ("Laguna" on some maps) Wash. These are the authentic names of these locations as known to all of us who lived in that northern Navaho country.

At the site of Kayenta there was nothing in the way of permanent Navaho hogans nor even remnants of Anahsazzi habitations when the Wetherills moved there from Oljato to build the first primitive dwelling in 1909. Spring water was available close to the surface and therefore the Wetherills could plant trees and start a small lawn to the east of their cedar pole and rock house. Then shortly thereafter, people of importance from Washington, D.C., were drawn into visiting this country by the news of the discovery of Rainbow Arch and Betatakin. As the name Kayenta began to be heard in Flagstaff, Babbitt Bros. took cognizance and obtained a permit to open a trading post there. About this same time a small boarding school and a stockman's headquarters had been established under the administration of the Western Navaho Agency. Perhaps because of this, travel to Kayenta began increasing from the west and Flagstaff instead of coming up the Chin Lee Valley from the south via Ft. Defiance from Gallup. Only a local with a truck and knowledge of the country could come in from Shiprock and the east or from Bluff across the San Juan River to the north.

Marsh Pass, about fifteen miles west of Kayenta, was the bottleneck for the whole northern Navaho Reservation from the west. This pass slipped through the dividing line between the great sandstone canyon formation of Tsegi with the rest of the north country, and the limestone rampart of far-flung Black Mesa which ended in the rocky fingers of the Hopi mesas far to the south. According to Dr. J. Walter Fewkes, there was an old government wagon road through Marsh Pass that had been used in connection with some of our cavalry expeditions of the late 1850's. Soon after 1910, John Wetherill and Clyde Colville began improving this part of the road bit by bit so that their official visitors might have less difficulty in reaching Kayenta. True, there were many weary miles of cross-washes and mud flats in both Long House and Klethla valleys, but these were nothing compared to the Chin Lee route which was practically mud and big washes all the way to Gallup. In wet weather or when the Chin Lee was "up" it was absolutely impassable, so all of us, as well as the Kayenta residents, began to use Marsh Pass although we felt privately that it was about the same as the old wagon road of 1850 of which Fewkes had written.

The view of Tsegi Canyon from the center of Marsh Pass was magnificent with the sandstone headlands rising in broken tiers above the dark green of the juniper slopes, but after or during a rainstorm nobody lifted his eyes from the road. Where the narrow muddy ruts crept along a sheer drop on one side, the classic exclamation of "Don't slip here, Tillie," by the wife of M. R. Tillotson, Superintendent of Grand Canyon National Park, became a by-word. I remember the Wetherills telling about their trip out one early spring with a badly burned young Navaho woman. She had fainted from weakness and fallen across the hot ashes of the fire on her hogan floor. Her chest was so burned that she was in agony. The Wetherills knew what the road would be like with the spring thaw underway, but thought they could get her through to the Tuba Agency Hospital. It took them three days and nights of camping between washes while digging the car out of the mud, to cover the sixty miles of road to Red Lake. Luckily from there to Tuba over the sand mesa road was only a few more hours. The woman survived her burns although scarred for life, and was able to return many weeks later to her Kayenta hogan.

John Wetherill had a way of driving distinctly his own. He would stop his car at the bottom of every steep pitch to put it into low gear and then jam his foot down on the gas until the car finally roared over the top. Something like resting a team of horses and then cracking the whip for a long steady pull. However, for a pioneer who had learned to drive when past forty, he did well, although some of his passengers who were good drivers themselves underwent a bit of mental anguish. With a look of relief, one of them said to me in my car, "*You* can change gears going up hill." If old John were living today in this era of automatic transmission driving, he might surpass us all. I was of the young generation then in those high-wheeled touring cars with cans of extra oil and gas on the running board, two spare tires on demountable rims padding the rear, and a thermometer on the radiator cap as a fancy touch. Each generation has its own habits and viewpoint, and this reminds me of an encounter that I had in 1921 with a typical old-timer out in the desert. Turning to the fellow beside him, that old desert rat mumbled, "This country sure's goin' to th' dawgs. Womenfolk runnin' around loose by theyselves an' wearin' britches an' boots!" Whereupon, without looking in my direction, he spat generously. I was wearing a man's felt hat, khaki shirt, corduroy breeches and high laced boots. This costume was comfortable, did not show dust and was accepted desert wear, but his personal disapproval was quite apparent.

The Wetherills of Kayenta were already an institution in themselves when I first knew them; scarcely anyone of prominence contemplated a visit to the northern Navaho country unless he was to stay with Louisa and John. Hosteen John and Estsan-otsossi [Asthon Sosi]—Slim Woman—as the Navahos called them, had been in that area for almost twenty years and their fame had spread far. He was known for his discoveries of Betatakin, Keet Seel and Rainbow Arch, and she for her knowledge and understanding of the Navaho people. Their home was a true outpost of civilization with an aura of stark simplicity. A traveler coming from any direction felt that at Wetherill's he had reached a real haven, and we were no exception to the rule after a long, rough trip from Grand Canyon. We had stopped at the trading posts at Cameron, Tuba, and Red Lake, shaking hands with the traders and exchanging news of the condition of the road and what other cars had passed, if any. The Navvies in the posts looked at us curiously for a few moments in silence, then resumed their trading or gossiping as Belecanas were of scant interest to them. Like most travelers in those days, we made it to the Wetherill's in time for the evening meal.

We sat at the long table down the length of the dining room with Louisa at the head and John on her right. Their partner since Oljato days was Clyde Colville, who always sat on Louisa's left. He was dark, very tall and good-looking, and some years younger than John. During the past years when John was away for many weeks with the different exploratory expeditions around Navaho Mountain and the San Juan, it was Clyde who looked after the place and did the trading. John never liked to trade; he preferred to discover cliff dwellings. Clyde was a good cook and turned his hand to that whenever they were caught with a houseful of guests and no regular cook in the kitchen. He was a bachelor and the three of them went on this way for years; in business they were known officially as the partnership of Wetherill & Colville. Louisa's two children, Ben and Ida (or "Sister" as she was called), grew up, married, and moved away. Sister died quite young in a tragic one-car accident and Ben, who had lost an eye when a little boy from the kick of a horse, died in middle age. To round out the home and to have some needed help about the premises, Louisa had adopted and reared two different sets of Navaho girls, sent them to the Kayenta school and saw to it that they remained bi-lingual. Betty and Fanny were the ones we knew best. Betty married a young Belecana trader, Buck Rogers, and they have grown children. For many years they owned a trading post on Highway 89 south of Cameron.

It is to be regretted that Ben Wetherill and Sister did not leave voluminous notes concerning the lore they must have absorbed during their long childhood years among the primitive northern Navahos near Oljato. Louisa came to the Navaho Reservation when she was grown and learned the language then, but her two children were a part of it from babyhood. It was noticeable at Kayenta when guests were present that Sister and Ben kept quiet when questions about the Navahos were asked. This was Louisa's staked-out claim and they did not dare jump it. In the family circle she was the supreme authority on the Navaho, and even John usually confined his talk to his exploration trips and the Anahsazzi cliff dwellings.

John was such a soft-spoken, unassuming man, that at first one did not realize the steel that lay under the surface. Old friends told us he had mellowed very much in the later years when we knew him. He let Louisa handle the paying guests and answer their endless questions about Reservation life. Silently smoking his pipe while his grey-blue eyes gazed at nothing in particular, he would sometimes speak up to mention the day when he had first led Fewkes to the great cave of Betatakin. Or it might be of the trip when he guided Byron Cummings and William B. Douglas for days over devious trails across Bald Rocks and through Redbud Pass only to have to spur his tired horse past Douglas in the final rush to be the first white man under the Rainbow Arch.

The Navvies accepted the trio of John, Louisa, and Clyde, as they had all grown old together. It was only in our time when Nahtahni, Indian Agent at Tuba, was trying to clamp down on the Navahos taking plural wives, that Louisa enjoyed telling this story on herself. In her zeal to help Nahtahni, she told every old Navaho who would listen that he should get rid of his extra wives or at least not replace any who died. But one old Navvy looking her straight in the eyes said, "Why do you tell us to get rid of our wives? You have always had two husbands."

Long after we were at Shonto and like all traders so tied to our post that we could not visit our neighbors unless their posts lay on our route to town, it seemed that something had ruffled the millpond of existence in the Wetherill partnership. No one seemed to know what had started it, but talk was that Clyde had grabbed a saddled Navvy horse and hit the trail for Black Mesa. Very shortly afterward John did the same thing, not forgetting to pick up an axe from the woodpile as he passed. There was not a trail or spring or hogan on this northern part of Black Mesa that these two pioneers did not know. But from Navvies riding down off of Black Mesa to Kayenta on their own errands of trade, the talk was that the two men never did get together. Clyde was always one spring or one hogan ahead of John. Finally, after a week, John came riding quietly down the trail, not forgetting to return the axe to the woodpile, and taking his accustomed place in the living room. His attitude was philosophic. A few days later Clyde rode in on another borrowed horse, and took his accustomed place on the left at the dining room table. The old partnership went on as before. What had been, had been.

When we stayed at Kayenta during our first visits, the Wetherills knew that Mike and I were skimping along on one of the lower grades of civil service pay, and furthermore that we were meeting people at Grand Canyon constantly who might be interested in coming over to Kayenta. So they gave us our meals for a moderate fee and any pack trips at cost. We slept in the yard with our bedding rolls to save money. The living room was the gathering place for everyone, centering around the well-worn fireplace, while from the frieze around the top of the wall delicately painted Yei-bichai figures gazed impassively. Navaho rugs overlapped each other on the floor, the old wooden rockers were swathed in them, and on the walls were a few priceless old bayetas. Black-on-white pots of Pueblo I and II were on the bookcase the shelves of which were filled to bursting with Bureau of Ethnology reports and official documents of every field of endeavor in the Southwest. Paying guests were accepted as part of the family circle because in those days no one ever got to Kayenta who was not worthwhile in some field of work, or at least deeply interested in the Wetherills and Navaho life in general. The contact with the outside world was the biweekly truck from Tuba with mail sacks and parcel post. The postmaster, Keith Warren, in the Babbitt trading post, said that the Kayenta post office was supposed to have the farthest haul from the railroad of any post office in the country.

Using Wetherills as a base, we pushed our red Buick over faint trails in all directions. Thirty miles or so to the southeast, skirting the shoulder of rugged Black Mesa, was the post of Chilchinbitoh. When we ground up to the door in low gear after shoveling our way across a few washes, the trader and his Navvy customers came to the door in surprise. Almost nobody drove there except the trader himself, or infrequently

Kleen-n'losi, the Indian Bureau stockman from Kayenta. After visiting awhile and buying a can of tomatoes with crackers, we asked if he had any "dead pawn." He had a few pieces, one of which was a heavy silver squash-blossom necklace, with no turquoise sets, worn smooth with age and usage. The price on the pawn ticket was just under twenty dollars. I wanted it badly for my budding collection but with the price of gasoline and food on the trip it took a bit of figuring. With the feel of those smooth old beads between my fingers as well as the solid weight of it, I decided I could cheerfully go hungry for a day or two in order to buy it. To the trader's delight (it was cash to him on an old debt) I did buy it and carried it home tied in a dirty piece of cloth.

Oljato, because of its past history, was particularly interesting to us. Moonlight Water is the translation of its Navaho name. To me, one of the prettiest place names in the whole Reservation. I did not dream then that I would own its opposite number and neighbor across forty miles of mesa and canyon—Shonto (Sunlight Water)—within a few short years. Around 1925 the Johnny Taylor family with their five young children were at Oljato in a post with living quarters they had built themselves from cedar posts and mud. Johnny had been running cattle around Cortez but the post-World War I slump in cattle prices nearly cleaned him out and he went to trading at Oljato with what little capital he could salvage. Although Oljato was north of the Arizona line in Utah, Kayenta was their nearest source of mail and supplies involving a journey of some thirty miles over shifting desert tracks. It was at Oljato in 1906 that the John Wetherills unpacked their wagonload of trade goods at headman Hoskeninni's request to start the first trading post in that huge land belonging exclusively to the northern Navahos.

The Taylors had not been out for several weeks so we took along their mail, and found for the last miles down Moonlight Wash that we had to make our own tracks as a rain had washed out all vestige of Johnny's route. Finally we caught a glimpse of Oljato to the right of the wash near some cottonwoods under the landmark of a red sandstone butte. We felt its charm of location as we stopped alongside the trading post where Janey Taylor insisted upon our having the hot noon meal with them even though we had practically materialized from nowhere as far as they were concerned. We knew her brothers Al Smith at Grand Canyon and Jess Smith at Tuba trading post, so we were able to bring her up-to-date on family news. With her youngest boy only five and the eldest twelve she didn't have time to get very far from that isolated trading post.

When we left Oljato we drifted over into Monument Valley following first this passable track and then that, as there was no direct dirt road. Monument Valley in those days had not yet been the locale of so many movies, and the only people braving the rigors of that route between the Tyende Wash crossing and the dugway beyond the San Juan River were locals, traders or ranchers. There was no shelter, food, or help between Kayenta and Bluff.

The day that Mike and I spent in the vicinity of the Mittens (sometimes called Tea Kettle and Coffee Pot) and Mitchell Butte in Monument Valley, we had the whole country to ourselves. Not a Navvy or a sheep was in sight, and nothing moved except a few stray white clouds in the northern sky. I did not know then that the Navaho responsible for Mitchell Butte being given that name would one day be a frequent customer of mine at Shonto trading post. But Hoskeninni Begay it was, who as a young buck out riding with his pal Klee-lahgai (White Horse) Begay had come upon the camp of Mitchell and Myrick. The latter two Belecanas had come down from the Mormon towns to the north in order to prospect for gold in the Navaho country. In a scuffle over a loaded gun, a beautiful new one which the young Navvies wanted to examine closely, Mitchell was wounded and managed to get as far as the base of that butte before he died. His body was found there later by a search party from Bluff. No one knows what became of Myrick as he was not in camp when this episode occurred. This happened in the late 1880's and word soon got around that it was not healthy to go prospecting for gold in the Navaho country—which was exactly as the Navvies wished. They cared nothing about gold for themselves, but they had heard of the fever it created in Belecanas and they did not wish their land invaded, nor to be infected by such an evil disease.

Where Gouldings is now, there was nothing. Keith Warren knew that a young couple from Bluff were running sheep just over the Utah line near the northern part of Monument Valley. He kept their mail for them for weeks at a time until they could drive in for it as well as groceries and household items. The Navvy trade in the store kept Warren informed as to how many sheep were in their flock and at what place they were watering, and in due time relayed the news that the young fellow was doing a little trading from his tent. Just staples like flour, coffee, salt, and sugar in exchange for goatskins, rugs, or a few stray coins. Apparently he did not need a permit as he was over the Arizona state line on land which Navahos claimed but about which there was some question. They lived in their tents and moved with the flock. Once a hardy tourist who had come down via Bluff told Warren that in the midst of that desolation he had been stopped by the sight of an angelic figure with long blonde hair running down the side of a sand dune, waving something in one hand. This was "Mike" Goulding, the wife of Harry, and she had a note for Warren to please send up their mail by the next car going through as they were camped near the road for the next week. These are the same Harry Gouldings who now live amid their de luxe guest accommodations on their section, more or less, of patented land.

In the spring of 1927, about forty years after Mitchell was killed in Monument Valley, I drove over from Grand Canyon to Kayenta to witness an event that we thought might be history some day: the landing of the first airplane in the northwestern Navaho Reservation. Scenic Airways of Grand Canyon were going to send over a two-seater to land on the mud flat (bone dry just then) east of Kayenta near Church Rock. John and Louisa Wetherill, a few Navvies and I were on hand early that morning to listen and watch for the little plane. The air was not too turbulent then as the heat of the day had not begun. The plane circled and made a good landing, with dust and small bits of sagebrush flying from the wheels. We were much more excited than the Navvies. To them, living on horseback, the automobile was still a great mystery and the only difference was that this was in the air. Louisa and John stepped into the plane bravely for a short swing over the country which just twenty years before they had entered with their horsedrawn wagons. Except for the little settlement at Kayenta, nothing had changed very much. Agathla still thrust its black volcanic spire into the sky in the midst of that solitude, and the Navvies still herded their bands of sheep near the waterholes. Soon the plane winged away for Grand Canyon and stillness returned to the wide flat south of Church Rock. The scent of crushed sage was still in the air as we climbed in the red Buick and drove slowly back to Kayenta. John and Louisa had little to say. That was a great gap to span in twenty years, from the day when Hoskeninni with his armed body guard of Navahos had ridden up to them and said that they could remain in his land to trade, until the casual flight of a plane from Grand Canyon into this same land. I could hardly grasp the full significance. We were quiet in our contemplation of the past and in our wonderment of what the future might hold.

Near Tsegi Canyon in the late fall of 1927 there was given a Mountain Chant—the Dark Circle of Branches in Navaho terminology. One of the most famous ceremonies of the Navahos, it is given only during the winter months and is very costly to the family having it as it lasts nine days with attendant hospitality for hundreds of guests. Only a wealthy family or one with extensive clan ramifications would put a

Mountain Chant on in grand style. Several important Medicine Men, even though they had to come from distant parts of the Reservation, must take charge of the ritual, including five or six major sandpaintings made on successive days and destroyed before sundown. On the last great night the ceremony culminates in the Fire Dance within the Dark Circle of Branches. Interspersed are such scenes of Magic as the Growing Yucca or the beautiful Feather Dance. Mike and I managed to drive down from Grand Canyon for this Mountain Chant by dint of his wangling a few days leave.

Louisa Wetherill had her hands full without us, although it was through her that we had received the message to come down if we could. She had written well in advance to a few of her influential friends, who were known as backers of such ceremonies. Evidently all of these had accepted, with checks enclosed for donations of flour, coffee, and sugar, for the Navaho family giving the ceremony. As the day approached, they began to arrive on schedule in Kayenta. Mrs. Harold L. Ickes (wife of the future Secretary of the Interior) was in Frank Allen's car from Gallup; Mrs. William Denman of San Francisco (wife of Superior Court Judge Denman of California) with another hired car and driver although she, too, had wanted Frank Allen; and last but not least, Miss Mary Wheelwright from Alcalde, New Mexico. It soon became apparent that none of them was absolutely delighted to see the others there.

The next morning, Louisa found that she had imperative business at home, so the three prominent guests left alone in their respective cars for the slow journey to the site of the Mountain Chant. The Medicine Hogan was large with a blanketed doorway, before which Mrs. Denman hesitated. As she had contributed abundantly through Louisa, she had no doubt of being a welcome guest and was only waiting for the appropriate moment to enter. Just then Mrs. Ickes joined her, saying that they might as well go on in as she had paid for the ceremony and the Medicine Man would not mind her bringing a friend in with her. While both were digesting this thought, Miss Wheelwright strode up with imperative mien under the small bunch of bobbing red cherries on her toque, and said without more ado that she had to enter immediately as the ceremony was being given especially for her. That this was quite a surprise to the other two, is an understatement. But after comparing notes and finding that they were all, willy-nilly, on an equal footing, they accepted the inevitable. Strange to say, they did not blame Louisa, feeling that she had the interest of the Navahos at heart and probably expected that one but not all three would accept the honor of backing this particular

Mountain Chant. But to my knowledge, never again in later years were these three in Kayenta at the same time for the same ceremony.

On the last night of the Mountain Chant within the great circle formed from cut cedar and piñon trees, we lay in our Pendletons as close to the performers around the huge fire in the center as we could get without being conspicuous. With Mike's black hair, and me snugly wrapped in blankets, with my Navaho dress and moccasins, it would have taken a close look in that flickering firelight to have spotted us as Belecanas. The young Navahos taking part in the Fire Dance proper were naked except for gee-string and moccasins. Their long hair was tied tight in the chonga knot and their bodies were well smeared with whitish clay as a protection against burns. Each brandished on high a long burning torch of pitch with a bright flame and black smoke, flailing the one ahead of him in the circle as they ran fast in ever-changing groups to the chant and the beat of the drums. It was barbaric to see these north-country Navahos, untouched by civilization along the railroad, giving their utmost to one of their most important and sacred rituals. The flames leaped up and up in the night sky and beyond their perimeter of light were only massed rows of dark faced, blanketed Navahos inside the high barrier of cedar branches. After the fire dancers finished and ran off, another larger group of Navvies wrapped tightly in their Pendletons but mostly hatless and with moccasined feet, began to chant as they went round and round the fire, single file, in a fast shuffling step. That particular song with its repeated beat to the shuffle of feet, stayed in my head for days.

When the Feather Dance took place we were lucky, as the basket in which the feather lay was placed close by on our side of the central fire. I understand that this dance is now almost unknown. It did not always have to be given in the Mountain Chant, as sometimes in late winter the Growing Yucca sequence was used instead, even in this cold northland. The Feather Dancer who presided in front of the basket was almost close enough for me to touch as he raised and lowered a light triangle of sticks tipped with feathers. At the appropriate moment in the chant, the young girl in ritual dress on his right moved her hands up and down in unison with his, while holding identical triangular feathered sticks. As the chant progressed with the Feather Dancer and his accomplice moving their arms, the eagle feather quill reposing in the basket began to rise very, very slowly until it stood upright on its stem, to stand there quite motionless. There was nothing jerky or wavering in its slow rise to stand upright, and if any black threads were used they certainly were invisible to me. The dancing flames from the huge fire were the background for both feather and basket, and all through the long chant the feather remained motionless standing on its quill end. As the song died away at the end of the chant, the feather sank slowly back until it lay once more flat in the basket as if a bit weary from its performance. If this was a feat of magic, it was perfectly done by these Navahos.

At daybreak when all was over and only large smouldering logs lay on the ashes within the circle of branches, the Navahos began leaving for home in wagons and on horseback. Many of the elders would never see the ceremony again. It was rather a time of sadness and withdrawal, so different from the spirit of the happy-go-lucky crowd leaving a three-day Entah with the prospect of another Entah in a month or so. The three cars with important Belecanas for Kayenta crept away for a hot breakfast at Wetherills. Mike and I tightened our belts a notch around our already thin waists, and started on the long homeward trek to Grand Canyon.

Of the Kayenta that the Wetherills brought to national renown, there is nothing left. The lawn with trees and the old rock and pole house with trading post have disappeared. For those who have read about Kayenta and the Wetherills, there is nothing to be seen except the grave on the mesa top. In death as well as in life, John and Louisa and Clyde are together on the mesa over Kayenta, buried under a slab of concrete. Their names have been traced with a stick in the wet concrete, and Ben's name is there in one corner. No fence surrounds the grave. Nearby is a simple stone monument with the names of John and Louisa with the dates of their birth and death. All about is bare ground with a little rock and sparse sagebrush, but in the distance is Comb Ridge and Agathla and the great north country of the Navahos in which they lived their lives.

226. The main road to Kayenta from the west in 1926, looking east through Marsh Pass, with the road in the foreground and at the right in the middle distance.

226

227

227. The trading post and warehouse of the Wetherills at Kayenta. John Wetherill supervises the loading of mules for our Tsegi pack trip. John, standing alone at the right, wears khaki breeches and his favorite leather puttees, Army issue.

228. Louisa and John Wetherill in their front yard at Kayenta, 1926. They were the only traders in the Western Navaho Reservation to have a lawn, until Shonto had one in 1931.

228

229

230

231

229. The Wetherill living room at Kayenta in 1927, with Navaho design Yei figures painted as a frieze. Bayeta rugs hung on the walls, and for light in the evenings a Coleman gasoline lantern hung from a nail in the ceiling.

230. The dining room of the old John Wetherill home in 1927. The walls were of upright cedar posts chinked with mud and plastered. Pole and dirt roof had lengths of unbleached muslin tacked under it. I understood from Louisa Wetherill that this room was one of the first built by them after their move to Kayenta from Oljato in 1909. Louisa's chair was at the head of the table, in front of the kitchen door.

231. The long, narrow hall led to guest bedrooms in the new addition built by 1920. Old Navaho gear of all sorts hung on the walls. On the mud floor lay sections of duckboard covered with cheap and durable Navaho rugs. Guests making their way to the one bathroom which opened off that hall often gave the effect of a rough day at sea as they negotiated that tippy and unpredictable footing.

232

233

234

232. South of Church Rock and Comb Ridge east of Kayenta was where the first airplane landing in northeast Arizona was made in the spring of 1927.
233. These Navahos helped get their cattle off the flat, in preparation for landing of the plane—to them a *chidi nahn-tai,* or flying automobile.
234. The Scenic Airways plane from Grand Canyon made a good landing in the skimpy brush. May 1927.

235

235. Not far from Church Rock to the north, the plane came to a stop near our reception committee—the Wetherill family, myself, plus a few local Navahos.

236. It was wonderful for me, in turquoise plush blouse and black velveteen skirt, to be with the Wetherills on such an occasion. Louisa had just said to John that she did not fit anymore her old Navaho name of Estsan-otsossi or Slim Woman, and that mine of Estsan-Nez, or Tall Woman, would last longer.

237. I stood around with my camera while the Navahos gossiped and the pilot tinkered with his engine. After a couple of hours the plane took off for Grand Canyon again.

236

237

238

238. The only road to Monument Valley and Utah from the south. The Laguna Wash crossing, north of Kayenta, was a terror of slick adobe mud at most seasons. The road in the foreground angles through the running water and up the cut bank opposite. The Navaho hogan on the nearby horizon was permanently occupied, as there was work for the men in helping dig out stalled trucks. 1926.

239

239. This main road north to Utah goes through the flats straight ahead between the red standstone Owl Rock, or Nasja, on the left, and the black volcanic peak of Agathla in the center. 1926.

240. The road to Oljato in September 1926. We are making our own tracks down the bed of Oljato Wash, as the trader had not been out for several weeks.

241. The Oljato Trading Post, run by the John Taylor family of Cortez in 1926, was the site of the first John Wetherill trading post in the Northern Navaho Reservation, started in 1906.

242. The road to Monument Valley from the south goes directly toward Mitchell Butte, named for a young prospector for gold, killed by a couple of young Navahos in the 1880's. One of the latter, Hosteen Haske, as an old man, was a good friend of ours at Shonto in the 1930's.

243. In 1926 this was the main road to the ridge in Monument Valley with Mitchell Butte on the right, and the Mittens in the distance. There was no post or settlement north of Kayenta clear to the San Juan except for a completely isolated trading post at Oljato run by John Taylor.

240

241

242

243

244

244. These buttes as they appeared in 1926 from the sandy ridge where today is located the Observatory Building, reached by an approach highway through the Navaho Tribal National Park.

245. Today a road goes down this sandy ridge toward the Tse-begay country, but in 1926 only sheep made their trails across here.

245

9. *TSEGI CANYON*

WHEN I SAW Betatakin in the fall of 1926, the golden leaves of the aspens under it had begun to drop after the first freeze. Mike and I had Wetherill horses and one pack mule, and a young chap from Bluff went with us who knew the Tsegi Canyon country and we figured the three of us could get along all right. We rode over from Kayenta and made camp on a cleared spot near the scrub oak thicket where John kept a log cache containing a few cooking utensils. It was cold that night, but from where our bedding rolls lay we were protected from the wind and could glimpse the great arch of the Betatakin cave. With the first light of day and without raising our heads we saw the square end-rooms on the western edge emerge from the darkness. This was where Dr. Neil Judd of the Smithsonian had camped in those snowy winter months of 1917 when he did the necessary reconstruction and protective work on the foundations and walls. That had been nine years before and not many people, mainly the few coming with pack outfit with John Wetherill from Kayenta, had seen Betatakin in the intervening years. In October the low sun gave us an excellent light on the little houses of stone masonry clinging to their steep ledges far back under that enormous curved roof. It was a perfect time of year for taking pictures and the more I climbed around to try this view and that, the more I fell in love with the beauty of Betatakin. Under the eastern end of the cave there flowed an unfailing spring of pure water, and not far above on a flat, protected surface were rather large pictographs of a long-horned mountain sheep and a human figure with upraised hands called by some a "Messenger of Impending War." Perhaps members of the Horn Clan as well as the Flute Clan had lived in Betatakin, as many modern day Hopis believe that their ancestors migrated south from these cliff dwellings to escape the warlike Utes and Navahos.

The entrance to Betatakin Canyon from the main Tsegi was so inconspicuous that no one would dream of the existence of such a huge cave and cliff dwelling just a mile away at the head of this box canyon. In a flat expanse of Tsegi near this intersection were the cornfields and hogans of Hosteen Ahnee-becloi who as a boy had hidden from

Kit Carson, and in our time of the 1920's was known as Old Man Grey Whiskers. One summer day in 1908 when Louisa Wetherill was riding around the country with John, she stopped in to rest at the Ahnee-becloi hogan. His oldest wife, feeling a spirit of kinship with Louisa, mentioned what she never would have to any other Belecana; that Anahsazzis had once lived in a huge cave in that side canyon whose entrance looked innocuous enough to lead nowhere. Louisa lost little time in telling this to John and before leaving for home, he rode up that side canyon between the thickets of scrub oak and the white-trunked aspen until the high arch of that cave appeared around a corner to his right. One look was enough to tell him that he had again made a major archaeological discovery. Within the next year Dr. Jesse W. Fewkes of the Smithsonian, Dr. Edgar L. Hewett of the American Archaeological Institute, and Byron Cummings of the University of Utah had been taken by John Wetherill to see this cliff dwelling which he had now named Be-tah-tah-kin. The translation of this Navaho word could be either Hillside House or High Ledges House, and other than Keet Seel, it is the only major cliff dwelling in the Southwest to be officially known and designated by its name in the Navaho language. Keet Seel means Broken Pottery or Shards but the neighboring Navvies did not name these cliff dwellings as such, simply referring to them one and all as Anahsazzi.

Tsegi, which means High Rocks or Cliffs, had changed in the six centuries since the Anahsazzis raised their corn in the fertile bottom land of the canyon where the water sank in instead of running off through a deep arroyo. As late as 1900 there were several lakes throughout the canyon, therefore on many old maps the name of Laguna (Lake) Canyon was used instead of the Navaho word, Tsegi. But as the herds of Navaho sheep and goats increased, overgrazing became common especially in the vicinity of water, and when a summer cloudburst did hit in upper Tsegi the water swept down this denuded canyon taking the four lakes with it and leaving nothing but a steadily deepening wash. Cornfields on the sides were left high and dry and sheep trails started fresh erosion. Tsegi became a perfect example of overgrazing and the destruction of cover with the resultant effect on the economy.

Keet Seel in the long canyon to the east off of Tsegi was a let-down to me after Betatakin, as perhaps it might be for anyone not an archaeologist. Beneath the shallow roof of the rather nondescript cave were the ruins of some three hundred rooms, the largest unexcavated cliff dwelling in the Southwest known at that time. In that sense Keet Seel was stimulating to behold, but we never thought of disturbing a stone or even scraping around idly as this was already in the Navaho National

Monument together with Betatakin and Inscription House. However, in more recent years vandalism has occurred at Keet Seel. The spring water there is quite alkali and after a couple of cold nights in camp, we were glad to pack up and move on toward the exciting prospect of little-known Bat Woman House. This high cliff dwelling had been seen by so few people that John Wetherill stressed the importance of our getting up to it. It seems that even J. Walter Fewkes had missed it when he visited so many of the other Tsegi ruins after 1910.

Bat Woman was different from the two large cliff dwellings of Tsegi in location and atmosphere although according to the carbon tests on ceiling poles it was inhabited during the same decades. While much smaller, it was still important enough not to be relegated to a minor category, with its well preserved rooms and kiva dominated by the symbolic white pictograph which John Wetherill had named Bat Woman. It could not be approached easily, for the trail, if one could find any, was terrible and we soon left our horses to proceed on foot toward the end of a steep and rocky canyon where the ruin lay high in the cliff side. We finally reached it with Mike, who was the lightest, climbing first up the wall of masonry into the first rooms of the cliff dwelling. Here we could see how many foundations and rooms had slid off into the depths, as the cave was shallow and sloped sharply downwards. Only the tops of tall trees were immediately below and I was chary of climbing to any observation spots as I did not wish to add myself to the debris at the base of the trees. The view was the whole sweep to the southwest over and above the Tsegi rim, instead of being confined to the immediate canyon as at Betatakin and Keet Seel. There was no shut-in feeling; it was a small but sheltered sky-high eyrie. I would like to have slept there and seen the daylight break over Tsegi, but we had not been able to find the spring upon which the Anahsazzi must have depended as it was probably covered over by the rock slides and rubble of past centuries. Our small canteens were becoming low, and John, the chap from Bluff, was anxious to get on with the horses as he was completely uninterested in Bat Woman. As we squirmed down the slope I could not help thinking of Byron Cummings doing the same thing in 1911 when he managed to take with him a whole pot and part of an original Anahsazzi ladder. On this trip Cummings had hired a Navaho known as Glad Hand because he was always shaking hands, to help him with camp chores and the pack burros. When they neared Bat Woman a couple of passing Navvies told of a nearby "sing" and off went Glad Hand. Cummings climbed alone to the ruin and returned with pack burros to Kayenta the best way he could.

In later years Cummings was under the impression that Glad Hand had died in the great influenza epidemic of 1918 when Navvies died by the hundreds in their lonely hogans. No doubt this information was given him in good faith by someone, but Glad Hand did not die. He simply chose this time to move to another part of the Reservation, find a wife there, and take up his existence anew. At Shonto in 1930 there were pawn tickets on the rack bearing the name of Hosteen Lichee. This Hosteen Lichee turned out to be a smiling, ingratiating little fellow always wanting to shake hands. His scanty brown hair worn in a wisp of a chonga had a reddish tinge which caused him to be designated as *Lichee,* red. Some of the Shonto trade tried to tell me that he was a brother of the Glad Hand who used to live around Tsegi, but one of the Tsayutcissi men said that it was Glad Hand himself. And he should have known because Glad Hand was now married to his full sister. After seeing a picture taken of Glad Hand before World War I, it was evident that we had the original back again in the Shonto-Tsegi district.

Hosteen Lichee, or Glad Hand, used to recount a story which I also heard from other Navvies, and which Cummings heard direct from Lichee along with supporting evidence. It concerned a well-heeled Belecana prospector or adventurer who had hired Glad Hand in the fall of 1910 to guide him in the remote upper Tsegi and Paiute canyon area. Apparently when the trip was over this Belecana gave him a new tent and other equipment besides his handsome gold watch. The next summer when he was out with Cummings in Tsegi as camp helper, he showed him these things where he kept them carefully hidden in a dry cave. Cummings knew that such Belecanas often gave part of their camping equipment as a farewell gift to their local guides. But a personal gold watch was something different. He began to think this over after his return to Kayenta where the story of this Belecana who was never seen again appeared to be widely known among the Navvies. No trader had seen this Belecana leave the northern Navaho country, but to make the tale still stranger, no white trader had ever admitted that he saw him on his way in to the Tsegi country. Yet that tent and gold watch were not a feat of magic. In addition, Glad Hand was known to have been a bit queer and to have been given to "spells" in spite of his affability, so the Navvies simply presumed that in one of his queer moments he had disposed of the Belecana and did not remember it clearly afterwards. Several of the Navvy trade at Shonto had spoken about it laughingly, when no one else was around. As far as we were concerned, little Hosteen Lichee was a friendly and inoffensive customer. Even at a distance, his small hat worn jammed down over his ears was a distinguishing mark, and Harry Rorick used to reach across the counter at Shonto when they were joking and trading together, and jerk it down further over his eyes. Lichee would just laugh. The other Navvies ignored him most of the time when he was in the post, as they did others who might be a bit queer. In Navaho the word *doh-halyan-dah* is frequently used in ordinary conversation without offending although the English equivalent is "crazy." In this sense when we say a person is crazy to do a certain thing, we do not mean to infer a psychotic condition. And among the Navvies around Shonto no stigma was attached to any degree of mental incapacity, only pity with sometimes a rather savage kind of humor. Lichee's Tsayutcissi wife was a large woman of commanding mien and a fine weaver who owned many sheep. There was a new baby in the hogan almost every year. Lichee seemed to obey her orders cheerfully, most of the time herding sheep.

246. This view of Betatakin shows why John Wetherill named it Hillside or High Ledges House, whichever translation is preferred for the Navaho word *Be-ta-ta-kin*. 1926.
247. Mike Harrison and I with a young chap from Bluff camped under Betatakin in September 1926.
248. Pictographs above the spring on the right hand side of the cave as they appeared in 1926.
249. After leaving Betatakin camp, the three of us ride up Tsegi to Keet Seel. Mike Harrison is at the left.
250. On another trip in 1927, a Navaho horse had bogged down in the Tsegi quicksand, and was too weak to be helped out.

246

247

248

249

250

251

252

253

251. Keet Seel in Tsegi Canyon showing the untouched condition in 1926 of most of that 350-room cliff dwelling.
252. We ask directions about the trail towards Bat Woman cliff dwelling and Skeleton Mesa on our way up Tsegi in September 1926.
253. Looking up at the site of Bat Woman cliff dwelling, with some low stone walls still clinging to the shallow ledges.

254

254. Mike Harrison climbs up into the main ruin, which seemed at best to have been a rather exposed and precarious shelter.

255

255. The pictograph on the wall of the cliff was named "Bat Woman" by John Wetherill in 1910. Dr. Byron Cummings visited this ruin in 1911.

256

257

256. On the lower ledges of Bat Woman, where slipping walls had been reinforced with upright poles by the Anahsazzi.
257. This is the greater part of the Bat Woman ruins. Since 1926 more of these crumbling walls have slipped down the cliffside. The Bat Woman insignia is near the upper right.

258

258. One of the few level spots among the Bat Woman rooms.

10. *SHONTO*

THE FIRST TIME I laid eyes on Shonto was from the back of a Navvy horse early in 1927. An Indian Bureau employee and I had been riding across country from one of the other posts when the sun and our stomachs told us it was about noon. Being close to Shonto, we dropped down into the canyon to see if we could hi-grade a cup of strong coffee from the trader. Although the weather was warm, a cup of hot coffee never went amiss when riding in that high, thin air. As we rode down the sand dune trail from the mesa on the west, we could see horses tied under the lone cottonwood tree by the spring. No Navvies were in sight, which meant that the trading post was open and that they were in there. Shonto was owned by Babbitt Bros. then and they had had plenty of trouble in keeping good traders there because of its isolation in that narrow canyon. One trader and his wife had been "spooked" out of there, as he frankly admitted. A single man trader or two had followed each other in swift succession, grown stale with batching in the confinement of that trading post hidden under the high cliff. Without a wife, family, or neighbors, such a man cared little about anything except making a showing on the books at inventory time. A man like this was behind the counter when we dismounted, added our horses to the group under the tree, and walked into the Shonto trading post.

After shaking hands and exchanging all the customary amenities, we asked how about some coffee. He indicated that we were welcome to build a fire in the kitchen stove and make some, as he could not leave the store. It was summer, so of course the fire in the trading post bull pen was cold; in winter this would have solved the problem speedily. After one look at the kitchen stove, a battered woodburner resting on three legs and a rock with a few sticks of cedar beside it, we gave up the idea of waiting for water to boil. Instead we bought a can of *chil-lichee* (tomatoes) and *bah-dakai* (soda crackers) which we ate while leaning against the counter. The trader looked a trifle sour as he had figured that if we had built a fire to cook a meal, he could have eaten with us. Incidentally, he was a nice enough fellow but burnt out on the confinement and Navvy trading in general. Later that winter when I drove to Shonto one evening with a couple of the trader's cronies from Tuba, he helped us start a hot meal and then gave his most precious secret to his friend Bill O'Brien. This was the key to the spring-house and what to do when there. Seemingly it was two steps down, then a ledge to the right, then another two steps down to a rocky crevice wherein reposed a gallon jug. In the heart of a federal Indian Reservation and with Prohibition in full swing nationally, this was indeed important news. Bill undertook the errand and in due time reappeared with the jug cradled under his overcoat, but soaking wet with icy water above his knees. In the pitch darkness and general excitement he had miscounted somewhere those two steps and stepped off into the spring. But some of the jug's contents—strong enough to tan a goatskin—and a roaring fire fixed him up, as it did all of us. In fact to me, the desert trail down the canyon and back the long fifty miles to Tuba across the snow-dappled mesas had never seemed so good.

Shonto was a gem in a setting of colorful beauty amid pink and white mesas in that great sweep of high country between White Mesa on the west and Tsegi, and between Navaho Mountain on the north and Black Mesa. Juniper and piñon trees straggled to the brink of the two-hundred-foot-high pink sandstone cliffs of the narrow canyon, and from a slight distance on either side the canyon was not visible at all in the expanse of mesa. As canyons go in that part of the Reservation, Shonto was small and intimate as compared with the grandeur of Tsegi and the oppressive height of de Chelly. The Navaho name of Shonto, Sunlight Water, identified the pool at the base of a promontory on the east side of the canyon, about midway in its ten-mile length. It was one of the best known springs, dependable and pure, in the whole northern Navaho Reservation, keeping the thirty-foot pool filled to a depth of several feet even in drought years. Navahos rode down the trails from east and west to water their horses, wash their wool for rugs, and have a cold, fresh drink themselves, in dry spells coming from as far as fifteen miles away. Burros would carry one- or two-gallon wooden kegs strapped to their packsaddles. Thirsty sheep and goats smelling the dampness of the pool could not be restrained by the small herders, and would stream down the rocky hillsides in an undulating flood of wooly backs above the clicking of stones and swirls of dust. There was movement and color galore around the Shonto pool as Navvies rode up on bay or buckskin horses with manes and tails whipping in the wind. The edges of bright-hued saddle blankets—often fringed and tasseled in rainbow colors of Germantown yarn—peeped from under all the saddles. A paint pony whose master was on the way to a Sing might be sporting a silver bridle which flashed in the sun. Pendleton and Beaver State blankets worn by both men and women glowed in patterns of scarlet, emerald green, and turquoise blue, with touches of black. All was crude color except the monotone pinkish sand background and the ubiquitous curs of nondescript hue. These curs would break out once in a while in a raucous free-for-all dog fight, which completely filled the canyon with reverberating yelps and ki-yis, while Navvies came to life with well-aimed sticks and stones to separate the combatants and I would stick my head out the trading post door so as not to miss the excitement.

During the months of 1928 when I lived at Tuba Trading Post with Marge and Jot Stiles, perhaps Shonto was in the back of my mind. It was not exactly for sale then but after Harry Rorick and I had married in 1929, we heard that Shonto could be "bought right." Harry had never traded before, but he had been born near Ponca City, Oklahoma, in what was then Indian Territory, and as he said, "Indians were nuthin' new to him." In fact, like Will Rogers, he was very proud of his one-eighth Cherokee blood, although with his white skin and blue eyes there was little evidence of this except for a tough resiliency and a devastating wit. He was frequently referred to as the Will Rogers of Shonto canyon. Harry used to tell how his family in previous generations had moved west from the Carolinas and made the "run" into the Cherokee Strip when it was opened in 1889, and he was very proud of Oklahoma.

Also at this time, Harry Rorick had thought he might go back into the cattle business with a small ranch layout in New Mexico where he knew the country well. But the outlook for cattle was still uncertain from the beating the business had taken after World War I; perhaps a well-located Navaho trading post might be better. Cattle and sheep could be bought and sold during the fall buying season from the Navvies, and we knew enough about rugs and silver and skins and piñon nuts to feel somewhat at home behind the business side of the counter. Trading post permits were strictly controlled by the Indian Bureau and limited to certain localities where they were held by established trading posts. Only members of the Navaho tribe had the right to open up a store wherever and whenever they wished. Rarely were new permits issued, and this is almost as true today as it was in the 1920's. All signs seemed to point in the direction of a trading post in the Navaho Reservation, and we liked Shonto. It would not run into much money because only the buildings (such as they were), permit, and inventoried stock would change hands. Not a foot of ground would go with it; that was Navaho land under tribal ownership. Traders were simply allowed to conduct trading post business at that spot, under supervision of the Indian Bureau Agent, and incidentally to live their lives there. It is a credit to the character of most traders in the early days that they created a need for themselves, an embodiment of their relationship with the Navahos, which only they could fill. In turn, this would be our job if we took over the Shonto post, when we would become a small part of the Navaho country.

In the winter of 1929-30 we took over the post from Babbitt Bros. in Flagstaff, with an agreement to purchase it later. Buildings and fixtures were to be about $5,000, with $2,000 down and a 6% mortgage, plus inventory of store goods which we figured might run $1500 more. No raw products were involved in the deal of course, such as skins, wool or piñons.

On a clear winter day we drove up the winding Shonto canyon to take possession of the post, with all our household goods heaped high on the new ton-and-a-half Ford truck that Harry drove, followed by the older Buick sedan stuffed to the top except for where I sat behind the wheel. Cat-suma, a stray kitten we had adopted, rode with us to his new home, there to start his own dynasty of slate-blue Maltese short-hairs. Shonto was still and quiet in the sunlight with a few Navvies hanging around the store, as news of a change of traders was getting about. The Babbitt trader with his worldly goods in two suitcases pulled out in an hour after turning over the contents of the cash drawer in return for our receipt. A few small brown paper bags hung on a nail had a Navvy's name on each with penciled notation of the amount of credit due him. These we would have to make sure were traded out by the right Navvy. We were left with a trading post heavy in pawn on the rack before wool season, and with the bullpen filled by what were mostly strange Navvies to us. There was not even time to unload the truck, but I did manage to grab an armload of Pendletons and pillows from the car and throw them on the stripped and rickety iron bed in the end of the old rock house. At least we would sleep warm that night, and Cat-suma with apparently the same idea lost no time in burrowing under one of the Pendletons, which made him feel at home.

Even though this was a month of slack trade, the store kept us busy because Navvies would spend hours in "trying out" a new trader. As I started in trading in the post right away also, they had two of us to work on, and a trader must never show impatience. Meals became as incidental with us as with the Navvies themselves. When we were too hungry to go any longer we cooked and ate, taking turns in the store. Between trading and in the evenings, we painted and repaired the very primitive rooms of the old rock house. Harry made the truck trips to town while I traded and held down the place. After several months when I did take the truckload to Flagstaff and drove slowly into town, it seemed to me that everyone on the street looked pale and sickly. I had been looking at reddish-brown Navaho faces for so long that they had gradually assumed the natural appearance of life for me.

Trade at Shonto was turning out to be as we had hoped, not spectacular but steady, if handled right. There were plenty of small-to-medium Navvy outfits who lived the year around within a ten- or fifteen-mile radius of the post. The canyons just north of us were known as goat country, which meant that there were many large herds of goats, and we would buy goatskins almost daily. There used to be a saying among traders that such a small post could break even on five goatskins a day. As a wool post it was fair—no big woolsacks on wagons, but steady batches of it brought on horseback in small sacks or tied Pendleton blankets. Then in the fall there were piñons *(neschi)* to be considered. That business was velvet, and Shonto had always been known as a fine piñon post, with piñon-covered mesas reaching to the horizon. The handling of these raw products would be our living and what would enable the post to pay out in perhaps five years or so, as was the general expectancy with posts in those days.

The big drawback to Shonto had been the problem of getting in and out of the canyon. The dugway that canted sharply down the western cliff directly across from the post was unused when we came to live there. And the shifting tracks down the canyon for six miles leading into the Kayenta road near Calamity Flats were impassable a great deal of the time except to an expert driver with good luck. Down over these tracks was the nearest connection with the Agency telephone line running between Tuba and Kayenta, with the nearest phone in the Red Lake post twenty-five miles away. As truckloads of wool and hides had to be hauled into town and tons of groceries and general merchandise hauled out to the post, our future road was a problem which we had to solve. One factor helped us temporarily. I was capable of taking loaded trucks in and out over that country while Harry traded and did a man's work about the place. No other trader's wife I knew of could do this—most of them did not even drive a car—for maneuvering a truck top-heavy with sacks of wool took plenty of muscle and "know how" on those desert trails. Privately the other women thought I was a bit of a fool to do such work.

Shonto district was also distinguished for being the last stronghold of the "long-hairs," those most conservative-minded Navvies who refused to alter their old customs among which was that of both men and women leaving their hair long. The older ones had never been taken into captivity as children by Kit Carson because their parents had made the fighting retreat behind Navaho Mountain, subsisting in those labyrinthine canyons as had the cliff dwellers before them. This had tended to make them tough and arrogant in their pride of race, as no Belecana had dragged them off to Bosque Redondo and lined them up for rations of Army beef. They had managed to survive in their own wild northern country to the south of the Colorado River. These were the Shonto Navvies among whom we had come to live, who knew no English or Spanish, nor wanted to learn any. Only the Navaho language was spoken all day long in the store, and canned goods on the shelves would be known by the color or picture on the wrapper instead of the printed name. They would come riding in over miles of rocky trails from the most isolated portion of the Reservation—Paiute, Tsegi, and Copper canyons, and Tall Mountain (Zilth Nez) to the north.

Early traders had built a tiny rock and cement lined hole at one side of the open Shonto pool, so that water could flow into this before being contaminated by the animals. It had a wooden lid, and the trader's perpetual chore was to see that the lid was put back on by the various Navvy families who also wanted to dip their drinking water from this enclosure. The trader or his wife, depending on the amount of the former's gallantry, had to carry this water in buckets a couple of hundred feet up the sandy slope to the post. When Babbitts took over the trading post at Shonto in the mid 1920's, they knew that in order to keep a trader there they had to provide him with a few more creature comforts. So they developed another spring site closer to the store and built a rock pumphouse over it, from which the water was pumped directly to a tank placed higher up in the sandstone cliff. The small gasoline pump could fill this 3,500-gallon tank once a day. In later years this proved to be quite sufficient for kitchen, bathrooms, and the small lawn. How fortunate we were to have this bountiful supply when other trading posts were having to haul water. When we moved in, there was only cold running water in the kitchen sink which was under a small south window. The plumbing was very simple: the water just drained out into a sandy depression under the window, where in summer the tomato and melon seeds would sprout and grow in profusion. In that wonderful dry air and sunshine there was never any disagreeable odor. This kitchen and another room were part of the original rock house with two-foot-thick walls which Joe Lee had built with some Navvy helpers about 1919. Each of the rooms was about 12 x 15 feet square, separated by a rock partition. Joe had traded in one room and slept in the other with the supplies. As the present kitchen had only the one window, Harry Rorick made another one high in the north wall by the kitchen stove. Then anyone cooking on the stove could watch the trading post door at the same time, which was very important. It was the best observation post we had.

In those primitive days there were two essentials for existence on the Reservation—water and Navvy trade. It was not idle curiosity to watch what was going on in the vicinity of the trading post. Since everything was barter trade at the outlying posts, a trader automatically took heed of what a Navvy wore or carried on himself or on his horse. A Navvy wearing a new shirt or hat that the trader had not sold him meant that the Navvy had ridden over to another post to trade. If he did not owe anything, all right let him go, but if he had heavy pawn in, this was a warning signal not to be ignored. He had probably sold some wool or a rug or pawned a piece of jewelry at a competitor's post where he did not owe anything. This might be Red Lake twenty-five miles to the west, or Kayenta twenty-seven to the east. Distance and time meant nothing to a Navvy when he wanted to travel to another trading post. I was always amused when Belecanas would ask me, "How do you tell these Navahos apart? They all look alike to me." I would reply truthfully, "Just the way we Belecanas tell each other apart."

The inventory of Shonto trading post in 1930 was typical of the small, isolated store absolutely dependent upon Navvy trade. The crude shelves held only essential items in groceries, enamel ware, yard goods, men's clothing, and Pendleton blankets. These shelves ran around three sides of the bullpen as the entrance door and two barred windows filled the front, while overhead from the rafters swung saddles, bridles, cinches, lengths of rope, and lanterns. No readymade women's clothing of any kind was sold, as our Navvy women bought the yard goods for blouses and skirts which they sewed by hand. Cotton velveteen came in boxes of about forty yards each, twenty-seven inch width, in standard colors of dark red, dark green, gold, and black. Local taste might demand shades of scarlet, purple, or midnight blue in addition. At Shonto we could not sell light blue velveteen or plush as it was said to fade white too quickly. Two and a half yards of velveteen were customary for a blouse, and skirts were made from seven to nine yards of sateen or Riverside Plaid cotton material. As our Navvies were relatively poor, they preferred practical colors for their skirts, such as dark reds and browns. The yards of cloth were gathered into a wide waistband of unbleached muslin of the Double LL Sheeting grade. They seemed to drape equally well around the thinnest or most voluptuous female forms.

Except for the old men who clung to their traditional pants of cotton cloth, sometimes flour sacking, cut in two pieces with ample fullness and slashed to the knee on the outside, the Navvy men wore Levis or ordinary work pants and shirts. Khaki shirts were not liked as well as blue denim or cotton plaids or checks in bright colors. For dress, there were the more expensive sateen shirts of scarlet, orange, or black, with button trimming in cowboy style which was then coming into favor with the younger element. Sometimes dark blue serge trousers and a plain white shirt were worn to an Entah ceremony by the young bloods, with cowboy boots, scarlet satin armbands and handkerchief, topped by a peaked black hat with turquoise and silver hatband, which made a most effective costume. A few of these items were kept on the trader's shelves for just such an event. Black work shoes for men in standard brands were beginning to sell in sizes, 5, 6, and 7. Our trade, although tall, had very small feet, perhaps from having spent so much time on horseback. A few boxes of hats, black preferred, were stocked in wide brim, very high crown styles. All in all, our trade was hatless and moccasined in 1930.

GROCERY, DRY GOODS, HARDWARE INVENTORY — SHONTO, SPRING 1930

2,000 lbs. Flour in 25 and 50 lb. sacks, retail $1.00 per 25 lbs.
500 lbs. Sugar, bulk, in 100 lb. sacks, to be weighed and sold by the lb. in paper sacks, 10¢ per lb.
5 wooden crates, 30 1-lb. paper packages of Arbuckle's Coffee, mostly round (in the bean), with some ground; retail 20¢.
100 lbs. table salt, in 1-lb. cotton sacks, 10¢.
5 cases (2 doz. per case) 1-lb. tins of Baking Powder (Lytona).
4 cases of Tomatoes, No. 2½ tins, 25¢.
2 cases Peaches, No. 2½ tins, 30¢.
2 cases Hard Candy, to be sold for 5¢ per ¼ lb. in paper sacks.
6 boxes Cotton Velveteen, retail $1 per yd.
8 bolts Cotton Sateen, retail 25¢ per yd.
5 bolts Riverside Cotton Plaid, retail 25¢ per yd.
3 bolts Double LL Sheeting, retail 15¢ per yd.
3 doz. Men's Cotton Workshirts, retail $1 each.
8 Men's Hats (Stetson, Mallory), retail $6 to $10 each.
3 doz. Levi's and pants, retail $2 to $3 each.
6 pair Work Shoes, retail $2.50 to $3 each.
2 Saddles, retail $75 to $85 each.
3 Bridles, retail $9 each, with bit.
1 Studebaker Wagon, retail $160.
6 Saddle and Collar Pads, retail $1.50 each.
6 tins Axle Grease, retail 35¢ each.
2 Coils of Rope sold by the foot for lariats.
2 sides of Leather, black and brown.
6 Wooden Water Kegs, small sizes, retail $2 to $4 each.
2 Lanterns, kerosene, $1.50.

The younger women had not yet heard of the *keh-ntsaigi* (high laced shoes) which commonly sold in trading posts nearer civilization, nor did they know of cotton stockings. The young men did buy work socks at twenty cents a pair, but the conservative ones wore black hand-knitted woolen stockings with instep strap and no heel or toe which were practical with moccasins. When new shirts and pants were purchased in the trading post at Shonto it was quite common for men to pull them on right over the older ones that they were wearing, especially in cold weather for the additional warmth. The women could not do this with their yard-goods purchases, although as soon as possible the new skirt would be added on top of the older and faded one. But I never did see a woman wearing more than one blouse at a time, possibly because it would have been too tight and uncomfortable. A velveteen blouse that was worn out in spots could be salvaged by cutting it down for a child.

On the shelf at Shonto next to the bolts of sateen and Riverside Plaid cottons, were packages of bias tape at fifteen cents of which the yardage was sufficient for one trip around an average skirt. Ric-rac braid was sold by the yard, from large cardboard rolls, at three yards for ten cents, and here Navvy women allowed their taste more latitude with pale pink, blue, or yellow ric-rac used against the darker hues of the skirt. We sold No. 8 thread in white and black for use with everything, although a few years later we had to stock No. 50 thread in black, brown, dark red, and white, for already the treadle sewing machine, *besh-nalkadi,* was making its appearance in a few hogans. This in turn began to change the style of the women's blouses by the addition of tiny tucks as decoration on the sleeves, together with real cuffs and fancy collars. Up to this time blouses, when sewn by hand, had two seams running the inside length of the sleeve and down the side of the bodice, with a comfortable six-inch slit under each armpit. The latter not only gave ventilation but greatly facilitated any necessary scratching. A cotton lining was made the same way for each blouse, the two being put in place and sewed back to back to make a simple and practical garment. The only buttons we sold were Navaho silver ones in dime and quarter sizes with ridged or stamped designs, and tiny peaked ones at twelve for a dollar that were sewn in long rows as ornamentation. Out of a box full of a couple of hundred of these latter, a Navvy woman might spend an hour in matching up a dozen that suited her. Patience was required in all such sales. Hooks and eyes, or snappers, were unknown, although safety pins were popular in medium and large sizes, either to close the collar or pinned in a spaced row down the placket as ornament by women too poor to own silver buttons. When our Navvy women picked out some of these from our little stock of notions under glass, that was the height of their frivolity. They never looked at the pocket combs or mirrors, leaving them to the returned schoolboys. I could understand the women not needing a mirror in the hogan, because after handling wool and skins and rugs in the trading post all day, I never felt like seeing myself in a mirror.

The actual taking of the inventory at Shonto when we bought the post was short and simple. We had been running it for Babbitts for some months and on the date agreed upon a couple of their men came out from Flagstaff. In a few hours the contents of the shelves had been checked off and a tally taken of the wool, skins, pelts, and Navaho rugs in bales on the dirt floor of the warehouse. This was before the reduction of the Reservation sheep and goat herds, and in the middle of the cycle of cheap wool and prolific rug weaving. A bale of good rugs did not run into much money wholesale: a well-woven 3 x 5 foot rug would be about six dollars and a good 9 x 12 foot rug not over twenty dollars. But Arbuckle coffee at twenty cents per pound and flour at one dollar per twenty-five pound sack helped to even up values for the weavers. Our big problem at Shonto, as at other isolated posts, was to dispose of these thousands of pounds of rugs which we had to buy even though we had no retail outlet. It meant grading them and trucking the bales of seventy or eighty pounds each in to the wholesalers we dealt with in Gallup or Winslow. Babbitts in Flagstaff never wanted to take rugs from independent traders as they had those from their own posts to sell. But Babbitts took our wool and skins and we did most of our merchandising with them as that was our shortest possible haul, two hundred sixty miles round trip from Shonto to Flag without any detours.

That road into Shonto was our problem. We had to make the big decision to put a little money and some Navvy labor into road work on the west dugway, blasting out one steep pitch of a twenty-two per cent grade and widening it so that it would be safe for anyone to drive in low gear. Luckily, being sandstone, it was never muddy nor slippery. Agent Walker knew this would help his field employees also in covering their territory, and he put his one and only road scraper to work, crossing the mesa from a junction near Begashibito with the old Kayenta road to the edge of Shonto canyon. The resultant road was a wonderful improvement—no more crossing of the rock beds after a light snowfall in what was a trackless sea of undulating white.

Our dream of Betatakin was still nebulous. We knew it was only about eight miles across the mesa to the east, because that had been an additional reason for our purchasing Shonto. Previous owners had not cared if Betatakin were one mile or a hundred miles away. They had other troubles on their minds. So did we in a measure, because, before Harry could ride the west rim of Tsegi canyon looking for a possible new approach to Betatakin, we had to make our own Shonto more accessible to Tuba and civilization. No need to plan on taking future guests to Betatakin, if they could not even find Shonto first.

After practically no rain in the summer of 1930, a cloudburst in September struck the canyon a mile above us. We watched the wash fill with muddy water racing past with four-foot waves in the center, tossing stumps and cedar posts about like matchsticks. We were vitally interested because our road to the outside world was completely cut off, not only down the canyon but across to the dugway on the west side. Some Navvies happened to be in the store, including old Calamity who had brought down a few wagonloads of cordwood to sell for sheepdip; the water was kept hot all day by a fire under the metal tank. He had stacked the wood conveniently near the road crossing of the wash. The wash rose and broadened as it rose, swirling around his carefully stacked wood. Calamity's eyes popped as his logs started floating off downstream, and his first reaction was to throw his rope and drag one ashore. A couple of young Navvies soon joined him and roped logs as they twisted and dodged away in the muddy current. In the end, however, with nine-tenths of his cordwood vanished from sight down the canyon, they were left with little but wet ropes. Next morning as Harry and a Navvy shoveled the cut-banks of the wash so that a truck could be gotten across in case of necessity, there was old Calamity sitting on his horse looking ruefully at the bare spot where his cords of wood had been stacked. This flood was the worst we ever saw in our years at Shonto.

So it became more and more evident that there was need for a road out of the canyon on the eastern side, instead of the precipitous horse-trail back of the post. Harry had done a little surveying and road work in former years for the Arizona State Highway Department, and he ran a line with his transit up the eastern cliff from near the government sheepdip corral. Agent Walker, short of funds as usual in those parsimonious days of Indian Bureau appropriations, helped with black powder and loaned his air compressor for drilling. As our share we paid for all Navvy labor at the regular Agency rate of two dollars for an eight-hour day. In addition, our Shonto Navvies gave one free day of labor for themselves, as they knew that their children would benefit from this project long after we were gone. Harry taught a few of them how to hold the jackhammer in drilling holes and how to put in the black powder.

The actual blasting he did himself after clearing the Navvies out of the area. The strongest Navvies vied for the honor of using the jackhammer, because that job paid fifty cents extra per day and they said the man who could do it was sure strong, or *bitzeel*. The Navvies respected us because they saw us working just as hard or harder than they did, month in and month out. Not too many Belecana traders had done this. As for me, my camera hung forgotten on a peg and I took no pictures of the road being carved from the pink cliff by Harry and his faithful Navaho road gang.

More frequent truck trips to Flagstaff were necessary as extra loads of fifty-gallon drums of gasoline had to be hauled out for use in the engine that ran the air compressor. For me it meant a 4 A.M. start and a return by midnight at best. It took about four hours in town at Babbitt's warehouse to unload, place orders, and load up again. Cartons of matches and things like that had to be carefully placed, for hours of swaying over the desert ruts caused a lot of friction. While the warehouse men tied the tarp covering on for me, there was time for my one hot meal of the day at the Monte Vista across the street. With none of the road paved it was slow going with a loaded truck, much of the way in low gear and compound low in the bad spots east of Tuba. At night, behind the wavering shadows in the road up ahead the jackrabbits had plenty of time to jump to safety. Sometimes I would stop a minute, and from horizon to horizon there would not be another light nor a sound, just the great dark sky overhead.

I grew to know every foot of the road and the bordering terrain, because desert roads shift from right to left in parallel tracks as the exigency of the moment demands. A half-hour's rain can make one spot impassable while it actually improves a nearby track over sand hummocks. Desert drivers kept this store of information unconsciously in the back of their minds. Occasionally in summer a tourist car would be stuck in the sandy ruts ahead of me, while men shoveled madly. Not daring to risk stopping and becoming stuck also, with a twist of the wheel I would pick the safest spot to make my own tracks around them. Choosing the right gear and split-second shifting was habit with us, there could be no mistake if the truck was to get through. Only those who have lived in isolated trading posts in the old days know the feeling engendered by the safe arrival of a truckload. Sometimes I was very late on the return trip and then a wavering light in the distance from the direction of Shonto would tell me that Harry was on his way to meet me, afraid that I had broken down somewhere. What a relief to change to the pickup while he took over the truck. When we reached the black void of Shonto Canyon, the pinpoint of light shining in its depths was the beacon of home. After a couple of hours' sleep, the regular day's work for both of us would begin again with the unloading of the truck. The memory of town grew dim in the routine of Shonto. To our Navvies town meant nothing, for most of them had never been there. Their name for Flagstaff was simply Kinthlani, Many Houses. We were their only contact with the outside world.

The pick-and-shovel work, putting the finishing touches on the road up the east cliff, was about over when a few inches of snow stopped work for several days. We did not realize then how lucky we had been with the weather, because the following year was the winter of the big snow which lay deep on the ground for months. The Navvies were happy as could be, having eaten well on their regular daily pay, and now they were ready to return to a little well-earned ease in the hogan. After the snow had melted in the ground, Harry was able to drive our truck to the top of the east mesa. It was a grand feeling of accomplishment and well worth the thousand dollars which the road had cost us. Now the Navvies could drive up and down into the canyon with their wagons, and the vast piñon-covered mesa east of Shonto was not so isolated any more. In later years, when unthinking tourists and government employees would cuss this rough, narrow road out of Shonto Canyon, I have wished that they could be told just why, how, and with what, it was built by us alone plus a handful of good Navvies, in that Depression year of 1930.

Once the road was in use, we actually missed the sound of Navvy horses on the old trail above the post, with their unshod hooves scratching for a toehold. We had expected that a Pendleton blanketful of wool, with horse attached, might fall right through our living room ceiling any time. But Navvy horses, born and bred in these rocky canyons, were about as sure-footed as goats. Now the trail was needed only for sheep and goat herds coming down to water, for Harry told the Navvy women to keep their flocks off the new dugways. He knew drivers of cars would have their hands full anyway without running smack into a huge herd of goats which could just as well be jumping from rock to rock on the hillside.

259. Navaho life outside the front gate of my home at Shonto Trading Post. 1930.

260. Sheep-dip time in 1931. The new stone house is at the right, with the living room hogan and three guest bedroom hogans in a row. These were used the next year in filming *Laughing Boy*.

261. Looking north up Shonto Canyon, with the trading post at the right under the cliff and new dugway down the sandstone cliff at the left, as it was in the late 1920's.

262. The view directly above the old trading post building, with Navahos riding up the horse trail on the eastern cliff.

263. The big flock of sheep and goats was waiting its turn at the dipping vat, while under the cottonwood by the spring, Navahos ate and napped. Their horses stood with resignation but the dogs scavenged endlessly.

264. News that the stockman from Red Lake would be there had brought an extra crowd of Navahos to talk things over with him that September of 1930.

265. A few customers lounge on the woolsacks in late spring. A rug-carding rack stands inside the pole fence at the right, where the dirty and coarser woven rugs were brushed over a bit by Donald or myself.

266. In the spring wool season of 1930, some Navahos from a distance had brought in their wool and were camped out near the Shonto pool for a good big meal. One had thrown a tarp over peaked poles for a shelter, something our local Navahos scorned.

259

260

261

262

263

264

265

266

267

267. Harry Rorick helping Bob Black Goats adjust a frame for the door on a new hogan. As it was to be twenty feet in diameter, it was started on six legs—a variation of the standard four-legged, or *deen-bijad* type. Actually in this case each "leg" was two stout cedar posts. 1930.

268. Strips of black roofing paper were laid over the layer of soft cedar bark. Loose dirt, several feet thick at the bottom, would be built up along the sides. Duggai Begay at the left, and Bob Black did this part of the work.

269. A coating of wet adobe mixture was smoothed over all after the metal and glass skylight was in place, both of which were our ideas and innovations in regular hogan construction.

270. These finished hogans were comfortable and cool in summer and snug in winter with an airtight stove for cedar wood. Shonto's old black iron "cannibal pot" swings from its crossed cedar pole support.

271. A contrast to our semi-modern ones, is this hogan on the mesa of the early forked-stick type, conical in shape with smoke hole facing east above the doorway entrance.

268

269

270

271

272

272. The interior of our large living room hogan, twenty-six feet in diameter, with five-foot-high stone walls supporting the heavy peeled poles of the high roof. Two small windows were put in the lower walls for views up and down the canyon. The smallest rug on the floor was one of natural tan and white wool that I had woven.

273

273. Looking north up Shonto Canyon in early spring of 1932. A little water from the melting winter snows still runs in the bed of the wash and no well-beaten truck tracks lead up to the trading post—summer travel of government and professional visitors and stray tourists had not yet begun. Navahos came and went on horses only.

274

274. Shonto Wash opposite the trading post in full flood after a cloudburst hit the upper canyon. September 1930.

275. Hours later, after the flood had subsided and our truck had made the first tracks out across the wash, Calamity rides dolefully home. Our dugway is at the foot of the cliff in the background, and the straight line at the right is the remains of an old brush fence that ran for miles across country to delineate the north-south boundary of Little Salt Clan and Tsayutcissi family grazing lands.

276. Shonto Canyon dried out, but it was days before we could go down it. In 1957 there was no wash, as tall cottonwoods and fenced fields showed the results of a check dam and erosion control work.

277. Among the five Navahos helping us build our new stone house was Starley Yazzie at the right in a peaked hat. Donald Tsayutcissi stands at the left on the wall, and the others were Bob Black and Cap Wolf.

275

276

277

11. *HOGANS AT SHONTO*

A FEW PEOPLE were beginning to visit Rainbow Bridge, the Tsegi cliff dwellings, and Canyon de Chelly, all now advertised by the Santa Fe Railroad Indian Detours and the Fred Harvey Company. They came in privately chartered five-passenger Packards or Cadillacs, driven by men familiar with the desert roads. They stayed overnight in any beds that a trading post had to offer and ate roast mutton, canned tomatoes, and dried apple pie at the trader's table. Big cups of strong coffee started them on their way bright and early for the next day's trip.

One morning on my way to town in the truck heaped high with bales of goatskins and sheep pelts, I could see a big car coming towards me on the sandy mesa east of Tuba. The driver had a hand out to flag me down, so I swung onto a firm spot and stopped. They also stopped and I got out of the cab of my truck, walking over to them in my khaki skirt and red velveteen Navaho blouse, with a bandanna snugly covering my hair against the eternal wind and sand. The man in the back seat took off his hat, bowed slightly, and asked if they were on the right road to Red Lake. I smilingly told him that they were not only on the right road but the *only* road, and all his driver had to do was follow my tracks for the last twenty miles back and they would be in Red Lake. It was as simple as that. The big boys with him sort of grinned, and then I realized why they all looked familiar to me. It was John D. Rockefeller, Jr., and his college-age sons who were taking a short trip through the Navaho country. As we had no way then to put up guests at all, Shonto was not on their itinerary. I heard later that Mrs. Rockefeller had remained in El Tovar at Grand Canyon; and that when the boys had been tramping around there in their woolen sport socks, she had washed these out herself and hung them on her portable clothesline because she said no one would do them as carefully as she.

In our part of the Reservation near Tsegi and Paiute canyons there was no place for guests to stay, so we thought it might be practical to build three guest rooms in the form of hogans. Hogans were comfortable for the Navahos in winter and summer, and easy to construct out of native materials. It had never been done before and our neighbors thought it queer—hogans for Belecanas, there was an idea at which to laugh. Even the earliest traders had put up tents or wooden shacks or a crude stone room, turning their noses up at the idea of living in a hogan.

The Shonto post was L-shaped in 1928, with the long back of warehouse, store, and our living room, smack under the towering cliff. From a distance it was almost indistinguishable from the cliff, for the pink sandstone had been blasted out, shaped into rough squares and laid up in walls right where it had fallen. The angle was formed by Joe Lee's old sandstone house. Under the tin roof of this there was a ceiling of vigas supporting split piñon slabs with at least a foot of dirt on top of them, which made fine insulation. But our local dirt being very sandy, sometimes a fine stream of it would trickle down onto the mashed potatoes or custard pudding on the kitchen table. Scampering chipmunks between the two roofs did not help the situation either. Finally we discarded picturesqueness and tacked strips of pale green oilcloth tightly between the vigas. We ate in the kitchen the first year, but after my mother made her home with us at Shonto and Donald ate his meals with us, we shifted to a long table, handmade by Harry, in the living room. Twelve people could sit at this easily. Also added was a sandstone terrace on the south side of this room, overlooking the new lawn and large shade trees. But we never ate out on it, because with sheep around us and Navvies camping nearby, there were always flies. Perhaps because we traders observed simple precautions, there was little sickness among us even though we cooked, ate, and worked under the crudest conditions. Visitors rarely understood this, as they thought we should eat as they did in their patios in Palm Springs or Santa Barbara.

Bob Black and Cap Wolf, son and grandson respectively of that fine old Navaho, Doh-eteen-begay, from Long House Valley, built the hogans for us. Bob was about sixteen years old and Cap about twenty; although neither knew a word of English, both were intelligent and excellent workers. They put up hogans of the four-legged or *Deen-bejad* type, about sixteen feet in diameter, for twenty dollars each. After this Harry added the necessary Belecana touches of tar paper over the cedar bark roofing layer, a metal and glass skylight and a cement floor. We had to haul the cement from Flagstaff and the sharp sand from under Black Mesa, as our own pinkish variety in which we wallowed was far too soft. The floor was attractive when painted sand color and strewn with Navaho rugs, and was completely encircled by the peeled cedar poles of the hogan walls and ceiling. With good beds and a few simple pieces of furniture, our guests seemed to like sleeping in a hogan, that is if they had not forgotten to stoop low on entering. Personally I had grown to like the plain sand floor in our small sleeping hogan of that first winter. It was snug and warm, retaining the heat of the airtight stove, and so easy to keep clean with a swipe or two of the broom towards the door. A vacuum cleaner salesman would have wasted his time coming out our way. The living room hogan was twenty-six feet in diameter with rock walls two feet thick and five feet high containing a wide fireplace and two low windows with views up and down Shonto canyon. Indian baskets, pottery, and Kachina dolls were interspersed among comfortable old sofas and chairs grouped around the walls. The center of the room was always left empty in true hogan style. Under the domed ceiling of intertwined cedar and juniper logs was always a world of silence with the sweet smell of cedar. It was a gathering place for our guests in the warm months of the year.

In winter everyone gravitated to the fireplace at the end of the living-dining room next to the trading post, where the fire was kept going day and night. The wide stone hearth sloped out gently to meet the floor and I could sweep all trash and dust right into the hot ashes. Close around the hearth were old rocking chairs draped with soft Navaho rugs, in which the Shonto cats slept in groups of twos and threes. It was quite routine to tip the chairs until several cats slid out before we could sit down. Their groupings changed from month to month as intra-tribal feuds developed and subsided, but none of them ever disputed the sovereignty of Cat-suma. He was No. 1 Cat at Shonto, and kept a chair to himself. Outside it was a still world of frozen sand with patches of snow on the north slopes under a brilliant turquoise sky. Wind from the north, cold and biting, swirled down the canyon past our protected location. Navvies with windblown hair and Pendletons clutched tightly about them would erupt through the trading post door to stand with outstretched hands over the red-hot stove in the center of the bull pen. Only at the end of winter would the shift come again to the strong southwest winds bringing their first clouds of yellow dust.

When spring was in the air, maybe around Easter, our first brave visitors would straggle in. Some came from the dude ranches of southern Arizona, and what a change of atmosphere it was for them. At Shonto nothing was consciously arty or Western, with a complete lack of wagon wheels and cow skulls strewn artistically in the foreground. This was the real West of a going business, with no frills, based on the economy of the Navahos in this primitive part of their Reservation. The Navvies were the important people, our customers month in and month out; the Belecanas, even VIPs, were only tolerated in comparison, though they were welcomed with courtesy, given all the comforts available, and wished Godspeed on their further travels. But it was the Navvies who were permanent.

Besides Agency employees, Park Service officials, Fred Harvey Company men from Grand Canyon, there came along in summer the stream of geologists, archaeologists, ethnologists—men like Gregory and Brown, Hewett and Cummings, Kidder and Morris. They were leaders in their fields, and we always enjoyed having them around. We would talk of sandstone strata, of erosion, of cave shelters and surface ruins, of shards and spearpoints. Their scientific approach to many problems was a stimulus to us with only our practical, layman's point of view. While we might not have exactly the same feeling as the Navvies regarding the Anahsazzis and this canyon world of theirs, still we might have been a step closer to them than we were to the professorial plane of thought. To some degree the Wetherills perhaps felt this way in their association with Fewkes and Kidder and others of the first "greats."

The Indian Detours may be a meaningless term nowadays, but to us in the late 1920's and the following decade it offered a type of sightseeing and service in the Southwest which has never been surpassed. The Indian Detour trips of the Santa Fe Railroad, with cars manned by drivers in Western outfits and girl couriers in Navaho blouses, silver jewelry, and hats with emblems, took tourists comfortably to remote spots of interest in the Southwest which they never could have found otherwise. Hunter Clarkson was the guiding spirit from his headquarters at La Fonda, in Santa Fe. From Grand Canyon, our friends in Fred Harvey Transportation liked to bring their parties to Shonto. So we felt, perhaps understandably, that Indian Detour cars coming as far as Chin Lee in the Navaho Reservation would be interested in stopping at a really isolated section of the Reservation, such as Shonto and Tsegi. But the one in charge of the couriers and the routing of such trips was not apparently interested in anything north of Cozy McSparron's at Chin Lee. However, after I talked with some of the girls who were the early couriers, they began to bring to Shonto small parties of individuals sincerely interested in seeing primitive Navahos. Some of these couriers were Marie Baca, Claire Bursum, and Henrietta Gloff. One of the most capable and tactful couriers, Zoe Berchtold of Santa Fe, came to Shonto many times with parties of stimulating and worthwhile people.

Mrs. Harold Ickes was interested in the Navahos for many years and even after her husband became Secretary of the Interior, she found time to visit us. In September 1933, she drove to Shonto with Frank Allen of Gallup for a few days in the prospective Wilderness Area of Tsegi and Navaho Canyons. Mrs. William Denman of San Francisco, an active member of the Indian Arts and Crafts Board, was a guest then also. The latter was sitting with Frank and me in the cool quiet of our living room hogan. Mrs. Ickes had disappeared somewhere. Although the dipping vat and corrals were only five hundred feet distant, the brawl, dust, and smell of the sheepdip could not penetrate the hogan's thick walls. Suddenly the crude wooden door was pushed open and Mrs. Ickes, stooping low for the entrance, made her dignified way into the room — every inch the great lady from official Washington. This made the following anecdote which she and her friend, Mrs. Denman, recounted with such glee in later weeks, all the more humorous. As Mrs. Ickes brought with her the excitement of the Navaho world of milling sheep and fighting goats immersed in the hot-tobacco-sulphur smell of the dip, her thoughts burbled ahead of her tongue as these words erupted, "You don't know where I've been just now — I've been down at the shitdeep!" A twist of the tongue can happen to king or commoner alike, and Mrs. Ickes was such an inherent lady that after a gasp of realization as to what she had actually said, she and Mrs. Denman simply linked arms and went out of the hogan together to — guess where? — the sheepdip. Their irrepressible laughter floated back to Frank Allen and me.

One possession at Shonto which survived all the years was a huge black iron pot, referred to by us as the cannibal pot. Perhaps Joe Lee had brought it by wagon from the Mormon country, anyway it had always been at the trading post and we had it sitting out in the sand of the back yard. One dark night a guest complained that she had lost the path to the outhouse and fallen into the pot; she did not look hurt at all, but was on the verge of tears. To save the situation, Harry said gravely that he would go right out with his flashlight to look at the pot and see if she had broken it. As he no doubt expected, this struck her as so funny that she laughed instead of crying, and by the next morning had forgotten her mishap. After this, we hung the iron pot by three chains suspended from stout cedar posts as we did not want to lose another guest in it some night. When I saw Shonto again in 1957, after many years away, the first thing that greeted my eye, and sitting in lone grandeur out in front of the trading post, was the black cannibal pot.

Starley Yazzie was the first Navvy in our neighborhood to become a friend. He was small and thin with a little grey in his hair which he wore long in the conventional chonga knot. Often there was a tiny turquoise bead tied in the white cotton cords to signify that he had had a recent Sing. He spoke good English and told us he was one of the first pupils in the small Blue Canyon school in the 1890's. A greyish peaked hat was always on his head as he rode down the horse-trail above the trading post in the early morning. He usually sang one of the appropriate old Navaho songs and we would hear him long before he came in sight on the rim. At evening when he rode up toward his hogan, the full-throated song with its quavering high falsetto floated down to us in the canyon. It made us feel that the petty worries of the day in the store were not so important after all. At least he was ridding *his* mind of them. The real thing was to feel in tune with the world around us; to find beauty in the sunset, in the pungent smell of fresh cedar smoke, and in the family welcome around their evening fire. This was part of the meaning of the Navaho philosophy—To Walk in Beauty—and in the songs we could hear it ring out exultantly. As Starley rode from our shadowy canyon into the last rays of the sunset, he was probably following the Trail of Beauty in his mind.

When I was trading alone in the store, Starley interpreted for me whenever I had something to say that went beyond the range of my trade Navaho. He was very good at this, even when it was something not particularly agreeable to one of his own clan relatives. Every day in a trading post there was heavy work to be done; cases of canned goods had to be opened and put on the shelves, and 25- and 50-pound sacks of flour stacked high. Arbuckle coffee in one-pound paper packages, in the whole bean or *numazigi,* was our biggest seller at twenty cents. This was ground fresh every day by the Navahos in their hogans in the grinder that was also used for corn, but even fresh grinding did not add appreciably to the aroma of Arbuckle's which was the cheapest grade of Brazilian coffee. Without the wooden Arbuckle crates, no trading post in the old days could have had kitchen shelves or a cupboard. Dust and sand got on everything in the post as it blew in, was tracked in, and was brought in with the pelts and wool. The wide counter tops of wood were worn greasy smooth; once a month or so we might scrub them with soap and water, thinking to remove some germs. Trachoma was so prevalent in those years that it was a habit never to put our hands to our faces, in the long hours of trading, where unlike in hospital work, we were not able to wash our hands, sometimes all day. Whatever was handled, was touched by all—not once but again and again. Head colds plagued the traders in winter for this same reason. Starley kept his clothes as clean as we did, and he was always washing his hair. In summer whenever I saw a black head bobbing up and down behind the big woodpile in our back yard and a voice singing "Onward, Christian Soldiers," I knew it was Starley taking a bath in our tin laundry tub with a bucket of spring water to the tune of this song learned in his Blue Canyon school days.

It was the one song he remembered. A Navaho sweat-bath may have been suitable for purifying purposes or where water was lacking, but on a hot day evidently he thought there was nothing as good as a shower bath with a whole bucket of fresh water.

In those days we kept neither cosmetics nor lingerie of any type for sale as the Navvy women around Shonto did not know such things existed. But Starley had seen some pink cotton shorts on our washline, and he told me one day in the store that his old lady would like a pair of those pink things. Whereupon I showed him the Sears catalogue and asked if she didn't want two pairs? No, she wanted only one pair, so that was that. A few weeks later the lone pair arrived and he carried them carefully hoganward. A month or so later, after I had forgotten the whole matter, Starley asked me to order another pair for her. Without thinking, I asked him what his old lady had done with the first pair. He sort of hung his head, saying apologetically, "She done lost 'em—she need another." Navahos like this type of humor themselves, and Starley enjoyed it as much as we did. I told it to lanky John Huston, the movie director, who was staying at Shonto with us about that time, and he loved it.

Although Starley always referred to his wife as his old lady—an expression picked up from some Belecana trader—we felt that she was quite a power in the hogan. They lived near Thief Rock to the south of us, but Starley's own family came from near Gray Mountain on the western edge of the Reservation. His nephew is Maxwell Yazzie, a counselor of the Navaho Tribe, and an educated and highly respected individual. When I talked with Maxwell recently, after an interim of many years, he still remembered me by my old name of "The Woman Who Weaves."

The Tohdoh-aidecon family lived above us on the west rim of Shonto. Tohdy, as we called him, was a meek, middle-aged man, and they were a poor outfit with a handful of sheep for weaving wool and about forty goats for meat and milk. Hardly a day passed that one of this family was not down in the store for five cents worth of *alkesdizi,* the bulk hard candy sold in all posts, or maybe a ten-cent sack of sugar which the Navvies refer to as *ashii-lakan,* sweet salt. Their pawn, consisting of several turquoise and silver bracelets, went in and out when redeemed by his wife's rugs. She was an excellent weaver, but often she was forced to weave quickies or "bread and coffee rugs," which of course we had to buy. They had a couple of small girls who wore shabby velveteen blouses with strings of red glass imitation coral beads around their necks. These beads had been brought into the Reservation during the war years, but by the 1920's no reputable Reservation trader would carry them in stock—too much nuisance value when mixed up with real shell or turquoise.

One day Tohdy came into the store, saying they had to have a Sing for his youngest girl and asked to pawn a shell necklace strung with bits of imitation turquoise. We would not hang it on the pawn rack, but let him have some coffee and flour against it anyway. He did not say what the Sing was for, and we supposed it was a routine ceremony for her bad dreams, or having seen too many snakes, or something like that. Then we heard from others that this girl of about ten had fallen on a sharp branch when playing in a piñon tree. Her abdomen had been punctured. The next time Tohdy came in, we asked him to let us send for the field doctor from Tuba. But shaking his head, he said that the Hah-tothli, Medicine Man, was in charge. Three days later when the Sing was over and the Medicine Man had collected his gifts and ridden away, Tohdy asked us to send for the doctor.

When the doctor arrived in due time at their hogan, he could see that the last stages of peritonitis had set in, after the girl's ordeal of nearly a week. What the family wanted was for the doctor to take her away to die elsewhere. Then there would be no chance of the hogan becoming *chindee* and they would be relieved of the burial. After sizing up the situation, the doctor refused to take the dying child on that long, rough trip. As he told us later over a cup of coffee at the post, that in this case he might not have been able to save her life even if he had been called days earlier. So the little goatherder, still wearing her brown velveteen blouse and red glass beads, was placed in a brush shelter under the night sky to await the end. Later her body was put in a crevice of the rocky mesa rim, while her soul was beginning to travel in the four-day cycle of the Navajo Trail of Beauty.

Her sister came in to the post more frequently when she was a little older, especially the summer when Mabel Rock worked for us. Mabel Rock was the school name of Mabel Tsayutcissi, who was Donald's full sister. Their mother was a strong and implacable Navaho of the old school, broad of face and with the muscled arms and shoulders of the steady weaver. When she hove in sight with a rug I always knew that I would get the worst of the trade, but I really liked her. Mabel never got beyond third grade at Ft. Wingate boarding school, and the summer she was 17—Donald said she was actually 19—decided that she would not go back to sit with those little children in the classroom. While she was mulling over this decision she would sit for hours in her room off the kitchen, looking through a Sears catalogue. Our magazines or the weekly newspaper meant nothing to her; Donald used to laugh and say, "She jus' dumb, thas all." The climax came when Harry scolded her for keeping her sister's greasy sack of mutton ribs in a corner of her room overnight. Mabel put her few possessions in a sack over her shoulder, and without saying one word to us, started walking down the canyon in her school girl clothes and shoes. It would be about eight miles over the canyon trails to her mother's hogan. Life went on as before in our kitchen except that Donald helped me with the dishes instead of Mabel.

It was not many weeks later when I saw the trading post door open slowly, and there stood Mabel in complete Navaho dress. Her long, full skirt of sateen and velveteen blouse were spotless, and over her shoulders was a Pendleton. In true Navaho style, she entered the post quietly, slipping around the right side of the bull pen as the women do, and with a shy smile for me, pushed up on the counter a small rug. It would be hard to guess that she had ever been out of the hogan or knew a word of English. With real warmth I said, "Why, Mabel, did you weave this yourself? How nice. This is a good pattern." She looked very pleased; and when I bought the rug she traded it out on materials, thread and needles, that I knew she wanted for herself. Surprisingly, she also purchased a little round ten-cent mirror. But other than a grudging, sibilant "yes-s," she would only speak Navaho. She had made her decision and was content. In the next few years her rugs became beautifully woven, partly because her mother was such an excellent weaver. The design with the Four Sacred Mountains in the corners with the zigzags to the Center of the World was a favorite of theirs. Years ago in the Western Navaho district this pattern was always called the Red Lake pattern because an early trader at Red Lake (Tonalea) had drawn the design. Later it came to be known as the Storm pattern, and was an easy rug to sell to tourists because it told a story. If Mabel had not shone at school, she was certainly shining in the hogan.

Donald had made his initial entrance into Shonto in quite another fashion. When we were first there, it was difficult for us to get to know the pawn, the faces of the regular customers, as well as those of the transient Navvy trade. So when this tall, long-haired Navvy whom we did not know, came in the post with a small sack of wool to trade out, Harry treated him like all the rest, using his limited trade Navaho. He seemed to be killing time and priced a lot of the merchandise before he sold his wool, showing that no new trader was literally going to pull the wool over his eyes on this deal. It took a full two hours for the transaction, and by that time he and Harry must have taken a liking to each other. Finally, he swung his sack of purchases over his shoulder and started out the door. Then he looked back for a second and asked in plain English, "Wha' time is it?" And Harry answered with a broad grin, "Why, god-damn-you! It's four o'clock." That was our first meeting with Donald Tsayutcissi and from then on he came in to trade regularly, eventually working for us and becoming like one of our own family. He was a real gentleman and a fine Navaho. Many of his Navaho traits we could have adopted ourselves to good advantage.

Donald liked to read, sitting in one of the rocking chairs, and picked out books that caught his fancy on my book shelves. He pored over one book in particular about the Navahos, written by a visiting college professor, which was supposed to be both erudite and authentic. I could tell from Donald's smile and his well-thumbed pages about Navaho customs and ceremonies, that he was getting a tremendous kick out of what this Belecana thought he knew about the Navahos. But I asked no questions. As Donald had gone away to school at Grand Junction, Colorado, and worked in the beet fields during summer vacations, he had a good understanding of spoken English. So I thought that the *Vocabulary, English-Navaho and Navaho-English,* by Father Berard Haile, O.F.M., of St. Michaels, Arizona, of which I had a first edition copy, would be of great help to him. Instead of that, it was hopeless. Try as he would with my assistance (which was probably quite inadequate), he could not master the phonetic spelling for written Navaho, much less English. He would say about the Navaho, with his finger under a certain word in the column, "Tha's not the way it soun's." I believe a question of dialect might have complicated matters also, because our Navahos spoke the pure language, different from those who lived near the pueblos and railroad towns whose parentage went back to Bosque Redondo days. But *I* used the *Vocabulary* of Father Berard, and it helped me tremendously.

When Donald began working in the post, he had to adjust his previous thinking as to values and mark-up in prices. He soon understood that no store could exist on a ten per cent margin, which he had thought should be enough. He finally saw that the thirty per cent and fifty per cent mark-up on many items of merchandise was necessary because wool and skins and piñons were taken against them, with the extra expense of freight and shrinkage in weight. Our freight rate in those years was one dollar per hundred pounds from Flagstaff with any of the Hopi truckers at Moencopie who did this work for the various trading posts. Just a few years earlier it had been one dollar and a half per hundred pounds for the one-hundred-thirty-mile haul from town. As Harry and I did all our own trucking over those miles of desert trails, I could appreciate that this rate was very fair. Donald, or H. T. Donald as he is known in business, has run his own post these many years now in Marsh Pass opposite the beautiful entrance to the canyon, and it is called the Tsegi Trading Post.

278. At an Entah in 1930 on the east rim of Shonto, this Navaho family is settling down to some goat ribs over the coals. The man with many silver buttons on his coat had stepped aside to be out of the picture.

279. The Medicine Hogan of new poles and cedar bark is back of the brush shelter where the family giving the Entah sit in the shade.

280. Horses were everywhere under piñons or tied to clumps of sagebrush, as this site was almost inaccessible. The Navaho at the right wears his prized possession, a black fur cap, though it was a hot summer day.

281. The patient, stripped and painted black, walks with his attendant following, to the spot where the Scalp has been ceremoniously buried.

282. After them, a few minutes later, the man's wife and another woman relative follow the same route. The woman's hair is unbound, the same as the men's. Their bodies are painted all over with black ashes or soft charcoal, and they are bare to the waist.

283. On the sandy flat near Shonto Trading Post the Navahos gathered during the last day of the Entah for games and horse races. We gave several twenty-five-pound sacks of flour as prizes.

284. Old Lady Little Salt huddling in her Pendleton stops to listen to Bob Talker's wife, probably to her often-endless string of complaints.

285. This is the "outline" rug in fine weave with shades of natural brown, gray, and black wool, that Byron Cummings liked so much. The weaver lived near Marsh Pass. 1932.

286. A typical and popular rug pattern woven in the district of Western Navaho between Kayenta and Tuba. Many of the good weavers of the Tsayutcissi family used this design of the Four Mountains bordering the Navaho World with the Lake in the middle, and the Sacred Arrows, and Whirling Logs. This was called the "Red Lake pattern" because a trader at that post had originated the design sometime after 1900.

278

279

280

281

282

283

284

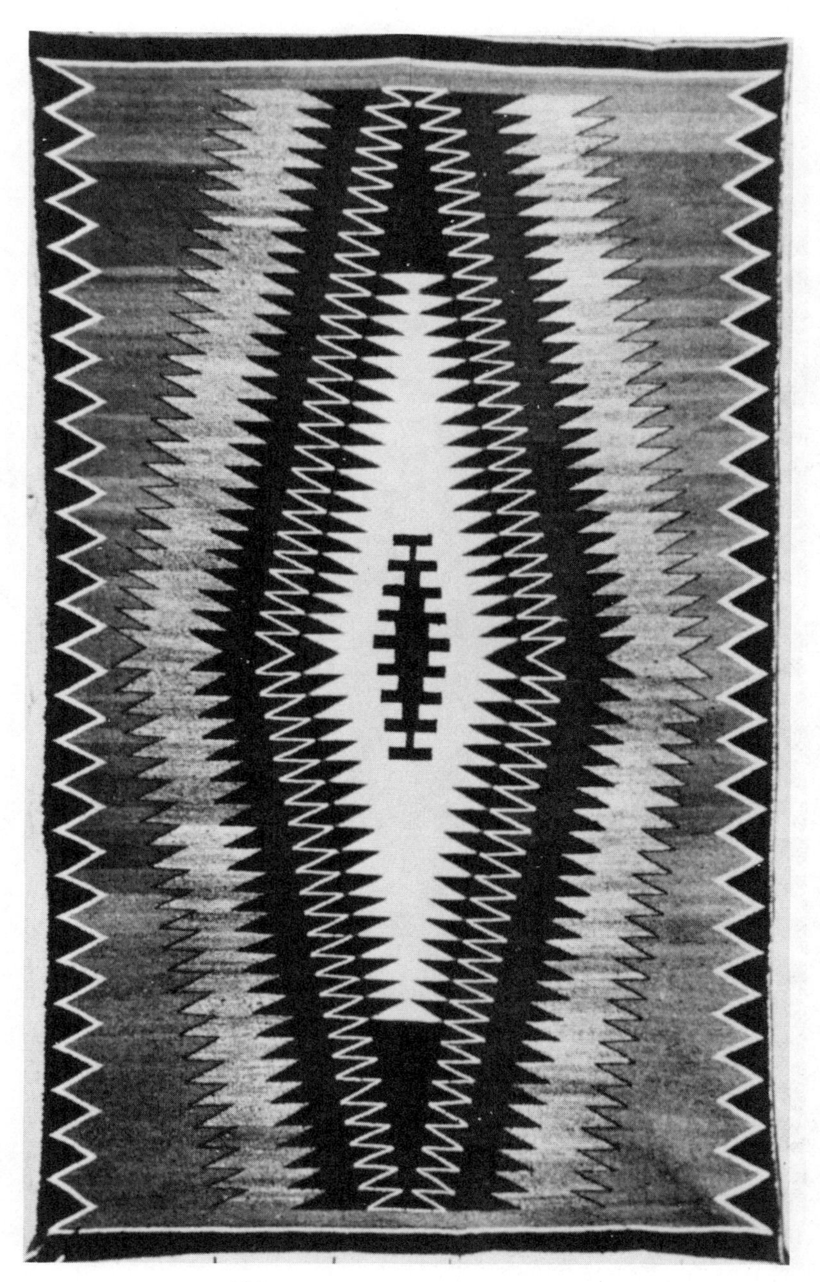

285

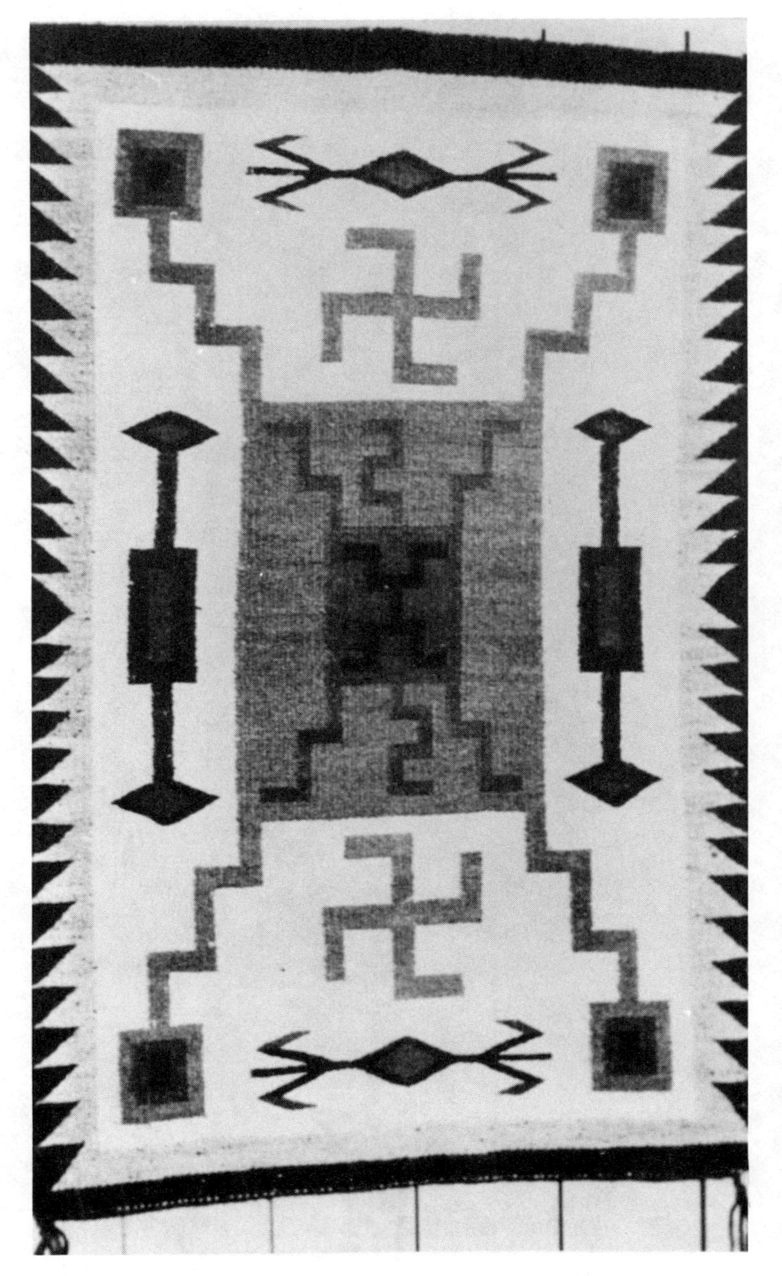

286

12. *SOME SHONTO NAVAHOS*

NEXT TO freighting-in supplies, our immediate problem was getting our mail and parcel post, which we wanted regularly once or twice a week instead of the old way of maybe once a month in the outlying posts. The former trader had arranged in Tuba for the Shonto mail and parcel post to be carried on the Kayenta truck and left at Calamity's hogan, for him to bring up to Shonto on his mule. Calamity was a haughty old Navvy whose hogans were close to the Kayenta road in the muddy stretch shown on the road maps as Calamity Flats. But instead of helping when a car was stuck there, he either stayed in his hogan or deliberately rode his horse away, so it got to be known as a calamity for one to be stuck in that spot. His family pawn tickets at Shonto were all in the name of Calamity; apparently the traders had forgotten his real Navaho name. This was the mail delivery that we inherited and maintained for several months, at the rate of one dollar in trade per trip.

Each Tuesday and Friday just before sunset, we would watch the western rim of Shonto for Calamity's head in silhouette slowly bobbing along on his little mule. Fifteen minutes later he would stride in the post on moccasined feet, shrug his old Pendleton loose and throw on the counter the bundle of mail and newspapers, with once a week a dozen loaves of bakery bread. A grunt accompanied this ritual, with a distinct air of disdain. Most Navvies having great respect for *nultsos*—a word covering letters, checks, and all printed matter equally—he seemed careful with the mail, although no one in his hogan could read, write, or understand a word of English. He stood sourly by the counter trading out his entire dollar's worth of credit each time on coffee, sugar, salt, matches and tobacco, which just about consumed it. Sometimes he brought in a small rug of his wife's, so dirty and poorly woven that it also was a calamity, but of course we had to buy it.

Frequently he would deliver eleven instead of the twelve loaves of bread, telling with expressive gestures how one loaf had been received broken open; no doubt it broke open right into Calamity's hands and stomach. One day he came in with the mail, giving us haughtier glares than usual with a long rigamarole concerning *akhan,* or flour, and *bah,* or bread. It seemed that the week before, a box with colored pictures on it of a kitchen, had arrived in the mail with a smashed corner. Now Navvies knew that cake flour was sold in small boxes for Belecana cooking, so naturally this box leaking a stream of soft whiteness from one corner was kept right in his hogan. But when his wives mixed up a tasty batch of Navaho fried bread with it, they could not break it apart with their hands—much less eat it. Something was *doh-haly-ahn* or crazy. He glared harder at us, and Harry and I suddenly remembered that the five-pound box of white kalsomine ordered for our kitchen walls had failed to arrive last week. But we never peeped and let him go on his way grumbling about Belecana flour in boxes. All Harry said was, "Boy, wouldn't I give a lot to have seen those old Calamity buzzards tryin' to set their teeth in that kalsomine bread."

Not long after this we could dispense with his services when Harry set up a small shed of corrugated sheet roofing with padlocked door, on the Kayenta road in an open, sandy flat. We could reach it across country from Shonto with the truck in about eight miles, and it would hold hundreds of pounds of parcel post. The Kayenta mail truck driver had a duplicate key. We heard that some tourists thought it a privy. Why there would be any need for such a thing in those uninhabited miles of sagebrush and juniper never entered their heads; at least no Navvy ever thought that. Then we painted SHONTO TRADING POST—KEEP OUT on it, hoping that some tourists would not think that this was a real trading post. We did not dare paint MAIL BOX on it, as that would be too much temptation for strangers in the midst of that isolation. It was a great convenience for us and it was never molested at any time although there was often merchandise in it overnight. This spoke extremely well for the honesty of the truck drivers and the Navahos in the vicinity.

In time the Navvies came to know that while maybe we spoke some of the poorest Navaho among the old traders of that day, they could not fool Harry on anything pertaining to their stock, nor could they slip sanded wool or a defective rug past me. When they tried it they ended by paying for it, and accepted the lesson with a grin. They saw we worked hard all the time, building hogans and the new stone house, besides the east dugway. All this gave them employment and wages in trade for improving what was essentially their country and not ours, and this was in Depression times. Good relations were thus created among the Navvy families who lived around us. Their hogans stood on the grazing area assigned to their family and clan, and except when marriage brought in a new husband, these people had lived for decades around Shonto; trading there after the post was opened and before that at Kayenta and Tonalea.

This is contrary to what many writers, who visit the Navaho Reservation desultorily, have to say about "drifting Navaho families" and "nomads of the desert." Maybe these writers do see a band of sheep being driven across country, but that only means going to or from a certain waterhole, or at most a shift between adjoining summer or winter ranges. The same families trade generation after generation in the same trading post which happens to be nearest to their family grazing grounds. If Navahos were "drifting nomads" over the sixteen million acres of their Reservation, as has been so glibly stated, there would be chaos for both individuals and stock. Just let a Tsayutcissi woman, for instance, push a band of sheep five miles too far north onto a Little Salt woman's range, and all hell would break loose. Every Navvy knows just about where their neighbors may be found. A good trader knows this also.

In the spring and early summer we lived with wool and when the warehouse could not hold any more, the accumulation of large sacks was rolled out and stacked against the front wall of the post. These nine-foot-long sacks would weigh about 300 to 325 pounds with long-haired Navvy sheep wool, after being tramped tight while hung in the wool rack. But the improved wool, tightly curled and greasy in appearance from the cross with Merino and Rambouillet rams, would run a good hundred pounds heavier. Wool bought in small quantities had to be handled and weighed over the counter, then emptied into our wool bin in the warehouse before being tramped into the sacks for trucking to railroad. Navvies would sometimes sand their wool or dampen it in the middle (It sure rained by our hogan last night, Hosteen!), but we could tell if the sack didn't feel right and would allow for that when figuring the poundage. Shonto was not known as a big wool post, although we bought from seventy to one hundred sacks each year, before the stock reduction program began, depending on whether we were "paying up" or not over that year's accepted price per pound. This was set according to the prospects of the wholesale market by the big owners of chain trading posts, and the independent traders went along with it. Keeping the sacks out front in a kind of terrace formation was good advertising as it showed the Navvies how much wool was being bought; of course any trader passing by could also tell this at a glance. The sacks made comfortable places on which to lounge, and Navvy men spent hours there.

Navvy women seldom lounged around the sacks, not because they were too busy with their sheep and weaving all the time, but because it was not considered good form. If they stopped to gossip or boil a pot of coffee, it would be in a group to themselves at a little distance from the trading post door. An old man, while sitting in the hot spring sun, might take off his shirt and go over the seams inch by inch, cracking any lice he found between his thumbnails. Salve for the various kinds of lice was a staple item on our shelves, the most popular being one for "blue lice" with next in order "white lice." It was the more slovenly families who had them of course, but others could pick them up quite easily by contact, and the clean families hated them just as much as we. The nits to be seen up above their foreheads could change hands easily while they leaned in earnest trading over our counter. We kept an eye on that. There was one old girl, very fat for a Navvy, who as soon as she got in the warm store would begin to scratch systematically from her head and armpits downward. Harry Nurnberger, who had traded at Kayenta for years, and traded for us occasionally in the store, used to say that after ten minutes of watching her, she had him following the same routine. The Navaho word for lice is *yaa,* and *yaa ahzay,* or lice medicine, was the salve in round tin boxes.

The word *ahzay* covered all kinds of medicines. Most posts kept a few remedies for sale such as Sloan's Liniment, Vicks, Mentholatum, Vaseline, and sometimes aspirin. Any cough medicine, *dohkoz ahzay,* if it were sweet and had a tinge of alcohol, would sell steadily in winter. The field doctor from Tuba left a box of simple medications in bulk at the posts as free medicine for the traders to give out at their discretion. Castor oil was a standby. Old Man Tsayutcissi, past 85, complained of digestive trouble one winter day and sent over a great-grandson for a small bottle of it. A few days later the little messenger brought back word that the medicine was sure stout and that the Old Man never felt so good. In fact he wanted another bottle. But here we used discretion, and refused; Harry thought we should leave something in him for springtime. A large brown bottle of iodine along with packages of sterile gauze was in the government kit, but the mercurochrome bottle was more popular with the Navvies because of its lovely red color. They seemed to have built up an immunity against blood poisoning. As they began to rely on us to do a little first-aid work, we saw all sorts of oddities.

A young Navvy we knew, walked in the store holding a rag over one side of his face which was covered with blood and fresh horse manure. Harry told me to bring a basin of clean, warm water from the kitchen, to which he added some mercurochrome. A horse had kicked the Navvy, but luckily the unshod hoof had grazed along his eyebrow, the sharp edge laying the skin open like a knife. This flap was hanging down over his eye onto his cheekbone, the whole wound filled full of manure. While the Navvy leaned over, he swabbed away the blood and manure with fresh pieces of gauze. Nobody thought of washing his hands in this whole procedure. After cutting some adhesive tape in tiny strips, Harry taped the skin loosely in place so that the air could get at it. We told him to come back the next day when maybe the field doctor could be there. Talking it over a little later with Donald, the remark was made by Harry that if the fellow had tried, he couldn't have landed in a heap of fresher manure. Donald looked sort of funny for a minute and then said that he had not landed in it at all, that he had to walk around looking for some fresh, hot manure to put *in* the wound. They knew that steaming horse manure had some therapeutic value. The field doctor did come next day and complimented Harry on his first-aid treatment. Whether it was that or the manure, the wound finally healed without even a scar.

The field doctor was supposed to cater to the medical needs of the Navahos and Hopis in Moencopie, within a radius of fifty or more miles from Tuba. There was a hospital there of some twenty beds with a registered nurse in charge, besides the field nurse who was also an R. N. But the Navahos had not begun to take advantage of these facilities. Babies were born in the hogans as of yore, with the simple aids of a rope from the hogan roof and warm, clean ashes from freshly burned cedar spread beneath the mother. Chants from a Medicine Man might overcome fear and uncertainty and bring mental peace. The doctor was a last resort in the case of a person severely injured or dying. That was all. It was discouraging to a conscientious doctor.

We traders were not supposed to come under this medical service, as it was only for government employees and the Indians. If we became ill or had an accident, we had to get out the best way we could to a doctor in the nearest railroad towns of Flagstaff or Gallup—a trip of from one to several days if road conditions were bad. We doctored ourselves as best we could and stayed on with our trade at the post. A trader, no matter how sick, could not just leave without first getting a responsible person to take his place. Navvy families would need food, and their silver and turquoise pawn had to be guarded.

One of the problems which had vexed the trader before us at Shonto was that someone was getting into the store for petty pilfering, but he could not find out how it was done. One night there was a Sing on the mesa a mile west of Shonto canyon and we drove up after sunset to see who was there and bring a small gift of coffee. The Navvy family was glad to see us but we left after a half hour or so. It was pitch dark as we crept down the dugway in low gear, and not a light showed in the canyon. Harry went first to the trading post door, with his flashlight in one hand and the key in the other. It was a shock when he saw it was not only unlocked but slightly ajar. We thought of all the pawn in the store as we went in carefully with flashlights held away from us. We could see some empty nails on the pawn rack and a bolt of yard goods pulled crooked; whoever was in the store had left hurriedly when the lights of our pickup shone on the dugway. After searching the whole building thoroughly and bolting the doors on the inside, we settled down to sleep. Next morning I drove to Red Lake to phone the Agent at Tuba, then hurried home. Some hours later, two Navaho policemen arrived in their rickety Ford touring car. We knew them both well: old John Daw of Red Lake, and Tilman Hadley of Tuba. They looked around the post and we told them of the two silver concha belts, three bracelets from the pawn rack that were missing, besides a bolt of brown sateen and a pair of men's work shoes. As usual, Navvy horses were tied outside, so the policemen borrowed a couple and rode right up the trail behind the post. Via grapevine, they had a pretty good idea as to where the goods had gone. Before dark, they were back with the stolen goods and a teen-ager whom we had known as a smart-aleck kid. Never having been to school a day himself, he aped the worst in the returning school boys. John and Tilman had gone direct to the parent's hogan above us on the mesa; the boy was there and confessed the theft, showing them where he had buried the goods under a cedar tree. The trial was a few days later in Tuba with the two policemen and a Navaho Judge (a Navaho, residing in that district, who was appointed by the Agent) present, as well as the Agent and ourselves. The boy was sentenced to reform school for a year and it did him good, because when he did come back to his hogan he kept out of mischief as far as we ever knew. The one we really blamed was a jack-of-all-trades in the family circle, who evidently had made a duplicate key to the trading post door. We put a new Yale lock on this door and changed the padlocks on the warehouse door also. No more break-ins occurred in our time, but that night if we had not returned sooner than expected, the store and all contents might have gone up in flames. That was usually done at posts when a trader had been killed, or when much pawn and goods had been stolen.

We followed the rule of closing the post at dark and never opening the warehouse at night. Many of the older traders living today kept to that custom. In the years between 1905 and 1930, about fifteen traders had been killed and their posts burned. Usually they were hit on the head while trading after dark, then the pawn stolen from the racks and the building set on fire. Perhaps in a sparsely settled community of Belecanas, where goods of such value were kept without any real protection, the record might not have been as good. At least in my time I always felt safe on the Reservation roads late at night, coming or going with a truckload of valuable merchandise across the lonely mesas around Shonto. Most of the Navvies knew me, or of me, and I relied on them. But right in those same years, a young Belecana walking across the northern Navaho country on his way to Utah, was killed perhaps for no other reason than his shirt and shoes. He had gotten off on the road to Kaibito, instead of the road to Kayenta as the Red Lake trader had directed him. No one would have been the wiser except that a few days later, the trader noticed a young Navvy wearing the shirt and shoes of the Belecana who had been in the post so recently. Sure enough, when Navaho policemen were called from the Agency, they found the Belecana's body where he had rested under the shade of a piñon tree. He had been hit on the back of the head with a rock. The young Navvy, tried in the Federal Court at Prescott, was given a few years' sentence.

The early 1930's were hard for the Navvies and the silver dime and quarter buttons disappeared from their clothes. They could not understand why wool was as low as five cents a pound one year, so they wove it into more rugs. This threw a burden onto the isolated trader who had to buy this great quantity of rugs and exchange at the wholesalers' in Gallup for more merchandise, part of which went against more rugs from the weavers at the post. It was an endless circle. Babbitts would not take any of our rugs, but Lorenzo Hubbell, Jr., would do so in part trade. Cash money spoke with a loud voice and the favorite saying around Shonto at noon as meal time approached was, "I can't leave the store now, he's got another nickel to spend."

Out of these hundreds of rugs handled, we selected a few dozen to sell at retail. Not always fineness of weave, but pattern or color could be the decisive factor. Natural grey, black, and white were always good sellers, and a little touch of red appealed to the average buyer. I liked the natural shades of brown wool but, except in old straight-line patterns, wholesalers did not want brown in a rug. The saddle blankets for home consumption were quite gay with Germantown yarn fringe.

We found one system quite by accident that seemed to work, human nature being what it is, and that was to hang an ugly rug, perhaps badly woven but with good pattern, high up on the wall of the store. Seeing that it was impossible to reach without the trader having to climb up on his shelves, that rug would be just what the customer wanted to buy. No other rug in the piles on the floor would do. After Harry had gone through the gymnastics of getting it down and the satisfied customer had departed, another hard-to-sell rug would be selected from the pile on the floor and laboriously hung in that same spot. It always worked.

About 1932, we had one lovely rug that Dean Cummings of the University of Arizona took a fancy to, and asked not to sell until he could buy it himself a little later. So we began to tell other travelers who admired it on the dining room wall that it was not for sale. It did not occur to us at the time, but in that Depression year it must have been the only Navaho rug on the whole Reservation that was not for sale. In the fall when the trader at Kayenta drove over for a visit, the first thing he mentioned was that so-and-so rug which was "not for sale" that he had heard about from tourists the whole danged summer.

In those days the stray tourists going from post to distant post carried such local news along with them. The Warrens, Wetherills, and Mangum, the Indian Bureau stockman, were our nearest neighbors to the east and they lived in Kayenta, about thirty miles away. Westward on our route to town was Red Lake, while north was only the distant Navaho Mountain trading post. Across country by fifteen miles of horse trail was Inscription House to the northwest. These were our closest neighbors and competitors, with the exception of the Cow Springs post that was practically on the outskirts of Red Lake. Except for the trader at Red Lake perhaps we only saw them once or twice a year. So when we drove over the mesas enjoying the endless vistas of blue-green sage and the play of sun and shadow over the bald rocks, it was probably of our Navaho neighbors that we thought. We noticed wherever fresh horse or wagon tracks led, what hogans showed signs of life, and whose herd of sheep had just crossed the road. If we met a Navvy we asked him where he had been and where he was going, and he did the same thing of us. That was the standard greeting in those leisurely days, and eventually all in the neighborhood would be informed. No radio or printed column of local gossip was needed.

From the front door of Shonto Trading Post looking across the sandy canyon floor bisected by the shallow wash, we sometimes watched open-mouthed at odd events that took place. On a warm August day even Donald Tsayutcissi stopped his work to watch with us as a tourist car came down the hill from the west and came to a full stop at the road crossing of the wash. A young man in bathing trunks (a sight never seen before in Shonto Canyon) got out and began to gingerly wade the inch deep clear water, lifting each foot high and putting it down carefully in advance. After he had thus achieved the crossing he returned to his car and drove it across toward the trading post. Donald shook his head and smiling said, *doh-haly-ahnde* (crazy). The personable young man turned out to be Dave Neumann on one of his first trips to the remoter parts of the Reservation, and evidently he had read never to cross a running wash without wading in to discover its depth. He showed much interest in Navaho silver and I was glad to discuss my collection with him which I had been assembling for many years. As it turned out, he evidently learned very assiduously, an article of his on Navaho silver being published in Santa Fe before many months had transpired.

Another time when Donald, Harry and I were taking an early morning breather in front of the post, a vision darted from our own front gate running down to the Shonto pool under the cliff. Clad in a brief bathing suit the handsome young Englishman, Moris Burge, took a soaring, flat dive into that scummy pool of unknown depth and unguessable contents. We were appalled. If anything had happened it would have been up to us to get him out over the long weary miles of desert roads for any medical treatment. But luck was with him and he surfaced in one piece and uncut. Donald had nothing to say, but Harry said under his breath, "Ol' Barnum was sure right, they's one born every minute." Moris was a nice young fellow, fresh from England, who was married to Margaret McKittrick at that time. She did a good deal of work at the Laboratory of Anthropology then, and within a year or so Moris Burge was the author of an article on Navaho silver published by the Indian Bureau, if I remember correctly. It was always nice to see newcomers in the Reservation take such an interest in the Navaho arts and crafts, and to sell them belts or bracelets or blankets. Well, as Harry used to say, that was what we were there for.

The routine of the trip to town seldom varied although it was never exactly the same. As at sea, wind or weather would lend variety and maybe force me to "change course" somewhere in those unending miles of desert tracks, called roads. In fact, getting out of Tuba eastward towards Tonalea in the old days after a sandstorm almost called for the abilities of a tracker. And when there was a level mile or two where time might be made, that is just where a flock of sheep would be meandering down the center of the road. There was nothing to do except creep along behind that bunch of tightly packed wooly backs, and hope that the leaders would take off after a bunch of grass in another direction. In the whole fifty-mile run from Shonto to Tuba I might meet one car and then it would be probably another local. At Tuba trading post I always stopped for gas, which was still brought out from town in the fifty-gallon drums. Earl Boyer was the trader there in the early 1930's and he thought he had a very dependable Navaho trucker. Even when residents of Tuba who bought all their gas from Boyer began to tell him of having engine trouble and joshed him about "watering his gas," he thought nothing of it. Then one cold morning he had to go out and wrestle a gas drum himself to serve a customer, and when he tipped it he heard the clinking of chunks of ice inside. That was enough for Boyer, and what he told that Navvy trucker was enough too.

There were two large Navaho clans around Shonto. One was the Ashii Altsissi, or Little Salt, and the other was the Bih-bi-tonih, or Deer Water people. The Tsayutcissi family was a powerful and widespread component of the latter. Roughly speaking, the Little Salts were more to the north between us and Navaho Mountain, although a few of the clan, like Long Salt, lived to the south of us on Black Mesa. The Tsayutcissis lived around us on the southern periphery, near Thief Rock and Klethla valley, and in winter took their sheep further south on Black Mesa. On the maps this part is marked Hopi Reservation but the Navahos used it. In earlier years, Hosteen Little Salt and Hosteen Tsayutcissi feuded so much over their grazing grounds that they built a barrier of piñon and juniper trunks which ran east and went for miles across the Shonto mesa and the canyon just north of the trading post. This delineated their respective territories and neither family trespassed; but by our time it had fallen into disuse as the old men had mellowed and their sons returned from boarding school.

Hosteen Tsayutcissi was a fine old man, an outstanding personality in his own right who believed in the Navaho way of life. As a small boy he had accompanied his parents with the group who went back of Navaho Mountain and thereby escaped the U.S. Cavalry. He became the head of an enormous family and was proud to admit that he had thirty-nine sons. As to his daughters, he said he had lost count of their number after one hundred. His hogan had probably contained three or four wives, as was considered suitable for a Navaho of his standing. That many women were needed to take care of the household duties. The older two might do the spinning and fine weaving, and help with the cooking. The younger ones looked after their babies, carded wool, and took their turn with the sheep and bringing water from the nearest spring. There were no idle hands, and as frequently two of the wives were sisters, they appeared to live and work together in harmony. But as the stockman who used to live at Red Lake with his wife said, "Boy, he kin have 'em all. One at a time is enough for me to argue with."

When Hosteen traded with us at Shonto he was quite old, hard of hearing and with dimming eyesight. On his high-crowned hat he wore a prized possession, an old pair of automobilist's goggles of leather and glass. He would come riding down the sand dune trail to trade the bundle of goatskins rolled behind his saddle. After tieing his horse under the cottonwood, he shuffled over to one of our front fence posts and made a stop there to relieve himself before being ready to enter the store. As he could not see very well himself, he took no heed of who might be standing nearby. I never knew whether it was we Belecanas, or age, that had that effect on him, but the routine never seemed to vary. Once inside the store he was all business and did not bother with others standing around in the bull pen, other than a superficial grunt and clearing of the throat. But one-by-one they would come over to touch hands gently in the Navaho greeting; whether he knew them or not, they knew him. I have often seen two nice-looking young women stop their visiting in a corner to go over and speak to him, whereupon he would politely return their salutation. Later he would ask a nearby man who they were, and invariably the answer would be that they were some of his granddaughters. Then all in the store would laugh, including the old man himself, who would shake his head as if that were too much to expect of him. How could he recognize all of his several hundred grandchildren as they grew to maturity? It was noticeable though how the Tsayutcissi resemblance, the blood strain, went down through the generations, perhaps due to isolation in this country controlled by the Navahos. Other clans were known for their infiltration of Pueblo or Mexican blood, from their habit of raiding and taking captives in former years.

Donald's mother had had a batch of children when she was one of Hosteen Tsayutcissi's wives, but she had left the old man and was living by herself, tending her own big flock of sheep, when we knew her first at Shonto. Many of her daughters resembled her, Lichee's wife and Phil Bryan's wife especially, also her youngest—Mabel Rock. However, Donald looked more like his father. Another son, Jack Tsayutcissi, the Hah-tothli (Medicine Man) and silversmith, was very handsome with fine regular features, besides being honest and hard-working. He had a full brother though, who had his same good looks but lacked the other attributes. His name was Ahnehing-njeun, or the Good-looking Thief; this name being actually carried on his pawn tickets. Donald's mother had a voice that carried and her "Ya-ah" when something pleased, or as often as not displeased her, could be heard all over the store. Whatever price Harry offered her first on a rug was always *doh-ihleen,* cheap, to her. She would say that Red Lake had paid two pesos more for her last one. Then Harry would tell her to take this one right down there—only a twenty mile ride. After this exchange and a few more "Ya-ahs" from her, they would settle down pleasantly to the business of trading out the rug. It was a profitable afternoon for her, the result of some weeks of work, and she made the most of it. They always parted the best of friends.

In winter when I had to stay in the store while the trade only gossiped around the iron stove in the bull pen, I would "card" rugs on the counter. To card rugs is to work over the surface with a wool card, giving a soft effect to an uneven weave or ugly pattern and removing bits of dirt in the wool yarn. It was hard work, but my right arm was strong and I did not mind inhaling the dust and smell of raw wool. It also allowed me to absorb the very essence of Navvy demeanor in a trading post. The quiet self-effacement of the younger women was noticeable; any other behavior after they had passed the giggling little girl stage would have been considered bold and far from decorous. When they entered, they walked around to the right side of the bull pen, because the right side of the hogan is the woman's side. They kept their Pendleton blankets pulled over their heads, not for warmth, but to protect them from any unseemly stares from young bucks in the store. A few old matriarchs, however, were a law unto themselves. They would sweep into the store, their wide hips and skirts filling the doorway, and go straight to the counter with their rug or sack of wool. Then after glancing around at all the men as if they did not exist and emitting a loud "Yah-de-luum" (equivalent to English "Oh, well"), they went right to trading. After all, most of the men other than blood relatives in the store, had been their husbands or brothers-in-law or fathers-in-law. It took more than these to faze such a Navaho dowager. The customers watched each other and their possessions like hawks because stealing was not looked upon as a sin, and we watched all of them for the same reason. Once Harry let a woman whom he had loaned an eight-inch sacking needle, (15 cents), slip it secretively into the bottom of her four foot cotton sack, without saying a word. Then after she had stuffed in all the groceries, he asked her for the needle. She just laughed and began to unpack the bag again; the other Navvies also laughed at the fact she had been caught.

In spring wool season and fall piñon nut or sheep-buying time, the hours were long in the store and warehouse, and the work hard. Our customers, swathed in bright Pendletons under their reddish-brown faces, would be going in and out of the door from early till late.

The Navvies ate in relays. That is, each group midway in their trading would buy a No. 2½ can of tomatoes and a box of soda crackers. We opened the can for them and passed out a couple of spoons and enamel cups, which in turn would be used by everyone in the circle on the floor before being returned to us—scrupulously shaken and licked clean. We stuck these under the counter on a shelf with the small brown paper bags on which the Navvy credit for goods sold was always figured. A trader in the old days couldn't operate without these brown bags and a stub pencil. If more than two cups or spoons were kept for circulation they were apt to slowly disappear, so the number was kept low, and of course year-in and year-out they were never subjected to soap and water. The Navaho trade never thought of such a thing—perhaps a spoon licked clean was more sanitary anyway than one wiped on a long-used dish towel. As to water in the store, there was none; the Navvies drank at the nearby Shonto spring. But in old posts a distance from available water, it was the custom to keep a pail of water with a long handled dipper in it for the trade to slake their thirst. This was sloppy business at best and an extra chore for the trader, so we were thankful to be freed from it all.

With three of us to wait on them we spelled each other off at noon to eat, when we were all tired and hungry. Suppertime was best; the store door was locked and we could relax by recounting the various incidents of the work day. After sunrise the wood fire in the kitchen stove was scarcely going before the first call for Hosteen came over the fence in front. Some Navvy had found he was out of coffee and that sad cry of *Cok-quay Etin* meant that one of us had to get a package from the store and hand it to him over the fence, because if we once opened up then we would get no breakfast. To boil coffee on a wood stove at that altitude of almost seven thousand feet took time and patience.

When the piñon crops were heavy on Black Mesa or around Paiute canyon, the post might buy about seventy thousand pounds of the nuts or a carload lot. The piñon trees produced in seven year cycles—two bumper crops, two fair, and three without—and some areas near us had a crop nearly every year. Then whole families of Navvies would make camp in that locality, with both old and young picking up the little brown pine nuts from the ground. First into small tins or baskets, then into the cotton sacks that held about eighty-five pounds of the nuts. These in turn went onto the back of a horse or into a wagon for the trip to the trading post, where the trader would weigh each sack on his scales with the balancing crossarm, computing the weight at the agreed upon price per pound. In the 1930's, we paid between twelve and thirty-five cents per pound, depending on the exact season and year. Most piñon nuts were shipped to the New York market via the wholesalers in Gallup.

287

287. This is a drought summer and Shonto pool at the left is low and scummy. Old Tsayutcissi, with goggles around the crown of his hat, sits his buckskin horse with dignity. The wife of John Smith (Ashii Altsissi Begay) holds her newest baby in the *awae-tsal* (carrying board) with deerskin thrown over it. Old Lady Black Goats (Slim's wife) with her usual infectious grin, sits on the horse in front of her solemn little granddaughter. 1930.

288. A Navaho with an oddly marked pony, probably an Appaloosa. The Navaho horses around Shonto were mostly bays or buckskins with black markings.

289. Very early morning in Shonto Canyon. The sheep dip is already under way. Steam from the vat of warm solution rises in the cool air of September.

288

289

290

290. Old Hosteen Tsidi, or Little Bird, looks at me as if I had lost my mind to be holding that "picture box" in his direction. He never wore a hat, but always a red cotton bandanna in the old style, with his shirt hung outside —the longer the better. His spotted horse waits for him in front of the warehouse door. The cottonwoods were pale gold, and even the dog hunted the warm sand in the late afternoon sun. 1932.

291

291. Harry Rorick taking a moment of rest outside the store.

292

292. A young Navaho girl sheepherder takes a minute away from her sheep to get something from the pack on her burro. In 1934 a new approach road from the west was built on top of the sand dune at the left.
293. These two bands of sheep, belonging to different women, seemed determined to mix. The women tried every antic to divert their attention.
294. The bands did mix and it took all the next day for the women to separate their flocks, one sheep at a time.

293

294

295

295. Bob Talker was a Navaho who lived just above us on the east mesa. He was a good worker, although he never allowed life and its necessities to worry him too much.

296

296. My kitchen at Shonto was in this small stone house built by Joe Lee as the first trading post. It was too cold for the snow to melt on the trees, and Navahos walked into the trading post with burlap sacks tied around their moccasins for warmth. 1932.

297

298

299

297. "Shorty" (Toh-do-ai-decon Bydanih) breaking the ice on Shonto pool so that his horses could get a drink. It had been twenty below zero that night.
298. "Shorty" drives his horses across the canyon to the hole in the icy pool.
299. On their slow way back to the side canyon where he kicked snow off the sagebrush for them in sheltered spots. There was nothing more for them to eat. Loss in horses was heavy that winter.

300

300. The very heavy wet snow of 1932. Donald Tsayutcissi carries an armload of wood into the house for the trading post stove whose chimney is sending up clouds of smoke.

301. This was the sand dune that the Indian Bureau bulldozed level and semi-surfaced with broken rock for a road out to town in place of the old steep dugway in preparation for building of Shonto Day School. 1934.

301

302

302. Mabel Rock, sister of Donald Tsayutcissi, just home from Ft. Wingate Boarding School, at the left. With her was one of the daughters of Toh-do-ai-decon, who lived above us on the west rim and had never been to school.

303

303. John Billy, a Navaho boy who had never been away to school and knew no word of English. He was chosen for the lead role in the film *Laughing Boy* for the long-shot scenes. 1932.

13. *THE PAWN RACK AT SHONTO*

THE THOUGHT of an Entah ceremony being given near his post was stimulating to a trader in the old days. It would break the monotony of summer and give him a chance to see Navvies who had not been trading with him recently, as well as the transient trade from more or less a fifty mile radius. Four or five days would be very busy with extra skins and rugs brought in to exchange for bright colored shirts and bandannas, besides the cash business.

In 1930 an Entah was held in Shonto canyon a half mile north of the post and we donated the expected amount of staple groceries which would augment their own goat and mutton to feed the visiting Navvies. Also to encourage races and games on the last afternoon, we put up prizes of a Riverside plaid shirt or a pair of Levis. The winner usually put it right on over the shirt or pants he was wearing so that nobody could steal it before he went home. Heat made no difference and the Navahos never aped the Belecana custom of exposing their skin to the sun. Men were seen on a hot summer day buttoned up in black leather jackets or wool-lined topcoats. They said it kept the heat out. One Navvy we knew wore an Army-issue sealskin cap all summer, for the same reason perhaps.

The Entah was for Yazzie San Begay, a relative of Starley Yazzie whom we were to know so well. As it was very early in the summer, we bought a lot of wool from Navvies who had sheared late. This made more heavy work behind the counter and my fingers were sore from opening pop bottles and picking up the nickels and dimes. Our Navvies would only buy the red or yellow soda pop and called for these by that name; it was warm for the bottles just stood on the shelf, but our trade did not expect anything else. The day of ice-cold pop was still in the future. Yazzie San Begay (Little Old Man's Son) we had noticed as a very thin young Navvy with a constant cough. A nice, friendly fellow like the rest of the Yazzie outfit. Now he could hardly draw a full breath as he was dying on his feet from TB. He went through the full three-day ceremony, sitting on his horse for hours or else stripped for the blackening, with his thin shoulder blades showing. I can still see the beautiful ketoh of heavy silver set with one green turquoise which he wore constantly, that was buried with him when he died a few months after the Entah.

Klee-ne-losi or Leads-a-horse, the Indian Bureau stockman from Kayenta, was the only other Belecana there. His Indian Bureau salary was one hundred dollars a month, plus a house and feed for one horse. He had driven up the canyon from Calamity Flats in his old government Ford pickup and having misjudged a sandy strip in the canyon had sunk right to his hubcaps in quicksand. Luckily he was close to firm ground and Navvies riding by to the Entah put their ropes on the car and helped him pull free. That Ford was an old wreck at best, held together mainly by bailing wire or "Mormon buckskin" as it was called colloquially in the Southwest. Klee-ne-losi spoke good Navaho and was well liked by the Navvies. One day he was near Marsh Pass and his ignition went haywire. While he was working under the hood, a group of young Navahos gathered to make a little fun at his predicament. None knew anything about a car's motor so he told them if they wanted to see something funny to stand in a circle and hold hands, with the one on each end nearest the motor to hold his finger on the metal top of the battery, and not to let go until he gave the order. This they gleefully did and Klee-ne-losi turned on the current of his weak old battery. It was enough to send that circle into the wildest war dance; no one could let go of the other, and the two by the car were frozen to the metal. After a few seconds of this Klee-ne-losi switched the current off and the line fell apart in all directions. They laughed as they rolled on the ground and then laughed some more, pointing to each other and saying how funny the other one had looked. He left them in high good humor as his motor finally caught and he chug-chugged away.

Klee-ne-losi made a good judge for the races together with a couple of older Navvies, men of distinction in the community. Harry was too busy in the store to leave, and I only attended the Entah in snatches. The races and chicken-pull were held on a long flat stretch paralleling the wash and I moved about, carrying my camera. The Navvies did not mind too much, although it was something not usually done by trader's wives. If strange Belecanas wanted to carry "picture boxes" around with them, all right, but they thought we should have more sense. Besides, in those days at Shonto no Navvy wanted to be photographed.

At the afternoon races, Shorty was a star performer. He lived just below us in the canyon with his wife, who was a daughter of Todhy, and their babies, in a neat and clean hogan. He had at least two dozen fairly good horses with which he occupied his time when not working in his canyon cornfields. Harry used to make acid comments about

Shorty "doin' nothin' but run cayuses," but maybe he secretly envied him. In the long summer evenings when we sat under the trees, we would see a bunch of horses galloping down the canyon in the moonlight. As the sound of their drumming hooves grew louder there would be Shorty riding herd, hatless, with his long black hair in the chonga knot. He was one Navvy who could not give up the horse age easily.

After the Entah crowd had faded away, we began to count the dime and quarter buttons we had taken in; this was real U.S. money except that a loop of copper wire had been soldered to one side, making it a button. Often this was carefully done so that the face sides, or patterns, matched. That it was against the law to thus mutilate coin of the realm was nothing to these Navvies. Our cash drawers would fill with these buttons at such times when the transient Navvies cut them off their clothes to spend. We tried to sell them back gradually to other Navvies, because the banks in town did not like them even with the wire filed off smooth. They would not stack in even packages.

Pawn became a ticklish question at the time of these Entah ceremonies or Squaw Dances in summer. Those Navvies who had not redeemed their silver belts or bridles with the spring wool clip would ask to borrow those articles now so that they might wear them for the three days of the dance. Harry said nothing doing; that it was not fair to those who had taken out their pawn and could now wear their ornaments with a clear conscience. Some Navvies fussed a little about this ruling, but managed to beg, borrow, or steal enough money, wool, or rugs to take out their pawn. Then we told them, as a favor, that they could pawn their silver ornaments again right after the Entah was over. The silver bridles would come right back anyway. There were about two dozen of them in pawn at Shonto all the time, with from five to ten dollars against each pawn ticket. Their owners felt that they were safer hung on a high nail over our pawn rack than they were in their own hogans. In our time, the silver bridles were only used for dress occasions, such as the great Entah gatherings in summer. Most were of plain heavy silver, filed or stamped in a simple design, with no turquoise. Loaning on the jewelry owned by our local trade was governed by the value of the piece, unless it was a wealthy family of good standing who would honor their pawn debt regardless of the actual worth of the pieces. When the pawn rack was heavy with belts, bracelets, necklaces, and bridles, with thousands of dollars worth of merchandise loaned out against them, the trader felt his responsibility. His thought was of the amounts owed him and not of the "drifts of color" as tourist writers love to describe the pawn racks.

Sample pawn ticket on bracelet:

WOMAN-WHO-DOESN'T SMOKE

flour and coffee	$1.45	2/19/30
sateen	1.80	3/15/30
	3.25	
rug pd	2.00	4/ 3/30
	1.25	
velveteen	2.50	5/20/30
	3.25	
coffee, sugar	1.10	6/ 5/30
	4.35	
wool	4.35	6/10/30
plus $2 to trade out	$0.00	

A few good bracelets of hers would be in and out of pawn all year round as she was an old white-haired woman who lived close by, wove good small rugs, and liked to do business in this way. Whenever she was in the store with perhaps only a goatskin to sell, she'd always look at her bracelets on the pawn rack and ask to have a sack of salt (10 cents) or a bag of candy (5 cents) added to one of the tickets before she wended her way homeward over the canyon rim. This was her way of keeping an eye on her possessions.

Sample pawn ticket on silver bridle:

HOSTEEN TSI-DI

black Stetson	$12.00	9/28
Pendleton	18.00	2/30
	$30.00	
wool	20.00	6/30
	$10.00	

His silver bridle would hang up high on the rack for another year, as wool was cheap, and they were a conservative family—didn't want to run their bill up too high. With a small amount loaned on it, they felt it was much safer there with the trader than wrapped in a rag in their own hogan.

Pawn ticket on a very old mountain lion skin bow-and-arrow quiver, made with separate compartments for each, and with the long, tufted tail hanging down as ornament:

HOSTEEN NEEDE-CLOI

flour, sugar, coffee	$7.25	1/27
wool pd	2.00	6/30
	5.25	
coffee, sugar	2.00	1/31
	$7.25	

Harry was always grumbling about it as moth-bait, because Neede-cloi did not want to take it out of pawn and it lay with its old red flannel lining under the pawn rack year after year. Though it probably dated back to the 1880's, Hosteen Neede-cloi in Tsegi Canyon did not want to use it any more, and I do not know what became of it.

Traders tried to keep out of Navvy family squabbles, but in isolated posts they could not help hearing a lot of what went on between their customers. Bob Talker, who had his hogan just above us on the east mesa, was married to a fine weaver, but she did not own enough sheep to furnish wool for her rugs, and was always looking sad and complaining. Neither knew a word of English, but when the store was empty she hung over the counter recounting with simple gestures her trials and tribulations with Bob. Even in the face of our silence, she must have felt better after unburdening her mind, as she left with a lighter moccasined step and a sweep of shabby skirts. Maybe an hour later, Bob would saunter in for his usual five-cent purchase of chewing tobacco. This tobacco came in long slabs for which traders had a cutting knife to make the 5-, 10-, and 25-cent slices. All old-time posts had this equipment and sold chewing tobacco in addition to Bull Durham with packages of papers for those who rolled their cigarettes. Nailed to the counter within easy reach of the trade was a box that we kept filled with smoking tobacco and a packet of papers. This was to make them feel at home and friendly towards the trader. I never knew one Navvy, even the poorest, to abuse this privilege of free tobacco. So Bob would roll a smoke and pass the time of day with us in a cheerful mood; little seemed to really bother him. But one day he was quite upset and concentrating on Harry, rambled on with his tale of woe, the gist of which was that he didn't see why his wife was so awful mad, just because he had gone off for a couple of days with another woman was no reason for her to keep harping about it. He droned on but not finding much sympathy in the air, he jumped bareback on his jughead and went scratching up the cliff trail towards home. Harry said simply, "Humph, mus' be goin' back for more." But in a couple of days who should come in on foot together but Bob and his wife, carrying a small goatskin. They traded out the two nickels for this in hard candy for her and chewing tobacco for him. The aura of peace was hovering over their hogan again, whether temporarily or not.

Doc Sklenka, the Indian Bureau veterinary, had charge of the sheep dip at Shonto where around 30,000 head a year were dipped in the drought cycle of the early 1930's. This was because in addition to our local herds the large goat and sheep herds of the wild north country were driven down to Shonto for the abundant water. Doc was a fine vet who has since passed on, perhaps to oversee the fattest flocks and greenest pastures of his vivid imagination. As our new hogans were finished, we had room for Doc and other guests as well. The equally new, unpainted privy was located directly behind the row of hogans; easy of access to be sure, but right where the entire sweep of southwest wind came behind it up the canyon. And in some spirit of generosity, Harry had cut the two holes in the board seat large enough to fit a giant, or at least it appeared so. The wind that came up through them at times would have launched a glider, and the lee side of any sagebrush would have been far preferable; but we were determined to be civilized, and our guests were game. One joked about putting a piece of the paper down behind and then seeing it float overhead; even the heavier sheets from the mail order catalogues fared no better. Doc put in a strong word of approval to backstop his friend Harry, saying it was the most comfortable seat he had found in a privy. With that stamp of merit, Harry felt emboldened to say that if any of the rest of us did not like it we knew what we could do—go build one of our own. So the subject died, although newcomers still made occasional quips about balancing on the brink. We really missed all this fun after the new house was completed with two regular bathrooms.

The routine of running a sheep dip could be strenuous for a conscientious veterinary. The old Navaho billy goats were a problem as their sweeping horns were too wide to go down in the trough. To keep them from hanging suspended upon the rim, the workers slipped their forked sticks back of the horns and pulled them smartly along, dousing the bearded head and slanting yellow eyes thoroughly with a bucketful of mixture at the exit of the trough. No wonder these old billies remembered this experience from year to year, and dodged it if they could. Doc watched a big iron-gray billy elude several Navvies and measure off to leap the six-foot-high pole corral. He grabbed a hind leg just in time and then the round and round started, although Doc was a 200-pound six-footer himself. Doc won and the old billy had another dip to remember. It was ignominious to be dragged through a bath that must have stunk even to them, when these old billies were accustomed to standing on a rock with kingly demeanor while they surveyed the nannies and kids in their flock. After a few days of this dipping the odor saturated the canyon, and only when sheep dip was over could the spicy scent of cedar and sage return to our clear air.

The winter of 1931 was the kind of which old timers could not remember the equal. We awakened one morning to a ghostly white world buried under a foot of snow with still more falling from the whitish sky. The sheer sandstone cliffs were a darkish pink while every twig of the cottonwoods, coated with snow, stood out in sharp contrast. Not the slightest sound could be heard as every bird and beast was huddled under whatever shelter was available; the Navvies remained in their hogans with their sheep close-packed for warmth in the corrals. Donald was staying with us and as a starter he broke trail to our woodpile out back, a huge stack of maybe twenty cords of wood. Soon smoke poured out of our three chimneys, and Navvies on the mesa above would smell it and know that at least the trader was not frozen. We had purchased the wood at four dollars a cord from Slim Black Goats that fall, when he drove in the yard with creaking wagon loads day after day—always calling to us in advance to tie up our dog, Queen. Once he was forgetful about this preliminary and opened the gate. As we stuck our heads out the door, we saw him make a long wild leap for the wagon just as Queen's teeth clicked behind his rear end. That skinny old long-hair had never used an English word to our knowledge, but right then his "Jees-suz C'ist" rang out over the canyon. As we could not be blamed for this type of education, I am afraid it must be chalked up against some previous trader.

After bacon, eggs and coffee, we went out to scrape the foot of snow off the roofs of our new hogans—from the rear they resembled huge marshmallows—as this was too much extra weight for them to support. There was no sun all day, so nothing melted, and we quit watching the thermometer as it hovered around zero. It did go as low as 20° below zero one still night. Old Luke Smith down at Cow Springs kept telling people for days that it had been 30° below at his store, then he discovered his thermometer had frozen and stuck there. As Old Luke always had to cap everyone else's stories, we let this one pass. It was still snowing a little the next day when we saw Shorty drive his horses in, slowly in single file, to Shonto spring. He pounded with a cedar post to break a hole in the ice for them to drink. The horses were weak from lack of food, but they needed water. After they took turns drinking, he broke trail for them again up a sheltered side canyon where he knocked snow off the brush. They could nibble on that; it was the best he could do to keep them alive. Our Navvies did not raise enough of anything to feed their horses, and the poor beasts had to exist like goats. That winter all the weaker ones died in their tracks, and that spring we missed many a good mare who had been in foal.

The penetrating cold never left the store those next weeks and we worked in heavy shoes and long woolen socks with our woolen jumpers pulled up around our throats. Our breath would show frosty in the store, although we lost no goods on the shelves from freezing. The bull pen would be warm from the heat of the rectangular iron stove in the center, stoked full of juniper and piñon logs. Navvies sitting on the floor were comfortable there, but standing behind that high counter of solid wood we did not feel a bit of heat from the waist down. Trading posts in the old days were always made in this fashion. Besides that, the flooring behind the counter was raised six inches, not only to make the trader appear larger than he was but also to enable him to see what the trade was up to in the bull pen. In a trading post cut off from the outside world, it was better to anticipate and avoid trouble than to have to face it. A good trader watched and listened to everything that went on in the store and if he stood high, he had a bit of advantage. Usually there were one or two Navvies about a post who were potential trouble makers—it would have been the same with Belecanas. We felt fortunate to be dealing with our long-haired trade, far removed from the other elements beginning to flood the more traveled roads.

Traders in outlying posts kept loaded guns, always hoping that they would not have to be used. A 30-30 stood in the corner of our living room, and a .38 was in the bedroom. Both were always kept loaded, as Harry used to say that there was only one safe way to have a gun around and that was to keep it loaded at all times and let everybody know it. In the store on a nail under the cash register, hung a handmade leather and buckshot billy with a wrist strap. This was just in case, as traders tried to avoid trouble at all costs. It was not only good business to do so but it made for peace of mind in the long evenings. It is quite a feeling to sit in a trading post alone at night, surrounded with nothing except miles of silent mesas hiding the scattered hogans. Unlike a ranchhouse, the trading post holds thousands upon thousands of dollars worth of merchandise and raw products, besides the intrinsic value of the heavily laden pawn rack. No fire or theft insurance could be carried on any of it as the premiums would have been impossible—no insurance company wanted this type of policy—so traders had to sweat it out.

Navvies stuck to their hogans at night but if they were in actual need of medicine or food, they had a perfect right to pound on a trader's door and ask him for it. That is the great difference—which most Belecanas do not understand—between the isolated rancher or farmer and the Indian Trader. The former usually live on their own land and have the right of private domain; their friends or ones on specific business come to see them during daylight hours, anything else being unusual. But a trader on the Navajo Reservation is only there by permit of the Department of the Interior, and he can expect any Navvy at any time for any reason whatsoever to pound on his trading post door. He has to answer and usually do something about it. The close-in posts kept their doors locked on Sundays as per government ruling. We tried to, but often a Navvy from the depths of Paiute canyon—where one day of the week is like the next—rode in twenty miles with skins and a rug to trade for necessary food. When he found the door locked and heard our cry of *Domingo* (Sunday), his look of agonized surprise was sufficient; we had not the heart to refuse him.

People have wondered why trading posts on the Reservation remained so barren and primitive, long after the pioneer reasons for such a condition have ceased to exist. Primarily it is because a trader could never own the land under his post and home. Red Lake (Tonalea) which has been a Babbitt post since the 1890's, is one example. Length of trading permits have changed under various Washington administrations from one to five years at the most. If the trader is long established and of good standing the renewal of his permit may become only a formality; still it always entailed some element of uncertainty. Even in the 1930's, the old traders were already talking of the day when there would be no more Belecana traders but only Navajo owned and operated posts. Navvies have tried it but many were put out of business by their own huge family and clan relationships. These demanded credit which the Navaho trader could not afford to give and yet could not refuse. That was, and is, the crux of the problem. It has been surmounted by some intelligent Navahos who operate posts owned, or backed, by a Belecana trader or wholesaler. In this way, the Navaho trader has had a valid excuse for refusing unrealistic credit. It was because we wanted to enjoy our life in the Navaho country and not merely exist that we put in the improvements at Shonto with much hard labor and very little cash. The new two-bedroom-with-baths stone house was completed and Harry ran a seven-mile phone line of our own—on 140 tall piñon posts—to connect with the Tuba Agency line through Klethla Valley. As the mail route to Kayenta now passed our door over the new road and dugways, a Fourth Class Post Office named Betatakin had been located at Shonto. I was the postmistress and we kept desk and storage space in a corner of the store for the handling of the bi-weekly mail. We wanted the name of Shonto for the post office but were refused because of another Shonto Springs post office in the state, so we settled upon Betatakin as that did not conflict with any other. Some over-zealous adherents of the John Wetherills tried to stir up trouble by insinuating we had done this to steal the name of Betatakin, but John and Louisa knew first-hand that we were disappointed in not obtaining the name of Shonto for it. We, as well as the Navahos around us, enjoyed the convenience of all this and people who were sincerely interested in the Shonto-Tsegi area and our primitive Navahos could now come in to stay with us in comfort.

The first real pay-off for our hard work came with a bit of luck perhaps, as it was in the Depression spring of 1932 when Navaho wool was only 4½ cents a pound at railroad, that some location men for Universal Pictures found their way to Shonto. Universal planned to make the first movie from Oliver La Farge's novel *Laughing Boy* and the background was to be authentic. "Laughing Boy" himself was a young Navaho from this north country of sandstone canyons and part of the book was laid here, so the location men had either Tsegi or Shonto in mind when they started out. But after seeing Tsegi from Marsh Pass they realized the impossibility of getting equipment into the canyon; besides, their budget was tight and they wanted to avoid the cost of building sets. As soon as they saw our four hogans in a row near the old rock trading post under the cliff, their minds were made up. They also needed a good-looking young Navaho for the role of Laughing Boy. He did not have to speak English but should be intelligent and photogenic, as sound would be dubbed in and regular actors used in the close-ups. Stress would be laid on the long-haired Navahos being real Navahos in their own land, and they needed about fifty of them with their horses—pay being five dollars per day. We sent out word for several young Navvies we knew to come to the post. This might take hours or days and while we were killing time in front of the trading post, who should ride up but John Billy. We had forgotten about him entirely. But here he was with his ready smile and flashing white teeth, regular features and long-hair in chonga. Walking gracefully over towards us he could have been Laughing Boy in the flesh. The Universal men sensed it right away and hired him for the role, although he had never been further than Kayenta or Tuba and had never seen a movie. Perhaps this was in his favor when the work began because with his simplicity and willingness to do as they told him, he was a success in his role. As an example of a well-adjusted individual, it neither gave him a big head afterwards nor changed his Navaho way of life in the slightest.

The movie payroll for those few weeks brought us badly needed cash business in the trading post also. But when we took into account the eighteen-hour working days, the wear and tear on our possessions, not to mention nervous systems, we felt we had earned it. We fed at least sixty persons, three hot meals a day, from our small woodburning cookstove and dutch oven outdoors with a good man camp-cook officiating. I had given up my bed and slept nights on a stack of Navaho rugs. Harry grumbled a good deal, and especially when a big black stallion galloped across our new lawn dragging two attendants with him. This stallion, the like of which had never been seen before in the Navaho country, was brought clear from Hollywood just to be photographed atop one of the sandstone promontories. We were glad when it was over and Shonto settled down once again to peaceful days. In later years we never solicited movie companies on location. When Monument Valley was photographed so often in that rash of Westerns showing cavalry chasing Indians and Indians chasing immigrant wagons, we were content that our canyons with their cliff dwellings remained untouched and remote. I never saw the movie itself, but at least Laughing Boy was a Navaho character played by a real Navaho in the country where he lived.

John Billy had settled down to married life with a nice-looking young woman when he was about twenty years old, after surmounting an obstacle in his path. Her mother, a grey-haired heavy matron, did not want her daughter to go because the two of them lived alone together; she drove a sharp bargain for her daughter since neither she nor John Billy had sheep or horses over which to do much haggling. The bargain was that if John Billy married her first then in due time he could marry her daughter and the three could live in the same hogan. She would be his older wife, hence the ancient taboo of never seeing his mother-in-law would not apply, and she could still be near her only daughter. So in the interim weeks John Billy had as his wife the old girl herself. They came down to the store to trade and she would graciously allow him to trade out half her credit on a rug she had just sold. Then outside in the sun, she would take his hair down and brush it with a tied bundle of stiff grass stems. It was plain he enjoyed all this fuss being made over him; maybe it was more than he expected from the daughter. His marriage to the daughter took place in due time and John Billy began to bring his young wife with him into the trading post. They would make their purchases in a hurry, swing on their horses and go trotting off happily towards their hogan. Life moved at a faster pace; the old girl was now herding sheep all day long on the mesa.

There was another personality who lived to the west of us with only an eight-year-old grandson for companion and sheepherder. Her census name was Tessie Green, but the Navaho name by which she was known everywhere was Shooting Woman, because when she was fed up with her last husband and put his saddle outside her hogan door as a sign that she was through with him, she did not stop at that. She waited until he came for his saddle and then shot him neatly through the high crown of the hat on his head. That was just in case he overlooked the first hint. She was a healthy old girl and good weaver, but in the years we knew her no other old man had suggested that he share her hogan with her.

When we first were at Shonto with no way to keep food cool in the summer months, we built a screen-and-burlap cage kept damp by a trickle of water. With our desert breeze blowing through this under our deepest shade, fruit, vegetables, eggs, and butter kept satisfactorily. But fresh meat could not stand the dampness, so from April through October or until the end of the blow-fly season we could use no beef. In early spring when sheep were thin, we ate young goats because they were fatter than the lambs and the flesh on the little ribs was really sweet and tender. Once at the table I made the mistake of telling some women guests that the meat they were guzzling so happily, was goat. They pushed their plates aside, and I thought from their expressions that they would have to leave the table. Queer how the mention of goat meat has a connotation in many people's minds with some odoriferous old billy. As they were still guests the next day, I fixed a nice hot curry with rice and trimmings, and after dinner they remarked that the meat in it had been really delicious. Later I could not refrain from telling them that it was from the same goat carcass, only hung under the tree one more day!

The rib sections were tied separately in clean flour sacks and hung in the thickest shade possible above our lawn. In the dry air, this meat that had been killed right and never refrigerated, would keep amazingly well for a day or two in summer. By June, when the young lambs were fat, we would ask some of the Tsayutcissi family to bring us in a carcass. By giving them a day's notice it could be killed in the early morning when the blood was cool and the muscles relaxed. The head would be removed and legs cut off at the knees, with the carcass cleaned out when brought in to us. A young Navvy lamb like this would weigh about twenty-five pounds, and the regular price in those years was two dollars in trade. In the kitchen we would cut off shoulders and legs for roasts and saw the backbone lengthwise to give two long sections of juicy ribs for roasting in an open pan. The shanks went to the cats, as their share. This was such habit that whenever the sound of sawing emanated from the kitchen, cats began to pop out of trees or bushes or wool sacks to converge on the door. Once in a while they were fooled by our sawing wood in the house and after gathering at the kitchen door in vain, they would realize the joke was on them and slink away in disgust to their interrupted siestas.

One thing that a trader had best know was the integrity of the

Navvy from whom he was buying sheep meat. Because while the carcass of a sheep that had died from some cause of nature just before it was skinned would look a little "off" it was more difficult to tell when a sick one had been killed just to save its meat in case a trader would buy it. Perhaps only one hind leg would be brought in to sell. But from the Tsayutcissis, the Little Salts, and some other families, we could depend on clean, healthy meat and often shared the carcass with them. We thought nothing of eating sheep meat month in and month out, but when the crisp fall days arrived and we bought a quarter of young beef from a Navvy, how good those first steaks did taste!

Anet-cloi Begay's wife would often bring us in a fat leg of lamb; she was Donald's half-sister, a handsome woman and a fine weaver. When sandstorms were bad in the spring, she rubbed her face with mutton tallow and then coated her cheeks and nose with powdered red rock. The effect was quite barbaric but it gave perfect protection to her skin. She would have her babies frequently although not with the clock-like regularity of her half-sister, Lichee's wife, or John Smiff's wife. Smiff was his pronunciation of his census given name of Smith, and we liked it. Her full sister, and in fact they looked like twins, was the wife of Ed Grass. That was his census name and although he had never been to school, he had learned to trace a creditable signature so he would not have to *thumb* his government checks. He was quite proud of this accomplishment and it was a symbol of the Navaho ability and willingness to learn. In those days we were not yet familiar with the words "adult education."

The Wetherill influence could be felt in some of our trade at Shonto where there had been association with them in former years. Duggai Begay (Whisker's Son), who was younger than Hosteen Haske, also had worked with John. He had gone on many a pack trip with Byron Cummings and John Wetherill around Tsegi and the Navaho Mountain district. He worked for us on the road, on the Betatakin trail, and helped with our hogans. His large, commanding wife saw to it that he kept busy and never missed the opportunity of a job. One day they rode up to the Shonto post seemingly without anything to trade or pawn. We wondered what was on their mind but after she hemmed and hawed awhile she ended by asking Harry Rorick bluntly if he didn't have a job for her husband? Duggai Begay sat calmly in his saddle, listening intently but saying nothing. When Harry shook his head, meaning no work, she grunted and said then they might just as well go back to the hogan. Her husband took all this in appropriate good humor and as they trotted off side by side, doubtless she was thinking up some additional chores to keep him busy.

At Shonto, Hosteen Haske (Hoskeninni Begay) as his name was then written on his pawn tickets, would stand and visit in the trading post for hours, leaning comfortably on the counter while eating apples and spitting seeds and core on the floor. Two small apples for a nickel were standard best sellers in most trading posts because for some reason the trade preferred these to one large apple for a nickel. He had only stumps of teeth left and was constantly talking therefore of how much his *bohwhosh* hurt, and why he did not dare put sweet candy in his mouth. The corruption of his important Navaho name of Hoskeninni (a large mesa near Oljato bears this name on all maps) into Haske—Navaho for angry or mad—by some previous Belecana trader at Shonto, gave him a great kick. He laughed with good humor, showing all his gums, as he repeated to me: *haske, haske* (always mad). His thin face with its aquiline nose and his tall slender physique are familiar to those who have seen the photo of him with little "Sister" Wetherill taken about 1909. Probably as the result of his long association with Louisa and John he felt at home with Belecanas whom he could trust, and we got along famously in spite of my pidgeon Navaho. I never sensed in him the latent dislike of Belecanas that I did in some other Navvies.

He loved to recount to me the days after the unpremeditated killing of Mitchell when he and Klee Lagai Begay and other members of their large families waited in silent terror in their hogans for the soldiers to come for them from Ft. Defiance. When the cavalry detail did arrive, the commanding officer wanted to hire a couple of local Navvies as scouts, needing men who knew this wild country well enough to help them find the culprits. As Hoskeninni Begay quickly volunteered for this job, he became one of the two Navaho scouts hired. He was paid fifty cents *(deen yal)* a day with plenty of food to eat, and he told me that he sure worked hard those next weeks riding with the cavalry and helping the soldiers look for himself. He felt real bad when they gave up the pursuit and he could not find himself for them.

Hosteen Haske as I knew him, coming and going in the trading post at Shonto, was a fine old-type Navaho and I had accepted him as such long before it dawned on me that he was actually the famous Hoskeninni Begay. I could never blame Louisa Wetherill for shifting the blame from him for an unfortunate incident on to certain members of the Paiute tribe whom she was known to hold in disapproval.

A Navvy who could not be said to be under the Wetherill influence, and yet was connected with the episode in Monument Valley with Hoskeninni Begay which culminated in the killing of Mitchell and Myrick in the 1880's. He was Klee Lagai Begay (White Horse's Son), probably the younger of the two when they had ridden up to the camp of the young prospectors. As we knew him at Shonto he had iron gray hair, an arrogant expression and a presence which displayed little love for the Belecanas. It seems that he had been accepted as the husband of Donald's mother after their meeting at an Entah, hence his entrance into the Shonto trading post scene. He always rode a good horse, dressed well and acted as a man of importance. However, we felt that he was not too well liked in our primitive and unpretentious Shonto neighborhood.

One day he rode in with his scalp laid open, where another Navvy had bashed him with an axe, half-supported by a young Navvy from the Tsayutcissi family whom we knew. He was dragged off the horse and stretched out with his head in the shade of a sagebrush. He was able to swallow a few aspirin which Harry gave him, and as our phone line was working we asked Tuba City Agency to send out the field doctor on an emergency. Klee Lagai Begay never moved as the hours went by and the sun sank lower—when I think of that wound and only a few aspirin for relief. Finally, about dusk, the field doctor arrived. Loading Klee Lagai Begay into the back of his Ford jalopy, he started back on the long, rough trip to Tuba City hospital, where the patient recovered fully in a few weeks.

His new in-laws seemed to feel however that he still had the faculty for getting into trouble with people, just the same as when he had grabbed the gun from prospector Mitchell in that long ago time in Monument Valley, according to Hoskeninni Begay's version. The local chit-chat had it that before very long his saddle was put outside the door of Donald's mother's hogan. As her position in the community was respected and secure, she was not one to countenance any trouble-making.

It was odd that we at Shonto in the early 1930's inherited these two Navahos, of Monument Valley historic fame, when they were old men. This could probably be attributed to the fact that our northwestern canyon district was the last stronghold of the primitive long-hairs. We liked them, and I had the feeling that they tolerated us with much less of the disdain that they felt for the average Belecana, be he trader or Indian Bureau employee.

304

304. An Entah ceremony in Shonto Canyon, 1930, for Yazzie San Begay. Mud Clowns under the direction of two old Medicine Men are treating the patient on the ground before lifting him high in the air.

305

305. Here they toss a small boy of the family, and one Mud Clown shoots an imaginary arrow into the air to kill the evil spirit.

306. Much fun is had among the Navahos after the serious part of the ceremony is over. It was easy at this location in Shonto Canyon to daub themselves liberally with mud.

307

A chicken-pull race up Shonto Canyon, with the "chicken" being pulled [illegible] shreds in the group ahead, while the other contenders are quirting their [illegible] to get into the fray. As our Navahos had no chickens, an old burlap [illegible] substituted.

[illegible] pull in Shonto Canyon, after the Entah for Yazzie San Begay, [illegible] white shirt on his horse directly to the right of the "chicken-[illegible] arm and hand with a firm grasp on the neck of the buried [illegible] a fifth leg of his overbalanced horse.

356

308

309

309. In one relay horse race, with changing of saddles, "Shorty," in white shirt, won the event.

14. *CLIFF TRAIL TO BETATAKIN*

JACK TSAYUTCISSI lived about ten miles from us on the edge of Long House Valley. One of the chants which he knew as a Medicine Man was the almost extinct Red Ant chant. Mary Wheelwright, who devoted much time to the study of Navaho mythology and founded the Museum of Navaho Ceremonial Art in Santa Fe, had searched all over the Reservation for some Hah-tothli who knew this chant. When we let her know that our friend Jack Tsayutcissi was the Hah-tothli she was looking for, she returned to Shonto that fall. They spent hours, with Donald as interpreter, sitting in rockers before the blazing juniper logs of our dining room fireplace. The soft, melodious tones of Jack's voice, mentioning the Navaho deities, would be interrupted by Miss Wheelwright's imperious voice repeating these same names in a Belecana accent with Boston overtones. Jack told us afterwards that he was surprised "she knew so many names." This recounting of the Red Ant chant lasted several days with time out for meals, after which they would return to the rockers soft with throw rugs and sheep pelts. The warmth and reassuring creak of the rockers were enticing, but it was an art to walk back of one without striking a crazybone.

Mary Wheelwright was so well known in the Southwest that with her death in 1958 an era had ended. As a spinster of inherited wealth and dedicated purpose, she felt she had special prerogatives. At Shonto she wished to sit on my right at the head of the long table. But that was my mother's regular seat and she did not wish to give it up, as she felt that the Baileys of New Hampshire were just as good early New Englanders as were the Cabots. So three times a day the game of musical chairs was surreptitiously played by Mary Wheelwright and my mother. As food was placed on the table, each would edge up without appearing to do so, to try to get within reaching distance of that one chair. Then with a little rush the one who had made it would sit down with a triumphant smile, while the other took the place on my left. Donald sat near Harry at the other end of the table; he said the food tasted the same wherever he sat.

The first time I ever saw Miss Wheelwright was at the Newcomb's trading post to the north of Gallup on the Shiprock road. It was in 1926 and Mike and I had driven all morning over terrible desert roads and were famished as well as tired. We asked Mr. Newcomb, who was trading alone in the store, if we could have a hot noon meal with them, introducing ourselves as National Park Service people from Grand Canyon. He said it was all right with him but that we had better speak to the Mrs. back in the living quarters. As we walked through, his wife came from the kitchen where we had heard animated voices, but in answer to our request told us as kindly as possible that Miss Wheelwright was there for a few days and that she did not like her to take in others while *she* was there. So retiring to the post, we purchased a can of tomatoes and a box of crackers, and ate this repast on the trading post floor alongside the Navvies in the bull pen. We were young and leading our own simple life, but realized there were ones who felt for various reasons that they had to kowtow to money and/or position. We never did it ourselves as we chose to believe that people of real worth did not wish it. This held true with me in the later years at Shonto, and to a high degree as far as Harry was concerned. Those of exalted position or many millions ate their meals at our long table, side by side with Donald or other Reservation employees, and seemed to enjoy it, often using this chance rubbing of shoulders to ask lots of questions in an informal way. It was the accepted way of life at Shonto, and by-and-large, we found the very wealthy and important to be the most simple and democratic.

Our first Christmas at Shonto when Harry, my mother, and I were alone, developed into one of those touch-and-go affairs where anything might have happened. A cantankerous Navvy by the name of Deschini started it by demanding that we open up and give him a package of coffee. We had told the trade that we would close the post on "Kismus" as all traders did, but to the few men who had worked for us we promised the gift of a new shirt. Some of these Navvies had already ridden in and accepted the gifts with glee, but none were around when Deschini appeared, as he had watched from the cliff for such a moment. He looked and acted very queer, and we thought it might pacify him to open the post long enough to give him a package of coffee at Kismus. We did not know until later that he had been chewing Jimson Weed (Datura) root which has that ugly stultifying effect. He shook his fist when I would not give him a second package of gift coffee and after making a lunge for me behind the counter, took a swing at Harry who was trying to get him out of the store peacefully but finally had to punch him in the jaw. This stretched him out for a minute, after which he disappeared around the warehouse toward the cliff trail. The news must have spread via sagebrush telegraph as Navvy men on horseback drifted in by twos and threes. I walked around between the Shonto pool and the trading post, shaking hands with some as soon as they got off their horses, and giving the remaining Kismus presents to our workers as they arrived. Things appeared peaceful but there was tension in the air as everyone knew that Deschini was lurking around somewhere. As dusk came, the Navvies mounted their horses and rode away but none sang their high falsetto evening songs of peace and beauty. Harry slipped out often like a shadow, making the rounds of the trading post. Next morning early I drove to Red Lake, phoning Mr. Walker at Tuba about the trouble. He sent a Navaho policeman out pronto who found Deschini in his hogan very much the worse for wear from his Jimson Weed binge and the KO on the jaw. For trying to maul a trader's wife and striking a trader, he was given a 30-day sentence of road work by the Indian Judge after a hearing in Agent Walker's office. Navvies had referred to him as Shash Begay, or Bear's Son, which is not a complimentary epithet, and he did not stand well among the representative Navaho families around us. Probably he was just a bully who tried to intimidate traders: one of those who in former years had made Shonto known as a bad place for a lone trader. But our Navvies had stood by us in a pinch, and soon it was a forgotten incident. As our business grew, Al Smith, Bill O'Brien, and Harry Nurnberger traded with us at times; but it was the faithful Donald who traded with us the longest and became such a welcome part of the Shonto family life.

We felt sorry for Deschini's wife as she was an old woman who kept out of his trouble-making and brought in her small rugs regularly to us. It was she who volunteered to weave a special order I had received from Jim McMillan of Spanish and Indian Trading Co. of Santa Fe, for a Navaho rug measuring 2½ feet wide by 32 feet long to fit a hallway. In the primitive Navaho fashion it was a feat to set up a warp of that length and narrowness, and get it even. She would come in the post and tell me with gestures how she sat with one cross-pole tied to the hogan door and a granddaughter sat with the opposite cross-pole tied to their sheep corral, while a little girl ran back and forth with the large ball of tightly spun woolen yard for the warp which was thus put in place. We advanced her credit for flour and coffee while she worked. The resulting rug was of good weave with a pleasingly repetitious pattern throughout its whole length; she had solved that problem very well. As had been agreed upon I gave her $35 in trade and I sold it to McMillan for $40 plus postage; this was in Depression years and the weaver and I both needed the business. What McMillan charged his customer I never knew, but Santa Fe had the outlet for such things that we lacked in our isolated posts.

Pairs of small rugs were also especially woven for us at Shonto by some of our conservative weavers, in contradiction to that statement so generally accepted that weavers would not make two rugs alike. They may have varied a few threads in the pattern so that the rugs would not be twins, as it is true that Navahos consider twins to be unlucky, but they gave the impression of perfectly matched rugs. As to twins, we never knew of any twin children growing up, although we heard occasionally in whispers of a Navaho woman who had given birth to twins. John Smiff's wife was one of these, and during our years at Shonto there had been two sets of twins, but always one of them had died rather soon. She was one of the weavers who did the pairs of rugs, about 2 x 4 feet, with touches of grey or black on a plain white background. As soon as a half dozen pairs had collected they were sent to Herman Schweizer of the Fred Harvey Company, who took all we could produce. Our weavers were among others who liked to put a Whirling Logs design from their Navaho mythology in their rugs—there being two of the log designs in the old Red Lake pattern—but later this design meant only the hated swastika to most people. So weavers had to be told not to use it any more, much to their amazement. World War II had not yet thrown its shadow over the horizon, and they never dreamed that their own sons would be fighting across the Wide Water. But by 1936 a rug with a swastika design in it could not be sold, unless to a collector knowing that such rugs would become rare items.

In the summer of 1931 our thoughts turned temporarily from routine trade to the high rim of Tsegi and that box canyon which held Betatakin. After talking with various Navvies who lived over that way, Harry found out that there was not even a goat trail down anywhere near Betatakin Canyon. They did not think that anyone could find a way over that layer of rimrock. Yet Harry on a Navvy horse began riding day after day until he was familiar with every bit of that Tsegi rim, while I traded in the store with sometimes Starley to help. Navvies would hang around in the afternoons waiting for his return, and he told them not to think he might get lost because he would no more get lost riding that country than they would themselves! He earned their respect by this and many referred to him as Ahkothle-san, or Old Cowboy. Harry had not been born and raised near Ponca City when it was in Indian Territory for nothing. One afternoon he rode in on a tired horse to tell us the exciting news that he had found a spot to get down into Betatakin canyon to the northeast of the cave. A rocky depression dropped off where the rimrock was not more than thirty feet thick, and below that there were no sheer drops. A large piñon with lopped-off branches could be propped in place as a ladder over this rimrock and the rest was easy.

With the help of some Navvies he got this tree trunk ladder in place and down they went into the canyon. There was no doubt that Harry was the discoverer of this route. It has been said in recent years that this was an old cliff dwellers trail, but that is not so. It was true that in this rimrock could be seen the pecked toe-holds in various places where the Anahsazzi had been but nothing that gave evidence of any practical mode of egress. Besides, it was this sheer rimrock that protected Betatakin from raiding parties over the mesa. To all intents, this promontory over the Betatakin cave had been of no import to either cliff dwellers or Navahos in the past centuries. When news spread that Betatakin could be reached without the time and expense necessary for a pack trip, we took our first few parties in via the tree-trunk route and they enjoyed being among the first to make this trip. As to the Navvies living in Tsegi, they were so surprised and delighted that Harry had found a way in and out of the deep canyon that they asked Agent Walker if he could help make it a horse trail. These were the Little Salts, Tom Hallidays (census name), and Hosteen Neede-cloi or Old Man Grey Whiskers, who wanted it for moving their sheep at certain times of year and also for access to the piñons on the mesa.

So Mr. Walker donated the necessary black powder and dynamite caps and we furnished the labor; Bob Black, Cap Wolf, and Pipeline, using rock drills and hammer, blasted out a passable horse trail under Harry's directions. The work went quickly, considering that first they had to rough in almost two miles of truck trail on the promontory for our pickup carrying the tools for the job. Finally the rimrock barrier was breached and the first Navvy horse crow-hopped down. To commemorate this, Harry pecked the date 10/31 deeply onto a rock surface, in true cliff dweller style, and it still appeared fresh and sharp in 1957. One of the Little Salts was the first to drive his flock of sheep up the trail, thus adding his bit to history. With the opening of the trail to Betatakin we drove our guests, clinging wildly to the sides of the pickup, right out to the head of the trail. Navvies would have the necessary horses there and our party rode the mile and a half down to the scrub oak thicket under the cave, with lunches and cameras strapped to the saddles. We would lie in the shade under the immense domed roof of the cave and imagine how the Anahsazzis came and went on their household errands, while we waited for the right angle of sunshine to strike the masonry walls of the little square rooms. There were no visiting hours and no one to bother us.

The responsibility for the party was always Harry's, but the guests we took in would never have thought of damaging or defacing any part of it.

Dr. Neil Judd of the Smithsonian took quite an interest in this new cliff trail approach to Betatakin. In 1930, the Smithsonian Institution had published *The Excavation and Repair of Betatakin,* by Neil Merton Judd, Curator of American Archaeology, at the United States National Museum. And a copy of this was autographed by him "To Mrs. Harry F. Rorick and all the ghosts at Betatakin. Neil M. Judd 5/15/34." Perhaps he felt that I, too, with my years at Shonto, belonged to that small coterie of those who had lived and worked under the spell of this beautiful ancient cliff dwelling.

We had the pleasure of taking persons immensely interested in Betatakin, but who for various reasons could not have made the pack trip which was formerly necessary. Mrs. Charles D. Walcott, widow of the long-time Secretary of the Smithsonian, enjoyed seeing it this way even though she was in her late seventies. And Marshall Finnan, Superintendent of Mesa Verde National Park, took a postman's holiday by coming over for a quick visit to Betatakin. Perhaps at first the Wetherills did not like sharing it with us, but they saw the logic of the development of the new trail and realized that before many years people would drive to the rim themselves and walk down. Which is just what happened, and we were the first to tell National Park Service that it was time for them to send a resident Ranger there. After summer guests had left the country, John and Louisa sometimes came over to Shonto for a friendly visit, saying our isolation in the canyon reminded them of their old days at Oljato. There was never the ill feeling between us that some of their friends tried to create, over our opening up of the trail to Betatakin.

The first National Park Service Ranger to be stationed at Betatakin was Bill Leicht in the summer of 1935, sleeping in a tent on the old camp spot near the scrub oaks and carrying his supplies down on foot from the tip of the promontory where he left his pickup. Bill was new as a Ranger but old as an outdoor man, being a geologist with some years in South American fields. He was a modest and charming person. We enjoyed his visits at Shonto for mail and groceries when he would join us for dinner at the long table or perhaps stay overnight in one of our hogans. Then our talk would range from the Orinoco river basin to the Anahsazzis in Tsegi and back to the Venezuelan primitive Indian tribes. Bill got along well in his quiet way with our Navvies and his car parked up there on the tip of the Tsegi cliff was never molested nor his camp site disturbed in any way. A mighty good record in any community. Then Bill Leicht was transferred to a desert National Monument and a young married couple, the Brewers, took his place. They preferred to keep house in one of our Shonto guest hogans until the Park Service Ranger station and quarters was completed on the rim at the head of Betatakin canyon. Water was the problem there, but by pumping from a small but steady spring under the rim, an adequate supply was obtained. However, in 1957 I noticed that some of the aspen trees at the bottom of Betatakin canyon were dying, perhaps due to being deprived of this precious moisture for their roots. On this same visit I was told by the competent young Ranger in charge that the trail down had been used by the cliff dwellers and Navahos in ancient times. He was interested when I told him who I was, and of the year 1931 at Shonto when Harry Rorick had found and surveyed this possible route down over the promontory cliff into Betatakin canyon. This was to keep the record straight and not for any personal aggrandizement, for Harry was not that kind any more than John Wetherill.

It was a little difficult for an educated, urban individual to quickly feel at home in the vast canyons and mesas of the northern Navaho reservation, for regardless of how important he was in his own sphere, he was only a dot when riding across the limitless mesas. He shrank as the horizons expanded and the dark-skinned people who live there did not seem interested in him nor his attainments. Their life was bounded more or less by the dim distances of their mesa land; most of them never had been to Flagstaff or Gallup. Among these primitive members of a proud race sufficient unto themselves in language and economy, such a Belecana felt restless and insignificant. He had trouble in making the mental break from all the multitude of things he took for granted in his modern world. Many thought of Montezuma Castle, Walnut Creek, and Wupatki as being more centrally located, and that Keet Seel and Betatakin were "so far off." Thus one seemingly very intelligent woman whom we had taken to Betatakin, stunned me with her last question. She had asked about the clothing worn by the cliff dwellers, the food they ate, and their pottery and baskets. But one thing was bothering her as she looked up at the sunny expanse of the cave, saying, "This is a perfect location with water and everything, but *why* did they build so far from the railroad?" I just looked at her in silence. Evidently with all her erudition, she had not been able to place herself in the world of the thirteenth century.

The mesa that sloped from Shonto up to the higher rim of Tsegi had rich soil where sagebrush grew high, green, and bushy. Hosteen Tsidi or Little Bird lived up this way with a cornfield or two in the low spots. Mounds of the pinkest sandstone strata broke through the surface here and there, and on these we would find the grinding holes of those Anahsazzis who had lived in their time nearby. As the natural depressions in the rock beds held both snow and rain water for their domestic use, shards were thick over the ground in these locations, where the lines of foundation walls were still visible. For miles these indications of the Anahsazzi communal life were so evident that it looked as if a real suburbia had existed at one time in what was then probably not considered to be an "isolated" neighborhood. With plentiful piñon nuts and fertile ground for their small-eared variety of corn, these sunny upland mesas with their natural rock tanks for holding water, must have appeared as a very desirable location to the Anahsazzis in search of a new home. We used to drive in the pickup truck round and round in all directions following faint wagon tracks towards corn patches or hogans, or perhaps on only a sheep trail. These trails were a little tough for an ordinary pickup but a few minutes of shovel work and swipe with the hand axe smoothed the way. When traversing the rock beds we were more careful as a high center there could be fatal; but the cars of those years had such clearance that we did pretty well even before the age of Jeeps. The high spot, figuratively speaking this time, of any such meandering over the mesas was to find an Anahsazzi pot. Whether big or little, beautifully or crudely decorated, it was always a thrill. Once when we had Fowler McCormick of Chicago out with us, he wanted to try and find a pot for himself. Curly Ennis had brought him from Grand Canyon, and the four of us went out for the day with the makings of lunch over a campfire to an almost inaccessible new place where foundation walls showed above the surface. None of us ever did any real digging, leaving that to archaeologists with their permits, but in looking around where wind or water had eroded the sandy soil, we would often spot the handle of a dipper or the side of a small pot. Sometimes these turned out to be whole pieces and we might as well pick them up before passing horses or sheep tromped them to bits. Mr. McCormick asked Curley where would be a likely place to look and Curly passed up the localities with broken shards to tramp along the edge of a recently cut bank. With his boot he tapped something brown, and beckoned us to come over. Carefully with his hands, Mr. McCormick loosened the remaining soil about the pot, and it came out whole. What a thrill that was, although the little pot was of the undecorated utilitarian variety of Pueblo I.

Small Navaho sheep-herders were continually bringing in a pot or a ladle or a bowl to us in the trading post, most of which were Pueblo I and II (as they were classified then) which abounded around Shonto. Frequently it was after a three-day windstorm in spring or a sharp summer cloudburst that the children's eyes saw these newly exposed pieces. Days later the small herder of goats would come into the trading post, stand on tiptoes and shyly push this acquisition wrapped in a scrap of grimy cloth onto the counter, without saying a word. It would be accepted in like silence and five cents worth of hard candy in a brown paper bag handed back, which was the routine exchange. The pot or ladle was then added to the growing collection over the sandstone fireplace in the dining room. There were regulations against selling any of the prehistoric artifacts found on federal land, and as long as I was at Shonto we never sold nor gave away a single item. Neither did we encourage the children to bring in more, as we felt that would not be right. Some black-on-white finely executed Pueblo II bowls had regular punched holes all over the bottom like a colander, and we understood these were rare in other communities. Sometimes grey, undecorated shards from the Shonto–Long House Valley area had a line of small perforations an inch below the rim of the bowl and perhaps an inch or so apart. Fewkes speculated about them and so have many others as to their especial use. To me the similarity was striking with the type of perforated bowl in which Nampeyo of First Mesa molded her pots. The holes near the rim were simply to take care of any excess moisture pressed out of the clay as the coils were formed round and round. The pottery makers of the Long House Valley district must have been numerous for centuries, judging by the tremendous spread of the shards, and the finding of these many remnants of the potter's working bowl or base. One of our Pueblo II ladles was greyish outside but with the most perfect geometric pattern of brilliant black on white covering the inside. Neither handle nor cup part had the slightest blemish from the centuries it had lain under sand and rock since the owner had last put it down.

Dr. Alfred V. Kidder came our way several times; of course the Kidder and Guernsey Report on Northeastern Arizona, 1919, was a most frequently consulted book on our shelves. This one time I hurried to show him a very large and beautiful Pueblo I olla which had been found a couple of miles to the north, right in Shonto Canyon. It was almost two feet high with a narrow, graceful throat, below which lay a band of black geometrical design giving the effect of a collar. I recounted how two young Navvies had told us about it and asked us to drive up to where some stone foundations showed under the sand dune of a tiny box canyon in the western side, saying the Anahsazzi pot was too big to get out of the sand. We told them to *wait* for us, but there was trade in the store and we could not leave for a couple of hours. When we did get there in the pickup and saw the large olla half exposed in the dampish sand against the remains of a foundation, it was evident that we were too late. The Navvies had continued to dig around it without compensating for the pressure of sand by removing the inside of the olla. The result was that it had split in three large sections. We handled these carefully and got them back home without any more damage, where we glued and taped the pieces together, and then placed it in a little cave in the sandstone cliff bordering our lawn. With its best side to the front, it looked beautiful and at home there in that natural setting just as if the Anahsazzi had set it down for a moment. But Dr. Kidder failed to share my enthusiasm, and flatly said that such an olla should be reposing safely in a museum.

One packtrip up Tsegi that Harry made with Curly Ennis from Grand Canyon, turned up something new in interest. Four complete skeletons of very tall men could be seen in the recent cave-in of a cut bank, lying four or five feet below the surface. As no cliff dwellers were of that size it was probably a raiding party from the north, who ran into a surprise attack from the smaller Anahsazzis. One skull was cleft in the back with the stone axe still imbedded. As Harry afterwards said, "There we were, pushin' those skulls around with the toe of our boots an' wonderin'. Probly a thousand years from now somebody will be doin' jus' that to our skulls, wonderin' who those old buzzards were and mebbe what they were doin' there."

On this same pack trip up Tsegi, Cap Wolf learned something new also. It had nothing to do with Anahsazzis or skeletons of which he would not come within touching distance. What caught his attention was the hard-boiled eggs I had put in the saddle bags. He had never seen eggs before as our Navvies had no place for chickens in their way of life. So Harry initiated Cap into the art of peeling, salting, and eating a hard-boiled egg. Cap said it sure tasted good. But a week later in the store when he asked to buy a couple of eggs from us to eat, it turned out that he thought the hens laid them that way—hard-boiled.

When we went to Shonto the Navvies knew practically nothing of modern improvements in living. The Kohler plant we installed in our spring house, whose motor ran steadily in the evening hours with first light *on* and last light *off* routine, was a source of wonderment to them. A little glass bulb hung on a wire giving off so much light! And when the first refrigerator ever seen in that part of the country was placed in our kitchen, their amazement knew no bounds. Shorty, who lived just below us in the canyon, would not believe that just wires could make it cold. Most of our Navvies had never tasted ice cream, but Donald had known it in boarding school days and wanted his young wife, the mother of four little children, to know what it was. So we sat her down in a chair in the living room with a saucer of vanilla ice cream. She tried it, licking a little at a time off the spoon, but soon put it down as too cold. Maybe it is an acquired taste. But the next winter when she and two of her youngest children died almost overnight in their hogan from pneumonia, I could not help but remember that in her short, work-a-day life, she had at least one taste of vanilla ice cream.

In the hogans around Shonto for mile upon mile and to all points of the compass, I never saw a stick of visible furniture up until at least 1935. There were no broken-down sofas, chairs, or stoves, in those days, because it would have required at least a pickup to move them and this was still the horse age. Many of our Navaho families did not even possess a Studebaker wagon—that symbol of wealth to a Navaho before World War I—but relied on their riding horses and pack burros to transport the household belongings in the shift between seasonal grazing grounds. Who would want to bother with a cumbersome bedstead or a chair with rickety legs, when the hard-packed earthen floor of the hogan supported the clean and warm sheepskins with their several inches of thick wool for reclining and sleeping comfort? Belecana furniture was neither envied nor wanted. There was nothing to get out-of-repair nor to display shabbiness. Sheepskins were replaced easily as needed.

A wooden crate that had held three dozen packages of Arbuckle's Coffee was convenient in the confines of the hogan to hold a coffee pot, an iron skillet, and enameled cups, but was not absolutely necessary. A few wooden pegs between the hogan logs keeping Pendleton blankets, hats and sundry articles of clothing out of the way, took care of that facet of simple living. When clothes were slept in—even the young men's hats were often tilted loosely over the eyes—and were practically the same for winter or summer, there was no need for an extensive wardrobe.

A few progressive men like Donald Tsayutcissi who had worked in the beet fields of Colorado after finishing eighth grade in Tuba City, thought there might be some betterment in using a cast-iron wood stove in a hogan instead of the traditional open fire beneath the smoke-hole. When we bought a new stove for the Shonto kitchen with pipes around the firebox to heat water for the boiler, Donald promptly asked for the old stove which we were glad to give him and we transported it to his hogan with our pickup. After a few weeks we asked him how his wife liked it. He shook his head in disgust saying, "She always burnin' her hands. When she don't see fire, she can't remember that that black thing is hot. She like to see flame and red ashes. I don' know, mebbe we don' use it much." After all, a small fire of hot ashes coddling a dutch oven with savory mutton stew or a heavy iron skillet for fried bread, was much easier to tend. And absorbing the warmth of the open hearth would be the family circle of elders and children on the soft sheepskins with their backs against the cedar logs of the hogan. Navaho children at an early age, like little animals, learned to respect "fire" as something that hurt. But otherwise in the hogan there were no breakables nor fragile objects requiring admonition of "don't touch" and it just might be that the placid, non-querulous nature of the Navaho child was enhanced by this lack of the constant "what not to do's."

After his wife's death, Donald ate and slept at the trading post, where he worked all day long anyway. The remaining two children, one a boy of seven, were taken care of by another woman member of the family. Almost two years went by before Donald announced that his mother had arranged a marriage for him, and that he would not be living at the post any more. The girl, quite young, was strong and attractive looking. They had the Navaho ceremony; and the Paiute woven ceremonial basket with the Trail of Beauty, commonly known as the Navaho Wedding Basket, was bought from us. These baskets sold from two to five dollars each, depending on size and weave, and after the ceremony were re-bought for one dollar less. That was the accepted custom among traders, and these northern posts kept a stack of them on hand. And another custom of the traders was to insist that the baskets be washed clean of the cornmeal sticking in the cracks, as they did not want ants or bugs attracted by this on their shelves. But some collectors have wanted the dried cornmeal left where it had adhered. There were other patterns woven by the Paiutes for Navaho use in ceremonies, such as the Star and Coyote Track designs. None ever had a snake symbol. My collection of about twenty-five of these odd patterns in Paiute-Navaho baskets went to the Museum of Navajo Ceremonial Art, in Santa Fe, in 1938, and are on permanent display there.

At Shonto, the day of electricity and telephone was followed soon by the *chidi nahn-tie*, or flying automobile. Using our truck with a drag after Navvies had chopped off the brush, a landing strip was scraped from the flat top of our west mesa, southwest to northeast with the prevailing winds, and Mr. Ruckstell of Scenic Airways at Grand Canyon flew a party of friends over for a perfect landing on the new strip. Frank Spencer's wife from Hopi House and Earline Shirley were among others, and they stayed with us overnight. Ruckstell and Harry wanted to see Betatakin from the air, so the next morning the three of us with Donald, Cap Wolf, Bob Black, Pipeline, and Jack took off in the tri-motored Ford. For that steady work-horse, the old "Tin Goose," was the first plane to land at Shonto. We swung over Tsegi, flying directly up the south rim of Betatakin canyon where we had a splendid view into the cave. Another circle to the south near Long House Valley and we were flying directly over Jack Tsayutcissi's hogans. The noise of our motors brought the women and children to the door, shading their eyes with their hands as they looked at the plane right over their heads in the sky. Jack got a great kick out of this and said, "Wait until I tell my wife I was up there looking down at her. She will think I am some liar!"

310

310. Jack Tsayutcissi, a good silversmith, and a well-known Medicine Man, who gave an important part of the Red Ant Chant for the records in the Museum of Navaho Ceremonial Art in Santa Fe.

311

311. In 1934, this road east of Shonto led to Betatakin or down into Long House Valley and on to Kayenta. The ground was rich and the sagebrush grew high and tough.

312

312. Harry Rorick and Cap Wolf blasting out the new top of the horse trail down to Betatakin Canyon in 1931. The view is to the south down Tsegi with Marsh Pass in the distance. This point on the promontory was about seven miles from Shonto.
313. On the opposite rim of narrow Betatakin Canyon, looking into the huge cave with the almost hidden small cave at the left. 1931.
314. Harry Rorick, Curly Ennis, and Cap Wolf on a little trip to upper Tsegi.

313

314

15. *SHONTO DAY SCHOOL*

In the Depression years of 1930-33, the Navahos became accustomed to the traders saying *Peso Etin*, No Money, in answer to their constant queries as to why wool and sheep and skins and rugs were so cheap. How could one explain the interlocking factors that caused the great Depression cycle? So if it was a fact—*Peso Etin* in Washington—they accepted it as they had the years of drought and famine, by tightening their belts. Then suddenly there was much money in the hands of Natahni, the Indian Agent at Tuba, that had to be spent right away. Strange Belecanas appeared out of the blue to set up Navaho CCC camps (Civilian Conservation Corps, a New Deal plan to alleviate unemployment) with which to begin work projects on truck trails, dams, and charcos. Money began to flow with streams of Nultsos or the green colored Government pay checks, and our ink pad was kept busy with the pressing of thumbs for the X—His Mark when we cashed them. Our Navahos could not understand why there had been no money one year and money to throw away the next year. What traders said now was *peso doh-haiyui*, much money, in Washington, while Navvies grinned across the counter and shook their heads. Incomprehensible. But being wise they accepted this phase too and worked at any job offered, trading out their paychecks for extra flour, coffee, sugar, and luxuries like canned peaches and pears. As the saying was, the wrinkles began to come out of their bellies. When they were well fed they began investing their small excess in hard goods—silver belts, bracelets, and necklaces studded with turquoise—because they knew that these things were not only exceedingly nice to wear now, but would be good for pawn in the next lean years. Like most primitive people, they never doubted that the fat years would be followed by the lean. That was nature's way and they lived close to nature, so close that they were really a part of it. Their life was regulated by the moon and the sun, the clouds and the rain.

The ebb and flow of Navaho daily existence with the sheep and the horses, children and trade, went on as usual. The days were busy with talk and laughter, with the baa-ing of distant sheep coming in for water or the noisy arrival of a truck. Cars came through on the road from both directions—quite a change from that first summer when no car but our own moved in the canyon. At night the spell of soundless quiet would descend on Shonto, held in by the brilliant stars above the dark canyon walls. When we had guests they felt this release from urban living, with no daily papers, little radio, and spasmodic telephone.

The spasmodic telephone of our Reservation system was not at its best one week end when Minnie Harvey Huckel drove out to stay with us accompanied by her secretary of many years whom we called Miss Katherine. No sooner were they settled down in our hogans than our wall telephone began ringing with the two longs and two shorts of the Shonto call. But above the static over the one hundred and more miles of Agency line nothing could be understood except that long distance was calling Mrs. Huckel. We all took turns listening at the receiver and repeating hopefully our questions, but it was no use. The small switchboard in the Agency office at Tuba City was closed until Monday morning so they could not relay a message for us. The efficient Miss Katherine had never been so frustrated; all she could report to Mrs. Huckel was that somebody somewhere was trying to call her long distance and Mrs. Huckel thought that Mr. Huckel, a top executive of the Fred Harvey company, might have been taken ill. However, we discounted that or a Harvey car would have been sent out with a message, so we waited until Monday morning for the hundred-mile round trip to Tuba. There, with the connection to the Flagstaff exchange, it was found to be only a routine call asking if Mrs. Huckel had arrived safely at Shonto!

Another time, the Grand Canyon had been vainly calling us to say that Byron Harvey, Sr., and his son, Stewart, were on their way out for a couple of days. But we were just as happy to have them roll through our gates, completely unannounced, which was much more of a surprise to them than it was to us. I had to scurry around to roast a leg of lamb and to bake a cake and it was while I was beating the cake batter in the kitchen that I overheard Mr. Harvey saying that it was his sixty-fourth birthday. So when the cake was ready to be iced I did something absolutely new to Shonto by twisting a brown paper bag from the store into a semblance of a pastry tube and writing HAPPY BIRTHDAY—BYRON HARVEY in large letters. We all had a laugh when I brought it to the table; although he was so pleased at my effort, it was probably the funniest looking birthday cake he had ever received. I think Vic Patrosso from El Tovar came with their party also, but it was Stewart who came into the kitchen and volunteered to show me the correct way to carve a leg of lamb as they were taught in the Harvey school. I was glad to see the professional way of cutting up the entire leg into perfectly-shaped even slices and would do it that way for a big group hereafter, although I did add that it might be wasteful for me as any uneaten slices dried out so quickly in our desert air. Harry Rorick overheard us talking and made the comment that of course I had to put in the last word. All of the Harveys were nice guests to have at Shonto and we always looked upon them as really belonging to the Southwest.

Another guest slipped quietly into Shonto, introducing himself as Dr. Hale from Pasadena. He was a tall, ascetic person and a conversationalist of charm and as the hours went by on our rock terrace I kept trying to find out his place in the scientific world without giving away my ignorance. All I could think of was Cal. Tech. but the name didn't seem to fit there. My efforts must have been amusing to him because he said finally with a twinkle in his eye that he was the astronomer, the one who had been in charge of Mt. Wilson Observatory for so many years. Of course recognizing the name then as one of the leading men in his field, I told him that he was the first astronomer of note to visit Shonto and that we were accustomed to settling for the usual archaeologists and geologists, although we had had Dr. Robert Millikan of Cal. Tech. with us recently. And that as it turned out was exactly the reason that Dr. George Ellery Hale had hunted up Shonto because Dr. Millikan had told him not to miss this chance of a glimpse of the unspoiled Navaho life about us while resting in the comfort of our simple accommodations. He stayed for several days, as had Dr. Millikan before him, relaxing in our primitive Navaho world. I can still see Dr. Millikan unwinding from the tension of his important mid-1930's work at Cal. Tech. as he watched us battle with our daily problems of weather, roads, water, mail, trade in the store, or just getting in a carcass of young lamb—all of which were of just as great importance to us.

It was wonderful for a few days, which was all the average person wanted to be cut off from his accustomed world, because he could not be a part of the Navaho land with its absorbing daily routine, as we were. Even the Kayenta mail truck went through Shonto (Betatakin Postoffice) twice a week bringing the Flagstaff weekly *Coconino Sun* and the *Arizona Republican* only a few days late; guests picked up these papers and threw them down after looking at the date. To us, any newspaper as yet unread was still news; it was more a question of finding that spare moment in which to read it. I always arranged them in sequence with the last date on top. This saved much time in reading as the murder was already solved and the world crisis had not materialized.

A great surprise lay in store for our Navvies—something which changed the whole life of the community across that lonely expanse of rock canyons, piñon and sagebrush. It was a prospective Day School-Community Center at Shonto for the Navaho children and their families. In 1933 an Indian Bureau man was sent to look over the isolated areas in the Reservation where such a center would be feasible. The day was chilly at Shonto when he arrived from Phoenix and settled down in front of the fireplace to ask me questions. How many families lived within a close radius? Were there many poor families nearby? And I told him that if that was what he was looking for, Shonto had more than its share of them, also that there was abundant water in the canyon which would be a necessity for the proposed center. He seemed pleased with the many things we had done ourselves to help our little community, such as the telephone line, the new trails and roads out of the canyon. After a good night's sleep in one of our guest hogans and a hearty breakfast, he went on his way. Within a week we were notified officially that Shonto was to have one of the new Day Schools. The time was drawing to a close when we would be alone in the canyon with the nearest Belecana twenty-five miles away.

Our real Navaho hogan guest rooms had seemingly made an impression on this man as well as on others who followed him. Why could not the idea be adopted for the construction of the first Day School? The small Navvy children who had never seen any dwelling except their own doorless, windowless, dirt-floored hogans would surely feel more at home in something that resembled these instead of a formal, Belecana-type building. This talk quickly reached the ears of the higher echelon. John Collier—always spoken of as John Colly by the Navahos—the Indian Commissioner appointed by Harold L. Ickes when he became Secretary of the Interior, himself had instigated this new plan for the placing of Day Schools in the Reservation, something that had never been done before with the Navahos. His daughter-in-law Nina, who was an M.I.T. graduate in architecture, came to stay with us at Shonto to make sketches and talk over the practical aspects of the project. Hogans were very adaptable, as they could be built all of logs or partly of stone, with or without chimneys or windows, and yet retain the over-all characteristics of hogans. The hogans designed for this Day School were to be copied in five other Reservation locations where likewise the juniper and piñon logs for construction were abundant. With us, native Shonto sandstone was to be used for all walls, with ceilings of juniper poles. This reduced the price of raw materials to be hauled in, while providing more work and pay for the local Navvies and giving them an incentive to participate in their new local school and center. The appropriation of thirty thousand dollars to build the Day School and Community Center seemed like an enormous amount of money to all of us at Shonto where we had been accustomed to stretching one hundred into doing the work of two hundred dollars. It was a windfall for our numerous poor Navvy families, each of which had one or more able-bodied man who was willing and anxious to do this type of work. Under a Belecana foreman they worked well and became adept at cement mixing and pouring, about which they had known nothing. A finishing carpenter was brought from town to hang doors and place hardware. For a whole year these families bought assorted groceries to supplement their steady diet of mutton and goat meat with fried bread and Arbuckle coffee and replaced their ragged clothes with new pants, shirts, and jumpers. Before this they had been dependent upon such work as we had for them.

The hogan-type rooms were grouped in twos and threes connected by covered cement walks, and modern windows let in the bright sunshine and plenty of fresh air. The little children smiled when they looked up at the juniper ceilings and felt at ease, it was not so frightening to be in school after all. The first resident teachers liked the layout of these rooms and found the living quarters very comfortable, and the Navvies were proud that their own kind of dwelling had been adapted and put to use by the Belecanas.

Our old-fashioned Navvy women took a long time to utilize the running water in the utility room for the washing of their raw wool for weaving; the small children were afraid to go to school at first. It was a matter of mental adjustment as always, to discard the old and accept the new; so the school only operated at a fifth of its capacity that first year, although it was easy for the children to get on the school bus in the morning when it made a circle route on each side of the canyon. But the children who did attend loved it, with that hot noon meal. The mistake made was in not having this day school attendance compulsory as in other rural areas. When a child of seven was asked by a stranger if he wanted to go to school, the natural response was to shake his head. And the parents of course did not realize how necessary it was for their boys and girls to go to school and learn English so that they could take their place in the new world they had to enter. This system was corrected later and each family was told that the children, unless excused for some valid reason, must attend classes at the Day School. The older women began to use the center also, riding in on the bus with their bag of wool or something to wash. They were adjusting to the wonders of the new environment.

We had to pass through that adjustment period ourselves. Instead of being the only one to whom our Navvies could turn in time of trouble or emergency, there was now a teacher and a stockman to whom they could go. They might never feel as close to them as they did to us who had shared their life during the past years, but it did spread the responsibility around a bit. They knew these Belecanas had been sent in by Nahtahni to help them. Our own seven-mile telephone line with its one hundred forty hand-trimmed piñon posts was now replaced with standard poles to Indian Bureau specifications, serving both the school and our trading post. The dugway on the west which we all had to use for our trips to town, had been replaced with a graded road which had been bulldozed right down the crest of the sand dune from the rim to the bottom where I had first ridden down on horseback. The Indian Bureau with some help from the Bureau of Public Roads had surfaced the dugway with crushed rock, and we were thankful for this great improvement which the Day School necessitated.

The entrance to the school property below our lower fence ran through what had been Donald's corn and squash patch during our first summers. Between it and the main Shonto wash was a spread of bright green grass, perhaps fifteen feet in diameter. In winter it was brown and frozen, but even in dry summers it was an emerald green and could be seen from the front of the trading post. One summer evening a university professor and his wife with their bedding rolls and camp outfit in their car, asked us where would be a good place for them to sleep. Harry told them of a good spot nearby where sheep and Navvies would not be running over them at sunrise, but they had seen that green grass and wanted to sleep there. Harry said he would not advise their doing that, but they had best roll their bedding out on the clean sand near the cliff as he had suggested. We became busy with other trade in the store and forgot about them, but in the early morning we looked around and there they were with their bed rolls and gear spread in the center of that green grass. Harry just smiled. When the store was open after breakfast they entered with a self-satisfied air and without any solicitation from us began telling about the fine night's sleep they had enjoyed on that green grass. Harry, without looking up from the papers he was shuffling, drawled, "I'm shore glad to hear that. 'Tisn't everybody likes to sleep on a cesspool. An' I been thinkin' lately those boards mus' be gettin' weak . . . that grass is too green." The university couple swallowed a few times and beat a hasty retreat, their motor roaring as they shifted gears to get out of that canyon fast. Harry said to nobody in particular, "Mebbe nex' time they'll listen to what a trader tells 'em."

With progress came other changes in Shonto Canyon, such as the disappearance of the pool of water next to the cliff. This was the one which had given its name of Sunlight Water, or Shonto, to the canyon and trading post. But the Indian Bureau ordered the pool filled in and a well with pump and overhead tank put in its place. Of course the water pouring from a spigot into a trough was much purer and cleaner than the wide pool lapping at the base of the pink cliff. But no more could we see what we had once before when young goats were playing on the almost perpendicular cliff over the spring and a youthful billy with pointed horns and white face was butted from his footing by an adversary. He plunged end over end, deep into the pool. When he rose to the surface, his horns and face were bright green with shining scum; he was really an apparition. An old Navvy woman standing under the cottonwood was bug-eyed. If she had not seen it happen, she would have been leaving that pool with the green goat as fast as her skirts allowed her. As it was, she and I looked at each other and the goat, and laughed and laughed. The little white billy with a final shake and a *ba-a* emerged from both scum and pool.

The thing I regretted most in my years at Shonto was that because we both traded and were on tap twelve hours a day, we could not go to as many of the big winter Chants in other parts of the Reservation as I would have liked. We knew of them and who was going to them, but our trade expected us to remain in the post. If I had been like some of the traders to whom business was business and Navvies something to be tolerated, that would have been different. But I liked the Navahos and was interested in their clans, their mythology, and the part that the various Sings and Chants, and particularly the one-day ceremonies, played in their daily existence. So I was frequently sorry at having to miss some of these Sings in the hogans of families we knew so well, but we tried to be good traders and an integral part of the Shonto neighborhood first and foremost. And who knows, perhaps our own Navvies wished it that way and liked us for respecting their right to privacy. They had heard enough of those who gave their Medicine Man gifts in return for which they had the privilege of sketching or photographing sand paintings. But that had been done by Navahos in the Gallup area along the railroad and was not for the proud members of the Northwestern Navahos, whose closest approach to this sort of thing was to allow Louisa Wetherill to bring one or two of her hand-picked guests to witness the sand paintings of the seldom-given nine-day ceremonies.

My life on the Reservation was coming to an end by 1939 and so were the old days of primitive atmosphere and isolation at Shonto. Perhaps we had helped in this change ourselves in the guise of progress, and after 1933 it became a very definite thing and we could not have stopped it if we had wished. John and Louisa still living under the spell of the old days, tried to stop it but went down under the wave. The glamor and charm of the untouched northwestern Navaho Reservation was giving way to CCC camps, truck trails, and pay checks to partially replace the vanishing flocks of sheep and goats and the general pastoral life. For personal reasons, of which my mother was one, I sold my half of the trading post to Harry for the minimum amount of cost to me. He operated it during the War years and sold out to a Farmington couple in about 1945. After paying off the mortgage and giving the details of the transaction, Harry added the really important news for me—that Cat-suma had died at age sixteen and was buried in a small dry cave under the Shonto cliffs.

When I saw Shonto in 1957 there was no wash with its trickle of water running down the center of the canyon. Groves of tall cottonwoods were there instead and lines of cross fences could be seen up and down the canyon guarding their healthy green corn stalks in their separate hills. Erosion control together with stock reduction had done their work. Through the trader's grapevine as I drove up the Chin Lee I heard that once again "Shonto could be bought." This time the figure being quoted was eighty thousand dollars for the same permit and the same buildings, with perhaps an added patina of age on the latter. My little spirea bushes and row of poplars had grown large against the cliff behind the lawn, where the old Joe Lee house with the tin roof was still doing duty. The old horse trail was visible winding up the cliffside and the front of the trading post was the same, bleak and bare, facing the expanse of pinkish sand. Shonto would change but remain unchanged . . . imperturbable, the same perhaps as with the Shonto Navahos we had known, and whose children and grandchildren now played around the post. The old generation was gone and with it their memories of U.S. Cavalry days, and their escaping the raids of Kit Carson; and now a new generation was grown who did not remember the years when tens of thousands of horses and vast herds of sheep and goats grazed over the Reservation supplying their owners with a pleasant pastoral mode of living. The young Navahos were already adjusting to the new, but something more was in store for Shonto which would bring the old leisurely way of life to an end.

In January 1961 an appropriation was granted for one million seven hundred thousand dollars to build a Boarding School at Shonto. This sum would have been unthinkable to us back in 1931, even though we always had dreams for the future development of that neighborhood. And if Hosteen Tsayutcissi could return to this earth for a moment he would most certainly exclaim *peso doh-haiyui,* much money, or *doh-halyahn-dah,* crazy, if not both. But this project will advance not only Shonto Canyon but the surrounding country with the necessary paved access roads to connect with Route 1 running east and west through Marsh Pass. And the children from the northern canyons can have their schooling while living in comfortable quarters comparatively close to home where their parents can ride in on week ends. All this is for the young generation and their children. For me, I would not trade it for having known the old Shonto, with all of its hardships, together with the fine old Navahos. The days to remember are those when only the sound of our truck's motor broke the canyon stillness, or when Starley Yazzie's falsetto tones of the Evening Song rose skyward as he rode up the cliff trail toward his hogan.

315

315. The new hogan-type Day School buildings at Shonto. 1934.

316

316. The "Tin Goose" from the Grand Canyon on the Shonto air strip. The Ruckstells, Mabel Spencer, and Earlene Shirley were among those in the party that flew over in this tri-motored Ford in 1933.

317

317. At the newly completed Shonto Day School, 1934.

SUGGESTED READING

Adair, John, *The Navajo and Pueblo Silversmiths*. Norman: University of Oklahoma Press, 1944.

Amsden, Charles, *Navaho Weaving*. Albuquerque: University of New Mexico Press, 1949, Second Edition.

Colton, Harold S., *Hopi Kachina Dolls*. Albuquerque: University of New Mexico Press, 1949 ,1959.

Crane, Leo, *Indians of the Enchanted Desert*. Boston: Little, Brown and Co., 1925.

Cummings, Byron, *Indians I Have Known*. Tucson: Arizona Silhouettes, 1952.

Dellenbaugh, Fred S., *A Canyon Voyage*. New York: G. P. Putnams Sons, 1908.

Dockstader, Frederick J., *The Kachina and the White Man*. Bloomfield Hills, Mich.: Cranbrook Institute of Science, 1954.

Fewkes, Jesse Walter, "A Few Summer Ceremonials at the Tusayan Pueblos," *A Journal of American Ethnology and Archaeology,* Vol. II, 1892, 1-159.

———, *Preliminary Report on a Visit to the Navajo National Monument, Arizona*. Washington: Smithsonian Institution, U.S. Bureau of American Ethnology, Bulletin 50, 1911.

Franciscan Fathers [Father Berard Haile, O.F.M.], *An Ethnologic Dictionary of the Navajo Language*. St. Michaels, Arizona, 1910.

———, *A Vocabulary of the Navajo Language, English-Navajo*. St. Michaels, Arizona, 1912, 2 Vols.

Gillmor, Frances, and Louisa Wade Wetherill, *Traders to the Navajos*. Albuquerque: University of New Mexico Press, 1952, Second Edition.

Gregory, Herbert E., *The Navajo Country; a Geographic and Hydrographic Reconnaissance of Parts of Arizona, New Mexico, and Utah*. Washington: U.S. Department of the Interior, Geologic Survey, Water Supply Paper 380, 1916.

James, George Wharton, *Indian Basketry*. New York: Henry Malkan, 1902.

———, *Indian Blankets and Their Makers*. Chicago: McClurg Co., 1914.

Judd, Neil Merton, *The Excavation and Repair of Betatakin*. Washington: U.S. National Museum, Proceedings, LXXVII, 1930.

Kidder, Arthur V., and Samuel J. Guernsey, *Archaeological Explorations in Northeastern Arizona*. Washington: Smithsonian Institution, U.S. Bureau of American Ethnology, Bulletin 65. 1919.

LaFarge, Oliver, *Laughing Boy*. Boston: Houghton Mifflin Co., 1929.

Lummis, Charles F., *Mesa, Canyon and Pueblo*. New York: The Century Co., 1925.

———, *Some Strange Corners of Our Country*. New York: The Century Co., 1906.

Matthews, Washington, *Navajo Silversmiths*. Washington: Smithsonian Institution, U.S. Bureau of American Ethnology, Second Annual Report, 1883, 171-84.

Mindeleff, Cosmos, *Navaho Houses*. Washington: Smithsonian Institution, U.S. Bureau of American Ethnology, Seventeenth Annual Report, 1899, 475-744.